DIONYSUS

AND

THE CITY

DIONYSUS
AND
THE CITY

MODERNISM IN

TWENTIETH-CENTURY POETRY

MONROE K. SPEARS

OXFORD UNIVERSITY PRESS
LONDON   OXFORD   NEW YORK

OXFORD UNIVERSITY PRESS

Oxford   London   New York
Glasgow   Toronto   Melbourne   Wellington
Cape Town   Salisbury   Ibadan   Nairobi   Lusaka   Addis Ababa
Bombay   Calcutta   Madras   Karachi   Lahore   Dacca
Kuala Lumpur   Hong Kong   Tokyo

FOR BETTY
WITH LOVE

ACKNOWLEDGMENTS

I WOULD LIKE to express my thanks to Allen Tate and to Whitney Blake for encouragement and helpful advice; to John Irwin for a fruitful suggestion; and to the John Simon Guggenheim Memorial Foundation for a fellowship in 1965–66, which enabled me to produce in happy circumstances a first draft later to go through many a painful revision. I owe a special debt to two books without which this enterprise would hardly have seemed possible in its present form: *The Modern Tradition: Backgrounds of Modern Literature*, edited by Richard Ellmann and Charles Feidelson, Jr. (New York: Oxford University Press, 1965) and *Continuities*, by Frank Kermode (New York: Random House, 1968). Thanks are due also to the editor of *Shenandoah*, in which one chapter of this book has appeared.

For permission to quote copyrighted material I am grateful to:

Alfred A. Knopf, Inc., for extracts from *Poems and Essays*, © 1955 by John Crowe Ransom;

Charles Scribner's Sons, for extracts from *Poems 1922–1947*, © 1948 by Allen Tate;

Eyre & Spottiswoode Ltd., for British Commonwealth rights to extracts from *Poems 1920–1945*, © 1945 by Allen Tate;

Faber & Faber Ltd., for British Commonwealth rights to ex-

tracts from *Collected Shorter Poems 1927–1957*, © 1966 by
W. H. Auden, *About the House*, © 1966 by W. H. Auden, *Collected Poems 1909–1962*, © 1962 by T. S. Eliot, *The Hawk in
the Rain*, © 1957 by Ted Hughes, *Lupercal*, © 1960 by Ted
Hughes, *Wodwo*, © 1969 by Ted Hughes, *Poems 1938–1949*, ©
1949 by Robert Lowell, *Personae*, © 1926 by Ezra Pound, *The
Letters of Ezra Pound 1907–1941*, ed. D. D. Paige (1951);

Farrar, Straus & Giroux, Inc., for extracts from *For the Union
Dead*, © 1965 by Robert Lowell, *Near the Ocean*, © 1967 by
Robert Lowell;

Harcourt, Brace & World, Inc., for extracts from *Collected
Poems 1909–1962*, © by T. S. Eliot, *Lord Weary's Castle*, ©
1946 by Robert Lowell, *The Letters of Ezra Pound 1907–1941*,
ed. D. D. Paige, © 1950;

Harper & Row, Publishers, for extracts from the volumes by
Ted Hughes as listed above;

Laurence Pollinger Ltd., for British Commonwealth rights to
extracts from *Selected Poems*, © 1948 by John Crowe Ransom;

New Directions Publishing Corp., for extracts from *Personae*,
© 1926 by Ezra Pound;

Random House, Inc., for extracts from *Collected Shorter
Poems 1927–1957*, © 1967 by W. H. Auden, *About the House*,
© 1965 by W. H. Auden, *Selected Poems New and Old 1923–
1966*, © 1966 by Robert Penn Warren;

Rapp & Whiting Ltd., for British Commonwealth rights to extracts from *Poems 1956–1967*, © 1967 by James Dickey;

Wesleyan University Press, for extracts from *Poems 1956–
1967*, © 1967 by James Dickey;

William Morris Agency for British Commonwealth rights to
extracts from *Selected Poems New and Old 1923–1966*, © 1966
by Robert Penn Warren.

M. K. S.

Houston, Texas
September 1, 1969

CONTENTS

DIONYSUS

AND

THE CITY

THE MODERN
AND THE PAST

MODERNISM IS, of course, an impossible subject. The thought of seriously undertaking to define any literary term is a depressing one, and modernism has special difficulties: whatever it is, and whether dead or alive, it is certainly too close for proper detachment. Writers on this subject are tempted to posture histrionically as mad and tortured moderns proclaiming the Last Days or as imperturbable traditionalists proving quietly that nothing has changed; and they are likely either to bore the reader by telling him what he already knows or to avoid the obvious so desperately that they present a distorted picture.

And yet modernism calls urgently and irresistibly for discussion. As the twentieth century approaches its last quarter, we see the literary *anni mirabiles* 1922–25 from a half-century's distance, and the beginnings of the cultural era as a full century in the past. In 1969 we can feel the gyres turning and eras changing: the moon landing obviously ended the first stage of the space age that began in 1957, and it is clear by now that the literary developments in this same period raise fundamental questions about the nature of the original modernism and their relation to it. The word itself has been so debased by advertisers and journalists that we wince when we use it, and in some contexts it has acquired a

3

period flavor: nothing is so stale as yesterday's modernism. But no other word can feasibly be substituted for this embarrassing one in the enterprise of trying to define the concept, explore it, see it in various perspectives, and thereby understand more fully the major changes that have taken place in English verse during the present century.

After attempting several kinds of definition against a broad background in the first three chapters, the present book focuses on British and American poetry and considers the emergence of modernism in the years 1909–14, the effect of rediscovering it upon a group of poets a decade later in the American South, and finally its relation to the second revolution of the mid-century in both criticism and poetry. Let us begin with a look at the word itself and its connotations, and then proceed to sketch in the basic chronology and consider briefly some definitions of the essence of modernism and its place in literary history.

DEFINITIONS

And yet what is Modernism? It is undefined. Henry James stopped before a certain piece of sculpture to apostrophize "the beautiful modern spirit"; but he did not attempt a definition where a more incompetent man would surely have done it.

John Crowe Ransom in *The Fugitive*, February 1924

The *modern* pertains to "the present and recent times" (*OED*) as distinguished from the past; this has been the central meaning of the word since the sixteenth century. What is designated as modern need not, however, be new or even very recent, so long as it is not felt to be obsolete or outmoded. The criterion is relevance, not time; and hence it is necessary to distinguish *modern* from *contemporary*, which refers to chronology alone. A work may be modern, we feel, though remote from us in time (Sappho, Catullus, Villon, Donne, Blake); conversely, it is apparent that much contemporary work is not in any sense modern. (To say this is not to imply an equation of modernity with value, though it appears to be a necessary component: Baudelaire, speaking of painting, said, "Modernity is that which is ephemeral, fugitive, contingent upon the occasion; it is half of art, whose other half is the eternal and unchangeable." [1] On the other hand, it is unfortunately true that art may be extremely modern and yet of no value.)

The seventeenth-century Battle of the Books opposed the moderns of that and the preceding century to the ancients of Greece and Rome. Dryden, in "An Essay of Dramatic Poesy," gave the moderns the best of it in drama, with Shakespeare as prime exhibit, and with modern progress in science as argument by analogy for the possibility of progress in other realms. Swift's "Battle of the Books," on the other hand, represents the moderns (including Dryden) as defeated by the ancients because they rely upon science and the venomous and cobwebby products of their own insides rather than upon the sweetness and light of humane tradition. From Swift's time to our own, the more extreme moderns have defined the meaningful past as extending a very short distance behind them; Allen Ginsberg's gospel is that Henry Ford was right, history is bunk and the past is irrelevant.[2]

In every context from interior decoration to religion, *modern* implies a contrast with the past, a break with tradition and convention. The twelfth-century Schoolmen who introduced dialectic into the new universities and broke with the tradition of classical humanism were called *moderni*. *Devotio moderna* in the sixteenth century opposed pilgrimages and excessive ornament and emphasized a stricter morality and personal piety. Modernism in various religious denominations has been opposed to papalism, fundamentalism, literalism, and traditionalism in general; it was

1. Charles Baudelaire, "The Painter of Modern Life," 1861, in *My Heart Laid Bare,* ed. Peter Quennell (N. Y., 1951), p. 37.
2. See below, note 4 to Chapter Seven.

condemned as a heresy by the Roman church in 1907, and the Vatican under Pope Paul has begun again to denounce neo-modernism.

When Matthew Arnold in 1857 entitled his inaugural lecture as Professor of Poetry at Oxford "On the Modern Element in Literature" (as Trilling [3] points out, it was an innovation to speak in English and on such a topic, even though only ancient literature was discussed), he equated *modern* with *rational, civilized, tolerant*, and he used the term achronologically, so that Periclean Greece, but not Elizabethan England, could be described as modern. Irving Babbitt, in *Rousseau and Romanticism* (1919) says of Goethe, Renan, Ste.-Beuve, and Arnold: "What all these writers mean by the modern spirit is the positive and critical spirit, the spirit that refuses to take things on authority." Babbitt affirms that he himself has tried to be "thoroughly modern in this sense. . . ." [4]

This honorific meaning survives, though it becomes increasingly rare in literature. Shakespeare used the word in the now obsolete sense of *ordinary, everyday:* "Full of wise saws and modern instances." Most subsequent literary uses have a stronger deprecatory overtone; there is an implied contrast between the unworthy present and the glories and certainties of the past. To cite a few examples almost at random, this overtone is clear in Fielding's play, *The Modern Husband* (1732), in Keats's fragment, "Modern Love," with its doubts that "ye may love in spite of beaver hats," in Meredith's quasi-sonnet sequence with the same title (1862), and in George Moore's *A Modern Lover* (1883). In "The Scholar Gypsy," Arnold spoke of "this strange disease of modern life / With its sick hurry, its divided aims." And in *Madame Bovary* (1857), the druggist Homais is a living parody of modernism in the honorific sense. From Flaubert on, most of the great modern writers have detested the popular modernism

3. Lionel Trilling, "On the Modern Element in Modern Literature," in *Beyond Culture* (N. Y., 1961).
4. Irving Babbitt, *Rousseau and Romanticism* (Boston, 1919), p. xi.

of the newspapers, with its shallow optimism based on the assumption of human perfectibility and automatic progress, its ignorance, superficiality, and contempt of the past. Thus Eliot's *After Strange Gods*, subtitled *A Primer of Modern Heresy*, begins: "*Le monde moderne avalit.* It also provincializes, and it can also corrupt." But if these writers in this sense reject the modern world, they do so with intense awareness and participation; they do not simply ignore or escape it. Baudelaire had already practiced in his own poetry the doctrine he expounded in his critique of the salon of 1861, "On the Heroism of Modern Life," urging painters to take as subjects the "pageant of fashionable life and the thousands of floating existences—criminals and kept women—which drift about in the underworld of a great city. . . ." [5] "The life of our city is rich in poetic and marvellous subjects. We are enveloped and steeped as though in an atmosphere of the marvellous; but we do not notice it." With appropriate irony, he asserts, "So there *are* such things as modern beauty and modern heroism!"

To sum up, it may be said that the self-conscious awareness of a break with the past may be felt in two main ways: as emancipation, a joyful release from the dead hand of convention, from stale pieties and restrictions; or as disinheritance, a loss of tradition, belief, and meaning. Probably both feelings always co-exist to some extent, in an ambivalence paralleling exactly the adolescent's feelings toward his parents (ontogeny repeating phylogeny again), and both feelings may well exhibit themselves alternately in the same writer. Much of the vitality of early modernism seems to come from the release of pent-up energies in iconoclasm, an exhilarating smashing-up of images and idols—as, for example, in Nietzsche, Ibsen, Samuel Butler, Shaw, early Pound, or, to take an extreme and late one, H. L. Mencken. In time, the sense of emancipation tends to grow uncertain of itself: Whitman's "Years of the modern! Yeats of the unperform'd!" becomes Hart Crane's "Years of the modern! Propulsions toward what capes?"

5. Baudelaire, op. cit., p. 128.

But sometimes the balance is precisely and ironically maintained, as in Eliot's account (1915) of Miss Helen Slingsby, after whose death "the footman sat upon the dining-table / Holding the second housemaid on his knees— / Who had always been so careful while her mistress lived." Similarly, Eliot's Miss Nancy Ellicott smoked,

> And danced all the modern dances
> And her aunts were not quite sure how they felt about it
> But they knew that it was modern.

She is no Lucifer, but "Matthew and Waldo" keep watch over her fall like Meredith's "army of unalterable law"—from behind the glass of the bookcase. With the later Eliot, of course, as with most of the great moderns most of the time, the feeling of disinheritance is dominant. Among the fragments at the end of *The Waste Land* one of the most poignant is that from Nerval's "El Desdichacho" ("The Disinherited"): *"Le Prince d'Aquitaine à la tour abolie."*

So much for a very sketchy indication of the range of meanings and connotations of the word *modern.* It would be an interesting study in semantic history, but is beyond our scope, to determine precisely when and how the general or descriptive term became attached as a specific historical label to the twentieth-century movement in the arts. Both meanings seem to be present already in such early titles as P. Meier-Graefe's *Modern Art* (1908) and T. E. Hulme's "Lecture on Modern Poetry," written in 1908–9 and published in 1914. The historical sense dominates in the description of *Rhythm,* a quarterly edited by J. M. Murry and others, 1911–13, as "The Yellow Book of the modern movement" (the original *Yellow Book* in 1894 had proclaimed that it would have "the courage of its modernness, and not tremble at the frown of Mrs. Grundy"), as in the titles of the *Modernist* (1919), the *Modern Review* (1922–24), and the *Survey of Modernist Verse* by Robert Graves and Laura Riding (1927), and it seems to be at least as important as the descriptive in most of the anthologies of *modern* poetry that followed Louis Untermeyer's first in 1919. The terminological problem is that the two meanings, descriptive and historical, can hardly continue indefinitely to coincide. (The same problem exists, of course, with regard to such terms as Symbolism, Romanticism, or Naturalism, though it is less confusing in these cases because the terms themselves have no time reference.) If modernism was a specific historical movement that reached its height in the 1920s, then obviously a time must come (if it has not already) when modernism will no longer be modern in the sense of *contemporary*. Or so it would appear, if modernism is a movement belonging to the same order as previous movements, and continuous with them. Before turning to this question of continuity, however, we must review the broad outlines of modernism as a historical movement and consider some of the attempts that have been made to define it.

In the largest sense, modernism as an era in Western culture has often been described as beginning with the Renaissance in Italy, with the Reformation, or with any of numerous later events from scientific and mathematical landmarks in the seventeenth century to revolutionary political ones in the late eighteenth. (The earliest beginning I have seen suggested was the title of an exhibition at the Institute of Contemporary Art in London, 1949: "40,000 Years of Modern Art." This made excellent sense as an indication of the link between modern and primitive art, but does not help us discriminate eras.) Plausible cases have been made for beginning with various mid-nineteenth-century publications as their centenaries have passed: *Moby-Dick* (1851), *Leaves of Grass* (1855), *Les Fleurs du Mal* and *Madame Bovary* (1857), *The Origin of Species* (1859), *Das Kapital* (Volume I, 1867). Northrop Frye holds that the "modern movement, properly speaking, began when Darwin finally shattered the old teleological conception of nature as reflecting an intelligent purpose." [6] The date that is perhaps most widely accepted, however, is 1870. This was the year the dogma of papal infallibility was pro-

6. Northrop Frye, *The Modern Century* (N. Y., 1967), p. 110.

nounced, the year Prussian militarism with its *blut und eisen* doctrines revealed itself in the Franco-Prussian war, and the year universal free compulsory education was introduced in England. These events marked the beginning of the end of liberal Christian humanism, already foreshadowed by Marx and Darwin.[7]

In 1870 Rimbaud was beginning his incredible three-year career as poet; Isidore Ducasse, "Comte de Lautréamont," died and his *Chants de Maldoror* was published. The masterworks of Flaubert and Baudelaire were thirteen years old. In 1873 Corbière's *Les Amours Jaunes* would appear, and in 1876 Mallarmé's *L'Après-midi d'une faune*. Dostoevsky had published *Crime and Punishment* (1866) and *The Idiot* (1869). Nietzsche's *Birth of Tragedy* would appear in two years. Ibsen had written *Brand* and *Peer Gynt*, and before the end of the decade would produce *A Pillar of Society* and *A Doll's House*. In the United States, the South had been defeated and the robber barons presided over a rapidly expanding capitalist society. Nineteen years after *Moby-Dick*, Melville had given up the attempt to make a career of authorship; his books all out of print, he worked as a customs inspector. Whitman fared slightly better, having expected massive public indifference; Emily Dickinson, secluded in Amherst, made no attempt to publish. Poe had been dead twenty-one years. Henry James had been writing reviews and short fiction for some years, and was soon to produce his first successful novels. In England, Hardy had begun writing novels, and in 1874 would publish *Far from the Madding Crowd*. G. M. Hopkins had renounced poetry, but in five years would write his first great poem in sprung rhythm, "The Wreck of the Deutschland." As to painting, Cézanne would exhibit at the Impressionist show of 1874, and by the end of the decade Van Gogh, prototype of Expressionists as Cézanne is of Cubists, would begin to paint.

There is, of course, no end to this kind of chronological citation; but perhaps these are sufficient to remind the reader of why

7. Cf. W. H. Auden, Introduction to *Poets of the English Language* (N. Y., 1950), V, xvii.

1870 is a plausible date to give for the beginning of modernism as an epoch in the cultural history of the West. For the beginning of modernism as a specific movement in the arts, 1909 seems a reasonable choice. Picasso and Braque, inspired by the Cézanne Memorial Exhibition of 1907, had independently painted Analytical Cubist works in 1908. Marinetti issued his *Futurist Manifesto* in 1909. De Chirico, immersed in Nietzsche, was incubating his Pittura Metafisica, and Kandinsky would produce in 1910 his first abstract watercolor. Schönberg wrote his atonal *Drei Klavierstücke* in 1909, and Ravel his *Gaspard de la Nuit.* Diaghilev's Ballet Russe gave its first Paris season in this year, with Stravinsky's *Fireworks;* in the next season they danced the *Firebird* to his music. T. E. Hulme and T. S. Eliot in complete independence of each other wrote, and the former published, verse that was distinctively modern; Pound, in London and meeting regularly (and separately) with Yeats, Ford Madox Ford, and Hulme and his proto-Imagists, published two volumes in 1909, *Personae* and *Exultations.* Joyce at this time had published only *Chamber Music* (1907) and a few stories and articles, but he had written *Dubliners* and had rewritten the first half of the *Portrait;* in 1909 he was back in Dublin briefly, negotiating to open a chain of cinemas. D. H. Lawrence published poetry and, the next year, fiction in Ford's *English Review,* which was the first modern literary magazine and had begun publication in December 1908. In 1909 Proust began work on *A la recherche,* and Freud lectured in the United States; Gertrude Stein published *Three Lives* and William James *A Pluralistic Universe.*

A new phase, or a new movement, had become clearly apparent in all the arts by the middle 1950s. Perhaps the best single date to give for it is 1957. Since this was the year of Sputnik, it has the virtue of reminding us that, as original modernism was related to the inventions of photography, radio, the cinema, the automobile and the airplane, so this second revolution was heralded by a new and accelerating wave of scientific and technological discoveries, from the atomic and hydrogen bombs to television,

the contraceptive pill, DNA, and other medical advances. Of
them all, however, Sputnik marked most clearly the beginning of
a new era, that of the conquest of space. In the arts the new
trends seemed in some ways to be a counter-revolution against
those that began in 1909, in others a renewal or continuation of
the original impulses. An important part of the central drive was
destructive, against both art and society. With Ionesco's *Bald
Prima Donna* (1950), the Theater of the Absurd began its as-
cendancy, fully established by Beckett's *Waiting for Godot*, performed in London in 1955. In England John Wain's *Hurry on
Down* (1953) and Kingsley Amis's *Lucky Jim* (1954) began a
new comic and anti-heroic trend in the novel. The most famous
protest against the social order was John Osborne's play, *Look
Back in Anger*, 1956, which gave a name to the movement, or
part of it. In poetry, the dominant figure was Philip Larkin,
whose *The Less Deceived* appeared in 1955; for reasons peculiar
to the British situation, he and the other poets represented in
Robert Conquest's anthology *New Lines* (1956) moved toward
restraint, wit, and regular forms. They were called The Movement, a rather pointless title except as indicating a general sense
that some movement was needed.

In the United States there was a widespread feeling, partly as a
reaction to the conformist pressures of Eisenhower's first term,
that it was time for a departure from orthodoxies. The most flamboyant result was the Beat movement, publicized incessantly in
1955 and represented in poetry by Allen Ginsberg's *Howl!*
(1956). This loose, emotional, personal verse, often sloppy and
often obscene, was the most extreme form of reaction against the
conception of poetry upheld by the New Critics, who had already been denounced by Karl Shapiro (*Beyond Criticism*, 1953)
and many others. In 1957 Jack Kerouac's Beat novel *On the Road*
appeared, and *Evergreen Review*, chief organ of the movement,
was founded. It is a curious fact that in 1957 appeared not only
Literary Criticism, by Cleanth Brooks and W. K. Wimsatt—perhaps the nearest equivalent to a *Summa* achieved by the New

Criticism—but the major works of the two critics who have dominated the scene in the following decade. (See Chapter Six.) The most important reason, however, for choosing 1957 as the date of the new movement is that this was the year Robert Lowell wrote his first poem in the new mode that came to be called "open" (or naked or confessional) poetry; and in retrospect it seems clear that this new mode is the most significant and lasting feature of the movement.[8]

Whether this mid-century movement is called post-modernism, neo-modernism, or anti-modernism will depend, obviously, on how we define modernism. Let us look briefly, then, at some of the more recent definitions. Edmund Wilson, in his immensely influential *Axel's Castle: A Study in the Imaginative Literature of 1870–1930* (1931), described modernism as essentially "the development of Symbolism and . . . its fusion or conflict with Naturalism." He thought of it as French in origin, and as homogeneous from 1870 through 1930. Though he found its great writers fascinating and admirable, Wilson believed modernism to be obsolescent, and he called urgently for a more socially and politically oriented literature. Richard Ellmann and Charles Feidelson, Jr., in the anthology *The Modern Tradition* (1965), interpret modernism very broadly as a distinctive mode of imagination going back at least to the mid-eighteenth century for its beginnings. Modernism is, they say, a paradoxically untraditional tradition, for it "strongly implies some sort of historical discontinuity, either a liberation from inherited patterns or, at another extreme, deprivation and disinheritance." On the other hand, they argue that the "modernists have been as much imbued with a feeling for their historical role, their relation to the past, as with a feeling of historical discontinuity." And they endorse Stephen Spender's view, in *The Struggle of the Modern* (1963), that the

8. This was also the date of Robert Penn Warren's *Promises*, marking the appearance of a distinguished older poet in the new mode, of Ted Hughes's first volume, *The Hawk in the Rain*, and of James Dickey's first mature work. These poets are discussed below in Chapters Five and Seven.

modern finds its character by "confronting the past and including
this confrontation within itself as part of a single total experience," or "vision of the whole." Frank Kermode, in *The Sense of
an Ending* (1968) and in a series of essay-reviews most of which
are now collected in *Continuities* (1968), argues for the essential
similarity of *palaeo-* and neo-modernism, though he distinguishes
between traditional and anti-traditional moderns in both movements. His thesis (to simplify drastically) is that apocalyptism,
the sense of an ending, is the common element in the two movements, "that certain aspects of earlier modernism really were so
revolutionary that we ought not to expect—even with everything
so speeded up—to have the pains and pleasures of another compa-
rable movement quite so soon." Irving Howe, in the introduction
to his anthology *Literary Modernism* (1967), argues for Nihilism
as "the central preoccupation, the inner demon at the heart" of
modern literature from Dostoevsky to Beckett. This thesis goes
only one step beyond that advanced by Lionel Trilling in his famous essay, "On the Modern Element in Modern Literature" (in
Beyond Culture, 1961, and also in the Howe anthology), that
modernism is essentially the drive toward freedom from society,
culture, and civilization and toward anarchic surrender to experience. (In *Beyond Culture* Trilling makes his historical conception
explicit: "What I am calling the modern period had its beginning
in the latter part of the eighteenth century and its apogee in the
first quarter of the twentieth century. We continue the direction
it took.") In sharp contrast, Harry Levin argues in "What Was
Modernism?" that the great moderns were "the children of Humanism and the Enlightenment" and that the anti-intellectual
strain is characteristic rather of what "I would prefer to call
post-modern," the epigones of the 1960s.[9] Cyril Connolly, in *The
Modern Movement* (1965), propounds a definition rather like
Levin's: "The modern spirit was a combination of certain intellectual qualities inherited from the Enlightenment: lucidity,

9. Harry Levin, *Refractions: Essays in Comparative Literature* (N. Y.,
1966).

irony, scepticism, intellectual curiosity, combined with the passionate intensity and enhanced sensibility of the Romantics, their rebellion and sense of technical experiment, their awareness of living in a tragic age." Again like Levin, Connolly assumes regretfully that modernism is now a thing of the past. Most of the recent interpretations that hold the movement of 1957 to be different from that of 1909 (anti-holist?) have been based on values very unlike those of Levin and Connolly, however; they have been denunciations of the central modernism that began in 1909 as a detour or dead end away from the main highway of tradition. Perhaps the most ardent proponents of such views are Graham Hough and Robert Graves among the British and Karl Shapiro in America. All three proclaim exultantly that modernism died and was succeeded by neo-Romanticism in 1957, if not before; and they have many followers.

The issues involved in these definitions are both axiological and historical. The question of whether modernism is radically new and incommensurably superior—or inferior—to the past, or whether, on the other hand, it contains so little novelty that it can be absorbed into a cyclical view of history, is not one that we can confront profitably at this point. We can, however, examine briefly what seems to be the chief historical question, that of the relation of modernism to Romanticism.

At the beginning, literary modernism was explicitly and polemically anti-Romantic. T. E. Hulme and Irving Babbitt (no literary modernist, but an important influence on others who were) show some of the political coloration of Charles Maurras and the Action Française group in their active campaigning against Romanticism. Pound, in part through Hulme's influence, denounced romantic emotionalism, vagueness, and sloppiness and preached the classical virtues of craftsmanship, economy, objectivity, precision. As they expounded it, the Imagist doctrine was primarily anti-Romantic, intended to produce hard, dry, classical verse. (In practice, much Imagist verse was literally neo-classical in the sense of being modeled upon Greek or Latin poetry.) Eliot, influenced first by Babbitt, later by Pound, and still later by Hulme's *Speculations* (when they were published in 1924), inveighed against Romanticism on moral and religious, as well as aesthetic, grounds and called for verse to be impersonal and traditional. Like succeeding "new" critics, he eschewed emphasis on simple emotion or the poet's personality in favor of close analysis to bring out the formal, rhetorical, and intellectual complexity of the poem; and he was sometimes guilty of prejudice against some Romantic poets.

There has been, however, a growing tendency in recent years to argue that the whole modern movement, in both poetry and criticism, is and has always been essentially Romantic throughout.[10] The anti-Romanticism which, as we have indicated, was so clearly apparent early in the movement is explained away as either a superficial disguise or a brief phase which was soon ended. To simplify, we may distinguish three versions of this argument.

The first is that of Edmund Wilson in *Axel's Castle*. Of modern poets in English, Wilson dealt only with Eliot and Yeats. His thesis was that they, like the other writers he discussed—Gertrude Stein, Joyce, Valéry, Proust, Villiers de l'Isle-Adam, and Rimbaud—based their work essentially on the French Symbolist aesthetic, and that the Symbolist movement was historically a second

10. E.g. Harold Bloom, *The Visionary Company* (N. Y., 1961); Richard Foster, *The New Romantics: A Reappraisal of the New Criticism* (N. Y., 1952). Sir Herbert Read, himself a fine poet as well as critic, consistently maintained that modern poetry, like all good poetry, is romantic in a psychologistic and organistic sense; see his *Form in Modern Poetry* (London, 1932).

An attractive and plausible version of this argument is that of Robert Langbaum, *The Poetry of Experience: The Dramatic Monologue in Modern Literary Tradition* (N. Y., 1963; originally 1957). Langbaum aligns Romanticism and modernism as a single developing tradition which he calls "poetry of experience." Romanticism, he says, was an attempt to *escape* from the faults with which the poetry has been charged: subjectivity, sentimentalism, inflated diction, formlessness. These faults he projects back upon the eighteenth century. But the book is lucid and suggestive.

wave of Romanticism. Modernism, according to Wilson, was merely a second wave of Symbolism. The French Symbolists, as Wilson interprets them, reject science and ordinary life either as Axel did (in Villiers's play), to pursue an ultimate aestheticism, or as Rimbaud did in real life, giving up poetry also in search of the primitive and a life of action. Wilson sees the same withdrawal from the world in the modern writers he considers, and he warns that it can lead only to these alternative routes, neither of which is satisfactory. Wilson's placing of Yeats and Eliot in this context had the effect of exaggerating their resemblance to the French Symbolists, and his interpretation of them as escapist seemed to be based on the assumption that the modern poet must accept a "scientific" version of reality and a goal of political action. But his extremely attractive and convincing presentation has, I think, made many later critics predisposed to see the moderns in his terms, as late Symbolist-Romantics.

The second version of the argument depends upon a revisionist interpretation of English Romanticism. It is not conceded that Romanticism was escapist; instead, the revolutionary, prophetic, and creative aspects of the movement are stressed. The beginning of both Romanticism and modernism, as Northrop Frye puts it, is Rousseau's

> assumption that civilization was a purely human artifact, something that man had made . . . and was at all times entirely responsible for. Above all, it was something for which the only known model was in the human mind. . . . The effect of such an assumption is twofold. First, it puts the arts in the center of civilization. The basis of civilization is now the creative power of man; its model is the human vision revealed in the arts. Second, this model, as well as the sources of creative power, are now located in the mind's internal heaven. . . .[11]

In all important respects, Frye argues, modernism is continuous with Romanticism; the anti-Romantic movement in criticism "is

11. Northrop Frye (ed.), *Romanticism Reconsidered* (N. Y., 1963), p. 10.

now over and done with," for "Anti-Romanticism, in short, had
no resources for becoming anything more than a post-Romantic
movement." This interpretation of Romanticism places William
Blake at the center—a procedure somewhat unhistorical, in view
of Blake's obscurity in his own time, but with the virtue of making the central Romantic a formidable and challenging figure,
whom no one can take less than seriously as artist and as thinker.
To stress the characteristics the other Romantics share with Blake
is thus to rehabilitate the whole movement. The interpretation
has a certain broad historical plausibility in placing the beginning
of both modernism and Romanticism in the revolutionary age of
the late eighteenth century, and it can be supported by the indis-
putable fact of Blake's considerable direct influence on numerous
modern poets from Yeats on. But Romanticism as thus defined
has nothing to do with the retreat from reality and the connotations of ineffectual dreaminess which are part of the meaning of
the word for such critics as Wilson. Furthermore, there is a certain blurring of necessary distinctions in simply taking modernism
as coincident with Romanticism. The innocent reader who approaches Eliot or Pound as he would Wordsworth or Shelley, in
the faith that they are all Romantic and therefore to be read in
the same way, will soon discover that he has been misled. The argument thus seems to lack operational validity. Or, to put it another way, while there are undeniably many respects in which
the two movements overlap, discriminating between them is more
interesting and likely to be more fruitful than simply observing
their very general resemblances.

The third version of the thesis that modernism is Romantic is
that which finds the essence of modernism in a special poetics of
the Image, and traces the continuous development of this doctrine from the English Romantics through both English and
French Symbolists to Yeats, Pound and the Imagists, and Eliot.
This is, of course, the thesis brilliantly propounded by Frank
Kermode in *Romantic Image* (1957). In contrast to the exponents
of the view just discussed, Kermode seems to disapprove of (at

the same time that he is fascinated by) the doctrine he expounds, which represents the artist as alienated prophet, seer, and magician, and the Image as mysterious and ultimately supernatural. Kermode is, however, scrupulously concerned to formulate a responsible interpretation of these very complicated issues, while some other critics have used his book in a different spirit for literary polemics. Thus the title, *Romantic Image,* is an accurate designation of Kermode's central theme; but it has led a good many people who have read it hastily or not at all, or who use it as grist for their mill, to assume that it proves modern poetry to be Romantic and Imagistic. Kermode in fact argues only that modern criticism (and the only critic he discusses at length is Eliot) is dominated by a special notion of the Image; he never suggests that modern poetry (and in fact the only poet he discusses at length is Yeats) can be identified with the small dead-end movement of Imagism. He does argue that Eliot's criticism is Romantic, carefully defining that term as referring to the "high valuation placed during this period upon the image-making powers of the mind at the expense of its rational powers, and to the substitution of organicist for mechanistic modes of thinking about works of art"; and certainly he implies that so to exhibit Romanticism, while professing the reverse, tends to discredit Eliot as a critic. Kermode wishes to do this, as he candidly states, in order to rehabilitate Milton and, more broadly, a poetic not based on the Image. To this end, he argues that Eliot's theory of the "dissociation of sensibility" is simply a back-projection of Symbolist doctrine into history: Milton "was the main sufferer in the great experiment of projecting onto an historical scale a developed Romantic-Symbolist theory of the Image." [12] There is, he argues, no substance to the conventional analogy between Donne and other seventeenth-century Metaphysical poets and Eliot and other moderns. To dismiss this resemblance as illusory is essential to disposing of Eliot as a Symbolist; and in spite of his evident love for Eliot's poetry, this is what Kermode seems to intend.

12. Frank Kermode, *Romantic Image* (London, 1957), p. 150.

Kermode's careful definitions and qualifications, as we have intimated, are abandoned by critics who use his work as a source for polemics. In *Image and Experience* (1960), for example, Graham Hough argues that Imagism is the "hard irreducible core" (and we note the conspiratorial overtones, as in "hard-core Communists") of modern poetry, and that it derives from French Symbolism: Imagism is "Symbolism without the magic." In contrast to Kermode's emphasis on the continuity of the moderns with nineteenth-century English Romanticism and with the Anglo-French tradition of Symbolism, with its English roots going back beyond Blake to the seventeenth century, Hough sees modernism as a revolution resulting from "an almost world-wide poetic conspiracy," discontinuous with the past and a "detour, a diversion from the main road." With a scarcely concealed xenophobia, he calls modern poetry hostile to the spirit of the English poetic tradition; not only is it French in origin, but it is dominated by "a distinctly American set of literary values." (From this definition it is only a short step to the tag of "Franco-American modernism" with which Robert Graves dismisses most of his contemporaries.) And Hough vigorously repudiates what he takes to be the modernist, or Imagist-Symbolist, poetic: "the collocation of images is not a method at all, but the negation of method . . . a poem, internally considered, ought to make the same kind of sense as any other discourse . . ." (p. 25).

At this point we are involved in a whole tangle of questions, all concerned somehow with various kinds of continuity or discontinuity. Since *discontinuity* appears to be the key term, let us see if we can clarify it.

DISCONTINUITY

T. E. Hulme's *Speculations* begins:

One of the main achievements of the nineteenth century was the elaboration and universal application of the principle of *continuity*. The destruction of this conception is, on the contrary, an urgent necessity of the present.

The achievement Hulme has primarily in mind is, of course, that of the nineteenth-century biologists and geologists in developing the theory of evolution. The assumption that man is continuous with nature is basic to Darwinism or Marxism; in literature, it manifests itself as Naturalism and the "disappearance of God." Hulme was prophetic in suggesting that a preoccupation with discontinuities was to be characteristic of the twentieth century, though he does not seem to have foreseen the anguish that was to accompany it. The special horror with which awareness of some forms of discontinuity fills us results from a contrast with nineteenth-century historicism: to take a mild academic example, the reaction of old-fashioned literary historians to the insistence of the New Critics that literature was *not* continuous with history was to denounce the new doctrine as immoral and heretical. Whether we like it or not, however, we recognize the perception of discontinuity, specific or generalized, as descriptive of our age and of ourselves, from Forster's "Only connect" to Yeats's "Things fall apart; the centre cannot hold; / Mere anarchy is loosed upon the world . . . " and Eliot's "I can connect / Nothing with nothing" and "These fragments I have shored against my ruins." The exploration of discontinuity is as characteristic of the twentieth century as the elaboration of continuity was of the nineteenth.

The shift is apparent in the sciences precisely at the turn of the century. Biologists studying inheritance became interested about 1900 in discontinuous variation, or mutation; they rediscovered Mendel's papers, and genetics arose as a separate science.[13] Planck's quantum theory, in the same year, revealed a fundamental discontinuity in the nature of matter and motion, or energy, and was the basis of many further theories such as Heisenberg's indeterminacy principle. The most significant of all was Einstein's special theory of relativity (1905), in which space and time were conceived of as a *continuum* (thus positing, in a sense, a new kind of continuity to subsume discontinuities). This *continuum*,

13. Charles Singer, *A Short History of Scientific Ideas to 1900* (Oxford, 1959), p. 490.

however, meant the abandonment of physical absolutes as the previous century's development of continuity meant the abandonment of metaphysical absolutes. All these formulations led to new concepts of the nature of reality: not only space and time, mass and energy, but cause and effect, observer and observed, were revealed as more complex and more curiously inter-related than had been thought.

As we have said, nineteenth-century acceptance of the principle of continuity led to the abandonment of spiritual absolutes and to the conviction that time and change are the primary realities. In his essay on Coleridge (1866), Walter Pater said:

> Modern thought is distinguished from ancient by its cultivation of the "relative spirit" in place of the "absolute." . . . Those sciences of observation reveal types of life evanescing into each other by inexpressible refinements of change. . . . The faculty for truth is recognised as a power of distinguishing and fixing delicate and fugitive detail.[14]

The parallel with the Impressionist painters—and, later, novelists —is sufficiently obvious. The idea of art as freeing man from crystallized perception, habit, and the like, is basic to such German Romantics as Schelling and Novalis (whose "Philosophiren ist dephlegmatisiren, vivificiren" Pater quotes in the conclusion to *The Renaissance*) and becomes even more prominent in the latter part of the century. It carries over into the early part of the new century in Bergson's emphasis—to be found also in Hulme and Pound—on the importance of immediate as against congealed experience, of avoiding abstractions, accepting the flux and constant metamorphosis. But the strivings of the modern artists toward spatial form, as in Cubism, Imagism, and the like, were reactions against this time-continuity obsession, which was bitterly attacked somewhat later by Wyndham Lewis in *Time and Western Man* (1927).

14. Quoted in Thomas H. Jackson, *The Early Poetry of Ezra Pound* (Cambridge, Mass., 1968), pp. 112–13.

The cinema was immensely influential as both symbol and—in the arts—cause of the new emphasis on discontinuity. Becoming popular soon after the turn of the century, it revealed that continuity (in its most primitive sense relating to physical motion) was an illusion, that static and discontinuous photographs can produce the illusion of movement. (Obviously, the revelation was itself illusory: it revealed nothing about the nature of reality, but only how an illusion was produced.) As in the ancient paradoxes, apparent continuity was analyzed into a series of disjunct discontinuities—but this time not in abstract verbal analysis but with what looked like photographic evidence. No wonder Bergson, in *L'évolution créatrice* (1907), bitterly opposed this cinematographic concept of change. Arnold Hauser comments, "The new concept of time, whose basic element is simultaneity and whose nature consists in the spatialization of the temporal element, is expressed in no other genre so impressively as in this youngest art, which dates from the same period as Bergson's philosophy of time." [15] The movies had other important influences aside from this focusing of attention on the phenomena of discontinuity. They were a step further in the direction of naturalism and documentation, bringing still photography alive; but they were at the same time a demonstration of how the camera can lie. From the beginning, the movie-makers were fascinated by the possibilities of trick photography; and so from the beginning the movies demonstrated the element of fakery and illusion in art, the distance between it and reality. *Montage*, speeding up and slowing down the motion, editing, double exposures, reversing—most of the basic forms of trickery were exploited early, so that film art as heterocosm, the creation of another reality, was at least as significant as its naturalistic use.

Four basic forms of discontinuity can be distinguished in modern literature.

(1) *Metaphysical discontinuity*. Hulme does not use this phrase, but it describes his position. Hulme's basic objection to

15. Arnold Hauser, *The Social History of Art* (N. Y., 1958), IV, 239.

nineteenth-century continuity was that it denied any distinction between the human and the natural. He argues for an absolute discontinuity between the organic world, the inorganic world, and the world of ethical and religious values; between them are chasms with no bridges. Only by understanding this can we "recover the real significance of many things which it seems absolutely impossible for the 'modern' mind to understand." [16] Hulme held "the religious conception of ultimate values to be right, the humanist wrong" (p. 70). At about the same time, Irving Babbitt was insisting on the discontinuity between natural and human—or, in the passage he loved to quote from Emerson, between "law for man" and "law for thing"—as the basis of his New Humanist creed. Eliot, influenced by both Babbitt and Hulme, posits a discontinuity between the natural, the human, and the supernatural. In his introduction to Pascal's *Pensées* (1932), he praises Pascal's "analysis of the *three orders:* the order of nature, the order of mind, and the order of charity. These three are *discontinuous;* the higher is not implicit in the lower as in an evolutionary doctrine it would be." He adds in a footnote: "An important modern theory of discontinuity, suggested partly by Pascal, is sketched . . . by T. E. Hulme. . . ." Similarly, Allen Tate in 1940 acknowledges Hulme's influence, affirming his belief in "a radical discontinuity between the physical and the spiritual realms." [17] This is the philosophical basis of Tate's attack on naturalism and positivism. In his later essays he attacks that angelism or gnosticism that arises from the corresponding error of ignoring the discontinuity between the human and the supernatural: "I call that human imagination angelic which tries to disintegrate or to circumvent the image in the illusory pursuit of essence." [18] Metaphysical discontinuity is, then, primarily a defense against naturalism and rationalism.

(2) *Aesthetic discontinuity.* Discontinuity between art and life has been asserted and denied variously in different contexts since

16. T. E. Hulme, *Speculations* (London, 1924), p. 11.
17. Allen Tate, *On the Limits of Poetry* (N. Y., 1948), p. 4.
18. Allen Tate, *The Forlorn Demon* (Chicago, 1953), p. 37.

Poe and Baudelaire, and has constituted a central preoccupation of the moderns. As a reaction against naturalism, moralism, and philistinism, many *Symbolistes* and decadents flamboyantly asserted this type of discontinuity both in art and in their personal lives: one thinks of Axel's famous "As for living, our servants can do that for us," of Dorian Gray, Des Esseintes, Dowson, and Wilde before the trial of 1895. In general, the moderns of the early twentieth century strongly rejected aesthetic discontinuity. Thus I. A. Richards, in *Principles of Literary Criticism* (1924), ridicules the "phantom aesthetic state" and insists that poetry is continuous with other forms of experience and hence open to inspection; Eliot insists that the poet is not a mysterious outcast, but a man like others, possibly a bank clerk, and that his art should in any case not express his personality. Both insist that the reader of poetry must be involved, an active collaborator, in contrast to the passively manipulated victim of the advertiser or propagandist; this might be described as the making of art continuous with the best of the reader's experience, or selective continuity. The notion of art as not mimesis but the creation of a heterocosm, a world parallel to but distinct from the "real" one, is sometimes a form of aesthetic discontinuity. But most of the great moderns have felt impelled to prevent the reader from escaping into the art-world by reminding him, sometimes wittily and sometimes crudely, that art is an illusion and a game (though the practitioners of *collage* and *trouvage* and of the anti-arts which consist in the absence of an art-work so that attention will be focused on random sounds or sights seem also to be saying that life is art if regarded as such). Brecht and many later playwrights refuse to provide a stage-world for the spectator to escape into because they want to maintain a rigorous continuity between the stage and the moral and political aspects of the audience's life; Auden, having asserted a kind of aesthetic discontinuity ("Art is not life and cannot be / A midwife to society"), and having called poetry a game, devotes himself with increasing rigor to making his poetry tell the truth.

(3) *Rhetorical discontinuity.* This is related to the preceding,

since rhetorical discontinuity depends upon the assumption of some form of aesthetic discontinuity. In its simplest form, it asserts that poetry, in contrast to prose, is discontinuous in structure; that it is either alogical or governed by a logic different from that of prose. Rhetorically discontinuous poetry is elliptical, lacking the transitions and connections of prose, its images juxtaposed without comment or explanation, and arranged in a non-rational order. As this description suggests, cinematic techniques illustrate a similar kind of structure and have certainly exerted a powerful influence; the other arts, too, exhibit parallel trends in breaking with the rational and conscious. Surrealism, following the logic of dream and the unconscious, is an obvious example, as is aleatory music, following the principle of randomness.

The basic notion of the poem as drama (rather than statement) and as gaining intensity by ellipsis was clearly defined by Pound as early as 1908, in a letter to W. C. Williams: "To me the short so-called dramatic lyric . . . is the poetic part of a drama the rest of which (to me the prose part) is left to the reader's imagination or implied or set in a short note. I catch the character I happen to be interested in at the moment he interests me . . . And the rest of the play would bore me and presumably the audience. . . ." [19] By common consent, Pound's *Cantos*, from 1917 to the present, is the most extreme and lengthy example of rhetorical discontinuity, though Eliot's *Waste Land* (in structuring which Pound also had a hand) is also often cited. In his introduction to his translation of St.-John Perse's *Anabase* (1930) Eliot stated most explicitly the doctrine that there is a specifically poetical order of images. He follows a French critic in arguing that any obscurity in Perse is "due to the suppression of 'links in the chain,' of explanatory and connecting matter. . . ." And he continues: "The justification of such abbreviation of method is that the sequence of images coincides and concentrates into one intense impression. . . ." "Such selection of a sequence of images and ideas has noth-

19. D. D. Paige (ed.), *The Letters of Ezra Pound 1907–1941* (N. Y., 1950), pp. 3-4.

ing chaotic about it. There is a logic of the imagination as well as a logic of concepts." *Anabase*, he argues, is poetry because its "sequences, its logic of imagery, are those of poetry and not of prose. . . ." Eliot may have been betrayed into somewhat incautious generalization here by his generous impulse to justify Perse; he has been severely taken to task for it by Yvor Winters and critics of similar disposition, who accuse him of advocating and practising "imitative form," the representation of chaos by chaos.

Donald Davie, in *Articulate Energy* (1955), makes rhetorical discontinuity his definition of modernism:

> . . . the break with the past is at bottom a change of attitude towards poetic syntax. It is from that point of view . . . that modern poetry, so diverse in all other ways, is seen as one. And we can define it thus: What is common to all modern poetry is the assertion or the assumption (most often the latter) that syntax in poetry is wholly different from syntax as understood by logicians and grammarians. . . . This is, surely, the one symbolist innovation that is at the root of all the other technical novelties that the symbolist poets introduced (1966 ed., p. 148).

As we shall see, Davie's assumption that the technique comes from French Symbolism is extremely dubious; some argue that the innovator is Wordsworth in the "Lucy poems," and others make the point that the distinction is always one of degree: insofar as the poet "nothing affirmeth," in Sidney's phrase, his syntax is never really that of discursive prose; he does not make a statement but tells a story or enacts a drama. The technique seems therefore dubious as a criterion of modernity, for much great modern poetry is syntactically orthodox, while parts of Aeschylus and Shakespeare according to this standard are post-Symbolist. But these are complicated matters, to which we will be returning in various contexts throughout the book.

(4) *Temporal discontinuity*. This is the type with which we began, whose esoteric version is Einsteinian time-space convertibility and whose exoteric analogue is the movies. The notion of spa-

tial form and of simultaneity, unquestionably very important in early twentieth-century modernism, involves both this and the preceding type of discontinuity. Before going on to consider historical discontinuity, the most significant and familiar form of temporal, the reader may find it convenient to have the four basic kinds summed up in tabular form:

Metaphysical: natural / human / supernatural
Aesthetic: art / life, or mimesis / heterocosm
Rhetorical: prose / poetry, or reason / imagination
Temporal: past / present / future.

I am tempted to add another category—Psychological—to cover both awareness of discontinuity in general and specific awareness of division within the psyche; this would include Eliot's "dissociation of sensibility" and other such formulations. But since we already have a table which is formidably, and perhaps speciously, systematic in appearance, it is probably best simply to note the relation without setting up psychological discontinuity as a category of the same order.

To resume, then, with the *historical* aspect of temporal discontinuity. Since the modern pertains to "the present and recent times," whatever is modern is, by definition, different from the past. But the art—and life—of the twentieth century seem to be more different from those of the past than has been the case in any previous age. A self-conscious awareness of a break with the past was a prominent characteristic of the proto-modernism of the late nineteenth century. Ibsen spoke of the "great chasm between yesterday and today" and declared a "war to the knife between two epochs"; Shaw had a passion for change and novelty, and was reluctant to acknowledge his debt even to such spiritual fathers as Marx, Ibsen, and Nietzsche. "To a large extent Shaw's ethic is one of discontinuity, of experimentation, of progress," says Ohmann, and he goes on to show that a deliberate cultivation of discontinuity is the basis of Shaw's style.[20] Toward the end of the century apocalyptic feelings of despair (or, very rarely, of triumph) become common among writers of the *fin de siècle;* Bergonzi has shown how important the expectation of *fin du globe* was in the scientific romances of H. G. Wells during this decade.[21] According to Virginia Woolf's famous statement, "on or about December, 1910, human nature changed";[22] as we have seen, the concept of biological mutation becomes prominent with the turn of the century; and the assumption that fundamental change in human nature is possible is essential to Marxist, anarchist, and other revolutionary political doctrines. (See Conrad, *The Secret Agent,* 1908. Obviously, any political revolutionary is advocating a kind of discontinuity.) From, say, 1890 to 1930 or later, the rejection of Victorianism was like an extremely protracted adolescence. There is always an analogy between historical change and the growth of an individual, since the present must emerge from the past as the adolescent achieves independence from his parents without losing touch with them, if all goes well. Since the beginning of modernism this process has become steadily more difficult and the gap between the generations has grown progressively wider. The feeling was very widespread that World War I marked the end of a major era, if not of civilization. But there is no need to belabor the obvious fact that a special kind of time-consciousness, marked by awareness of a break with the past, has been a prominent characteristic of the modern psyche.

There have always been some moderns who, in their ignorance or silliness, have been glad to accept historical discontinuity because they were certain that the past was irrelevant and that we therefore need not trouble ourselves with relating it to the present. Some beautiful early specimens are preserved forever in Swift's *Tale of a Tub* and Pope's *Dunciad.* But the present cen-

20. Richard M. Ohmann, *Shaw* (Middletown, Conn., 1962), p. 43.
21. Bernard Bergonzi, *The Early H. G. Wells: A Study of the Scientific Romances* (Toronto, 1961).
22. Virginia Woolf, *Mr. Bennett and Mrs. Brown* (London, 1924), p. 4.

tury has seen this position adopted by an increasing number of people who seem neither ignorant nor foolish. Their argument is based, directly or indirectly, on the recent history of the natural sciences, in which the past is increasingly insignificant in comparison to the present and the future. Thus the statistical generalization could be made in 1965 that of all the scientists who had ever lived, three-fourths were then alive; and of the total of scientific knowledge then in existence, two-thirds had been discovered since 1945. In 1969, I have seen the same generalization with the first fraction changed from three-fourths to nine-tenths; I am not sure whether a different method of calculation was being employed or whether the proportion is thought to have increased that rapidly. At any rate, the number of scientists and the amount of knowledge both continue to increase with incredible speed; and this is the psychologically significant point. Since the *rate* of change in science and technology accelerates constantly, the future is in many important respects unpredictable and unimaginable even at short range.

Futurism, apparently the first movement in the arts to be based explicitly on the acceptance of historical discontinuity, flourished from 1909 to 1915. It chief spokesman, Marinetti, argued that science and technology had brought about a complete change in the human psyche and sensibility, so that art must undergo the same kind of radical and violent change; he therefore called for the demolition of museums and libraries.[23] But Futurism, though it had a considerable impact on painting and sculpture, influenced English poetry chiefly in leading the pioneers of modernism to clarify their positions. Pound, Hulme, and Wyndham Lewis campaigned actively against Futurism in London from 1912 on; they ridiculed its romantic worship of the machine and of speed, danger, action, noise, and violence ("Automobilism") and started their own short-lived movement, Vorticism, to supersede it. Hulme called Futurism "the deification of the flux, the last efflo-

23. See Marianne Martin, *Futurist Art and Theory 1909–1915* (Oxford, 1968), p. 389.

rescence of impressionism"; Pound objected to Vachel Lindsay, for whom Harriet Monroe was full of patriotic enthusiasm, that he was really "of Marinetti's people"; and in his pamphlet of 1917 Eliot paid tribute to Pound for having "perhaps done more than anyone to keep Futurism out of England." [24] Others react differently to the same conviction of absolute discontinuity. While the Futurists gladly abandoned the past to embrace a triumphant future, the Dadaists (1916–23) felt that the loss of the past made both present and future meaningless, though often funny. Most Surrealists have reacted similarly, perceiving the break with the past as rendering the present absurd, with varying shades of grimness and wit. But since their central belief is that rational and conscious meaning is unimportant, this has not made them unhopeful of the future: most of them see the liberation of the Unconscious as the essential task of our age, and some believe that progress is being made. As we shall see in Chapter Seven, there is a definite link between these groups and the new practitioners of the anti-arts who rose to prominence in the 1950s.

The most spectacular recent argument for certain kinds of discontinuity has been that of H. M. McLuhan. Though we cannot here do justice to McLuhan's complex and much-debated ideas, we can indicate briefly how they relate to the categories we have been discussing. Even the expectation of continuity, McLuhan contends, is a manifestation of the Gutenberg mentality; the modern sciences and arts all assume discontinuity. A page of a newspaper exemplifies this basic modern discontinuity, for it is a mosaic of items juxtaposed at random, rather than a series of items ordered in linear fashion, to be apprehended in temporal sequence. Instantaneous apprehension of a total configuration, a unified field, is characteristic of the modern Electric Age, as opposed to the older successive apprehension of individual items in a prescribed order. Modern culture is aural, tribal, and concerned

24. Hulme, *Speculations*, p. 94; Pound, quoted in Harriet Monroe, *A Poet's Life* (N. Y., 1938), p. 368; Eliot, *To Criticize the Critic* (London, 1965), p. 174.

with relations, in contrast to the visual, individualistic, mechanical culture of the Gutenberg Galaxy. McLuhan's argument is, then, directed primarily at justifying *rhetorical* discontinuity, or alogical structure; his attitude toward *historical* discontinuity is more complex, for he argues that to accept discontinuity with the Gutenberg tradition of Western culture is to reaffirm continuity with an older and larger tradition.

McLuhan posits a major change in the Western psyche: not a mutation, but a fundamental change produced by the effect of electronic media. With absolute certainty, he proclaims the doom of Western civilization as we have known it. But he differs from other apostles of historical discontinuity in that he does not anticipate a future of radical novelty, but rather a return of the West to the great tradition from which our Gutenberg episode was, in the long perspective, a mere temporary deviation. (In this, as in many other respects, McLuhan tries to have it both ways.) His argument for discontinuity is based on analogy with scientific method and generalization from the presumed results of applied science (the effect of electronic media on the human psyche). He does not argue that the past is irrelevant: his essential thesis is that the future into which the new media are taking us so rapidly is not unknown, but a return to the tribal and aural past of the pre-Renaissance West, and what has remained the psychic norm outside the West, as in Russia, China, India, and Africa. McLuhan is thus no Futurist. The combination of a tribal and aural culture with modern science and technology in the Electric Age will surely be a new thing, however, though McLuhan does not stress its novelty.

To recapitulate, we may say that of the two basic reactions to the notion of historical discontinuity, the most extreme form of the first is Futurism, taking the break with the past as emancipation from the dead hand and looking forward to a triumphant future, free and untrammeled. McLuhan, with his faith in automatic salvation by television, seems usually to feel this kind of optimism. As we have seen, Ibsen, Shaw, and many other very early

moderns exhibited similar attitudes, though in them, as in the
Sunday newspapers and the man in the street, optimism always
alternated with apocalyptic dread and fear. (Bergonzi's study of
the scientific romances of H. G. Wells reveals this alternation in
Wells with particular clarity, from awed contemplation of the
technical marvels of the future to visions of Armageddon and
Doomsday.)

Most serious writers and artists of the present century have exhibited the other reaction, however, regarding the break with the
past as disinheritance or Fall. This historical catastrophism has
been a central theme of modern art, and the concomitant view of
the present as a waste land, now that civilization is destroyed and
human nature changed, becomes, with its wrenching sense of loss,
the dominant myth. Of course, people in all ages have felt that
the present was a sad decline from the past, that they lived in
changing times when things were especially difficult. Living in
the present is always hard, and the grass always looks greener in
the past. But modern artists feel this with a special intensity and
make the feeling central to their work. This is true not only of
the conservative art of literature, but of the other arts. According
to Harold Rosenberg, the most radical of modern artists—the action painters—hold that past art is irrelevant because the present
age is sterile, meaningless, and mechanical.[25] The late Sir Herbert
Read, one of the most eloquent and indefatigable defenders of
modern painting and sculpture, said that he had always regarded
modern art as "an art of protest—protest against a barbarous civilization that is indifferent to all spiritual and aesthetic values." [26]
And certainly most practitioners of the arts of the Absurd seem
to imply a similar view. All the arts, then, from the pioneering
moderns down to the latest manifestations of anti-art, testify massively to the artists' awareness of a tremendous change; many
works depend for their central meaning on a contrast, explicit or
implied, between the meaningless present and an earlier world of

25. Harold Rosenberg, *The Tradition of the New* (N. Y., 1961).
26. Herbert Read, *Letter to a Young Painter* (London, 1962), p. 64.

order and significance. As mystic wound, this is second in importance only to the belief that God has disappeared; both are the ground of enormous metaphysical pathos as well as personal suffering. The break with the past is a myth, with all a myth's power and overcharge of significance. The most superficial version was the Lost Generation glamour of doom popular in the 1920s and again, less glamorously, after the atom bomb was discovered. The great moderns tend to blame nothing so recent, but a much earlier Fall—though in history, and the result of impersonal forces; this breach with the past may be conceived of as either the "vast aboriginal disaster" itself or its consequence. In any case, the major writers do not attribute the innocence of Eden to the *belle époque* before the Fall; what they are sure of is that men and times are very bad now. As we have said, such a mythic belief is very different from the conviction that present and past are absolutely discontinuous. Perhaps the most accurate way to put it would be to say that the great moderns are haunted by the fear of discontinuity and obsessed by the problem of relating past and present. This attitude is the polar opposite of that which would dismiss the past as irrelevant.

To return now, briefly, to the word *modern*. The term may well be of doubtful use in reference to literature, since it is so strongly redolent of advertising and other commercial uses, and since the analogy with painting is so overpowering. It no longer raises hackles as it used to, but perhaps has lost color and sharpness through this diffusion. My concern, in any case, is not to rehabilitate the term but to clarify the ideas involved. Rather than generalize in the hope of arriving at a satisfactory abstract definition, I propose to suggest a definition in the next two chapters by describing two symbols which seem to me to represent the essential qualities of the movement. Both are, appropriately, very old, yet both have acquired new meaning and urgency. They arise naturally in this new significance out of the historical perspective with which we are concerned, and in discussing them we will be considering background and origin as well as definition.

CHAPTER TWO

THE
NATURE OF MODERNISM:
DIONYSUS

IF ANY GOD personifies modernism, it is Dionysus. His most recent epiphany, at this writing, is *Dionysus in 69;* a few years ago he appeared in Henze's opera *The Bassarids*, which was also a modern version of Euripides's *The Bacchae*. Dionysus presides metaphorically over most of the recent trends in theater, from cruelty and absurdity to audience participation, nudity, and the tribal rock musical. On or off the stage, he is apparent in two contemporary figures: the black militant, violently releasing dark and repressed forces both in society and within the psyche, and the rock musician, with his female devotees and his orgiastic cult of collective emotion.

Dionysus was resurrected for the modern world in Nietzsche's *Birth of Tragedy* (1872), which presented a view of the Greeks very different from the conventional one with its emphasis upon the noble simplicity and calm grandeur embodied in the serene proportions of Greek sculpture. Revealing the incompleteness of this Apollonian picture, Nietzsche restored Dionysus—reduced by the Romans to jolly Bacchus the wine-god—to his true and awesome importance. Apollo's sole norm, Nietzsche points out, is the *sophrosyne* of the individual: the "classical" wisdom of modera-tion, self-knowledge and self-control. Excess and *hubris* come to be regarded as belonging to the pre-Apollonian era (the age of Titans) and the extra-Apollonian world (the world of the bar-barians). "It was because of his Titanic love of man that Prome-theus had to be devoured by vultures; it was because of his ex-travagant wisdom which succeeded in solving the riddle of the Sphinx that Oedipus has to be cast into a whirlpool of crime: in this fashion does the Delphic god interpret the Greek past." [1] The essence of Dionysus, Nietzsche says, is the shattering of the *principium individuationis* for which Apollo stands: in Dionysiac rapture and awe walls are broken down and the bonds between man and man and between man and nature are re-forged. No longer the artist, man becomes himself the work of art. The indi-vidual forgets himself in the Dionysiac vortex; art is devoted to truth rather than illusion.

The effects of the Dionysiac spirit struck the Apollonian Greeks as titanic and barbaric; yet they could not disguise from them-selves the fact that they were essentially akin to those deposed Titans and heroes. They felt more than that: their whole exis-

1. Translated by Francis Golffing, in *The Modern Tradition*, ed. Richard Ellmann and Charles Feidelson, Jr. (N. Y., 1965), p. 555. Nietzsche had an immense influence not only on writers but on painters, from Papini and the Brücke school to Francis Bacon. Werner Haftmann (*Painting in the Twentieth Century*, London, 1965, I, 178–79) describes the profound in-fluence of Nietzsche on De Chirico, whom he quotes: " 'Art was liberated by the modern philosophers and poets. Schopenhauer and Nietzsche were the first to teach us the profound meaning of the absurdity of life, and to show us how this absurdity can be transmuted into art. . . .' " De Chirico's world, Haftmann says, "recalled to the disturbed modern mind the dark, Dionysian, daemonic aspects of Greek antiquity which had been forgotten since Winckelmann. In the ghostly figure of the *manichino*, the ancient gods reappeared disguised as demons, replacing the idyllic worlds of Ovid and Virgil with a nightmare whose hermeticism and magic strongly ap-pealed to the modern sensibility."

tence, with its temperate beauty, rested upon a base of suffering and *knowledge* which had been hidden from them until the reinstatement of Dionysos uncovered it once more. . . . And now let us imagine how the ecstatic sounds of the Dionysiac rites penetrated ever more enticingly into that artificially restrained and discreet world of illusion . . . let us imagine how the Apollonian artist with his thin, monotonous harp music must have sounded beside the demoniac chant of the multitude. . . . Indiscreet extravagance revealed itself as truth, and contradiction, a delight born of pain, spoke out of the bosom of nature (pp. 555–56).

Tragedy, Nietzsche maintained, was born of the Dionysiac experience of music and died of Apollonian rationalism. But, though he likes to assert "Dionysus versus Christ" and call himself "the last disciple and initiate of the God Dionysus," the genius of the heart, he does not want to do away with Apollo completely. It was the image of Apollo that kept the Greeks from the lust and cruelty of the barbarian followers of Dionysus.

Psychologically, Apollo and Dionysus represent a permanent opposition, a timeless polarity. This significance was clear in ancient Greece. As E. R. Dodds puts it, Dionysus and Apollo each ministered in his own way to the anxieties characteristic of a guilt-culture:

Apollo promised security: "Understand your station as man; do as the Father tells you; and you will be safe tomorrow." Dionysus offered freedom: "Forget the difference, and you will find the identity; join the θίασος, and you will be happy today." He was essentially a god of joy. . . . And his joys were accessible to all, including even slaves. . . . Apollo moved only in the best society, from the days when he was Hector's patron to the days when he canonised aristocratic athletes; but Dionysus was at all periods δημοτικός, a god of the people.[2]

2. E. R. Dodds, *The Greeks and the Irrational* (Berkeley and Los Angeles, 1951), p. 76.

As a symbolic dyad, Apollo and Dionysus can be used to describe any time or place; English literary history can be put, not very implausibly, in terms of their alternating reigns. Thus a Dionysian Renaissance is succeeded by an Apollonian eighteenth century, and a Dionysian age of revolution and Romanticism is followed by an Apollonian Victorian age. The special appropriateness of Dionysus as a symbol of literary modernism, however, goes beyond such large and mechanical generalizations. As Robert Langbaum says, Nietzsche, reversing Aristotle's definition of tragedy ("an imitation not of persons but of action"), turns Greek tragedy into a poetry of experience, meaning by this term the Romantic combination of the dramatic and lyric genres into the new genre that replaces all others.

> Nietzsche's Apollonian-Dionysian dichotomy corresponds to our distinction between the poetry of meaning, which the reader understands through judgment, through contemplating the images or events as objects complete with their own meaning—and the poetry of experience, which the reader understands through a combination of sympathy and judgment, through finding by an effort of creative insight his own life in the otherwise incomplete images or events. . . . For Wordsworth and Coleridge, then, as for Nietzsche, the poem exists not to imitate or describe life but to make it manifest. It is this purpose of evocation that unites the poetry of experience—from the romantic poems of Wordsworth and Browning, with their individualized speakers and objects, to the symbolist poems of Yeats and Eliot, with their archetypal speakers and objects (*The Poetry of Experience*, pp. 232–33).

Blake's revolutionary doctrines may be described as centrally Dionysian (the wisdom of excess, the liberation of the god within, the horses of wrath, and so on), and so may the sense of the numinous power of nature exhibited by later Romantics. The rejection of Christianity and the proclamations of neo-paganism made in so many varied tones of defiance, joy and despair by poets from Shelley through Swinburne are part of the same pat-

tern. At about the same time as Nietzsche, Walter Pater explicitly worked out a similar Dionysus-Apollo formulation, stressing
the subjective and centrifugal quality of the Dionysian as against
the objective and centripetal Apollonian.[3] It seems likely that
Pater as well as Nietzsche influenced Yeats, who in many ways is
profoundly Dionysian. Before proceeding to look specifically at
Yeats and other poets, however, we must return briefly to the
subject of Dionysus as symbol of modernism in general.

Dionysus had much in common with other "dying and reviv-
ing gods" of vegetation; but he was unique in being the only
Greek god who was born of a mortal mother, died and was resurrected, and was celebrated in mystery cults which involved the
ritual eating of the flesh and drinking of the blood of a sacrificial
victim (goat, bull, or human) who incarnated the god. These
similarities to Christ were revealed fully in Frazer's *Golden
Bough* (1890),[4] which summed up much earlier work in anthro-
pology and comparative religion. Frazer demonstrated the importance and universality of myth and magic, and provided the materials to show how they are related to the collective and
archetypal patterns of the unconscious mind; Jung soon after
began his psychological studies of this relation. It was Freud,
however, who first mapped out in *The Interpretation of Dreams*
(1899) the Dionysian realm of the Unconscious, or, more precisely, of those parts of the psyche not accessible to consciousness
nor subject to reason. Dionysus does not figure literally in
Freud's book, as he does in those of Nietzsche and Frazer (whose
writings, by the way, Freud did not know); but he seems the appropriate symbol for the forces unleashed by these three founders
of modernism. We shall add a fourth founder in a moment, Karl
Marx; and he, too, is aptly represented by Dionysus.

3. Pater's essay ("A Study of Dionysus") was published in 1876, and seems
to be independent of Nietzsche; see Gerald C. Monsman, *Pater's Portraits*
(Baltimore, 1967), pp. 17–21.
4. Revised and enlarged edition in 12 volumes, 1907–15. The most complete
account of Dionysus is in Part V, Vol. I (London, 1912).

Dionysus evokes the sense of dark underground forces mysteriously stirring, from Freud's Unconscious to Marx's masses, from Lawrence's Dark Gods to the sleeping giant of *Finnegans Wake* and Yeats's gods and Sidhe: "In Irish mythology there is a world of gods . . . who were driven underground by man long ago. . . . This myth of gods buried under the tyranny of consciousness, nature and reason, in Joyce the Finnegan concealed under the blanket of HCE, corresponds to the Greek myth of the Titans. . . ."[5] Celebrating an occasion when he and Delmore Schwartz "drank and eyed / the chicken-hearted shadows of the world," Robert Lowell evokes its Dionysian quality: "Underseas fellows, nobly mad," they welcomed "Joyce and Freud, / the Masters of Joy. . . ."[6]

Kermode's brilliant *Romantic Image* presents as its central symbol the Dancer, fascinating, subtle, and enigmatic, but also dated, *fin de siècle*, and mysteriously both dead and alive. Dionysus is, I think, a better symbol for modernism, for he suggests the dynamic energy and profound disruptive force of the revolution, and he is by no means obsolescent, but more in evidence than ever since the mid-century revolution. Dionysus, too, was a dancer; but his was the collective mania of possession or intoxication, and it spelled the "doom of orthodox *sophrosyne*." Nor was Dionysus an artist, and this again is symbolically appropriate, for the drive beyond art to the apocalyptic and eschatological has been a central one. Dionysus alone is not an adequate symbol. For our purposes, however, all necessary complements can be summed up in the City symbol which is the subject of the next chapter.

THE END OF LIBERAL HUMANISM

One dividing line between Victorian and modern "lies between the poets for whom the ideas and hopes of liberal Christian hu-

5. Northrop Frye, *Fables of Identity* (N. Y., 1963), p. 228.
6. "To Delmore Schwartz," in *Life Studies* (N. Y., 1959).

manism are still valid, and those for whom they are not. Thus Browning, Hugo, Longfellow are Victorian; Hopkins, Baudelaire, and Whitman are modern." [7] After the turn of the century, this rejection manifested itself with increasing intensity in the flamboyant and protracted revolt against all things Victorian. Since Victorianism, as summed up, for example, in Tennyson's "Ulysses," with its "self-reverence, self-knowledge, self-control" and its exaltation of the eternal striving of the individual will, was highly Apollonian, the revolt was at least superficially Dionysian, continuing the protest of neo-pagans and aesthetes like Swinburne and Wilde against Victorian pomposity, respectability, and hypocrisy. But breaking away from the Victorian family to follow the Way of All Flesh (as in Butler's novel, published posthumously in 1904) and observing the disappearance of both paterfamilias and God as ultimate father-image, inverting Victorian morality with Wilde and subsequent paradoxologists, exposing Eminent Victorians (1918) with Lytton Strachey and other iconoclasts, ridiculing Lawn Tennyson, gentleman poet ("Proteus" episode of *Ulysses*, published 1918), reducing Life with Father to affectionate absurdity (Clarence Day, 1935)—all this was only the visible iceberg-top of a larger and more profound phenomenon. Nietzsche, Freud, and Frazer, the three we have described as founding fathers of modernism, proclaimed not only the disappearance of God (already intimated by Darwin and the geologists) but a view of human nature and the human psyche radically different from that upon which Western bourgeois humanism was erected. Probably Karl Marx should also be described as a founder; most historians would certainly think so. In addition to his direct influence toward extremism in politics, from the Communist Manifesto of 1848 on, Marx, in demonstrating how economic and class interests determine beliefs and actions, showed, as did the other three, the limits of individual freedom and rationality and the inadequacy of Apollonian moral wisdom.

7. W. H. Auden, Introduction to *Poets of the English Language* (N. Y., 1950), V, xvii.

It is not reason, negotiation, or intelligent self-interest that will establish the just society, as Marx sees it, but class war and the dictatorship of the proletariat.

Though it is hardly possible to go farther in rejecting the values of liberal Christian humanism than Baudelaire and Flaubert, for example, had already gone in the mid-nineteenth century, the stream of rejection had swelled into a tide by the *fin de siècle*. Thus the feeling was widespread, well before the first World War, that the whole era that began with the Renaissance was ending; Hulme's fulminations against the "sloppy dregs of the Renaissance" were symptomatic, and Spengler's *Decline of the West*, the fullest intellectual embodiment of the attitude, was completed by 1914 (though not published until 1918). The war was a vast acting out of what had been revealed, in very different ways, by Nietzsche, Freud, Frazer, and Marx: man is not a rational animal able to understand and control his world and himself, but a mysterious being of unknown heights and depths, subject to forces both within and without that he comprehends only in part. Naturally, then, the imagination of the pioneering modern artist tends to be apocalyptic, seeing both the end of a cultural era and the end of all things; and in this light his interest in political ideals is likely to be limited.

The New Humanism of Irving Babbitt and Paul Elmer More was partly a rear-guard action, an attempt to rehabilitate the moral and intellectual ideals—bourgeois, individualist, Apollonian—of the Renaissance era. (Babbitt's first important book, *Literature and the American College*, was published in the same year—1908—as H. L. Mencken's influential popularization of Nietzsche, *The Philosophy of Friedrich Nietzsche*.) At the same time, however, the New Humanism was a repudiation of the era as incurably infected by Romanticism, in the name of a broader ideal which was presented as a consensus of classical, Christian, and Oriental wisdom. This latter impulse was parallel to a similar one in modernism.

When the dominant tradition of the West was repudiated,

there was a natural tendency to turn for enlightenment and spiritual sustenance to the East, and also to other traditions remote in space and time. This tendency was most spectacular in the graphic arts, when African, Egyptian, Oriental and other influences swarmed in upon the break with the naturalistic and mimetic tradition. Diaghilev's Russian Ballet, from 1909 on, was a vivid revelation of the power of the primitive and Oriental in the arts. Similarly, in the mid-century movement, interest in the East is prominent at every level from costume to the serious study of Zen or Hindu philosophy: San Francisco's geographical position as gateway to the Orient is certainly responsible for much of its importance as cultural center of the movement. But to return to the earlier moderns, we need only remind ourselves of Eliot's study of Oriental philosophy and of the Oriental aspects of *The Waste Land* (the Wheel, the Buddha's Fire Sermon, the Indian setting and the Sanskrit words in the last section) and the *Quartets*, of Pound's *Cathay* and his use of Confucius and the ideogram, and most of all, of Yeats's lifelong preoccupation with Oriental philosophy and literature, ranging from translation of Noh plays and Upanishads to dealings with Mme. Blavatsky and experiments in visiting the Mahatmas in Tibet through astral bodies to the profound speculations of "Meru" and *A Vision*—we need only recall these high points to be aware of the massive importance of the East in modernism. In *The Bacchae* of Euripides, Dionysus returns to Thebes from Asia, and his Bacchae are Asiatic; the cult of Dionysus apparently in fact originated in Thrace and its invasion of Greece, reflected in the play, occurred as late as the seventh century B.C. Hence Dionysus aptly symbolizes the exotic quality of modernism, its rejection of Western post-Renaissance humanism and its search for a wider tradition including the Oriental and the primitive.

To sum up, Dionysus, twice-born, is acquainted with mortality as no other god is; but is also less humane. He presides over tragedy and dithyramb, as over the seasonal death and resurrection of the vine, but his rites involve blood sacrifice and formerly cannibalism. He appears to the Greeks not as a magnified but familiar human shadow thrown on the clouds, like the Olympian deities, but as more mysterious and disturbing. Against the Apollonian tradition dominant in Socrates, Plato, and Aristotle, with its emphasis on the normal and rational, the cultivation of the aristocratic self-sufficient individual, the criterion of sanity and health, he represents the claims of the collective, the irrational and emotional and abnormal; of the feminine or androgynous or perverse; of intoxication and possession, surrender to non-human forces; even of disease. Hence, once more, he is a fitting embodiment of the modern concern with these matters, from Conrad's *Heart of Darkness* (1899) and Mann's *Death in Venice* (1911) on through Forster's *Passage to India* (1925) and many other avatars to the recrudescence beginning in the latter 1950s.

The fiction of Thomas Mann is an extensive and profound exploration of the end of liberal humanism. Mann once remarked that his whole career could be described as the process of freeing himself from the middle class. His first novel, *Buddenbrooks* (1901), was his most explicit and detailed portrait of bourgeois family life; but the theme is never absent from his subsequent writings, and his attitude toward it is always ironic and deeply ambivalent. *The Magic Mountain* (1924) is, I think, the most complex and searching treatment—so complex that any brief statement about it will necessarily be inadequate. Settembrini, the humanist, exponent of the Enlightenment, of everything modern and progressive since Petrarch, with his organ-grinder's moustache, his florid oratorical culture, and his belief in human goodness, plainly represents the bourgeois liberal humanism of the West since the Renaissance. His opponent, the Catholic Communist Naphta, as obviously represents the new extremism, the absolutist and apocalyptic attitudes that are characteristic of modernism. Naphta's suicide is meaningful chiefly in relation to his significance as Mind without Life, just as Peeperkorn's relates to his significance as Life without Mind; though Peeperkorn appears as Dionysus, the single character closest to representing the Dion-

ysian in the sense we have been describing is Naphta, Jesuit exponent of Nietzsche, of paradox, and of every form of the extreme.
The Magic Mountain is also the fullest fictional embodiment of
the theme of disease, sickness, as an instrument of knowledge—
the theme that underlies the whole science of psychoanalysis. In
The Magic Mountain, Hans Castorp's "dream poem of humanity"
envisions the union of the Apollonian and Dionysian, the recognition of the dark and awesome forces in the Homo Dei, lord of all
contradictions, "between mystic community and windy individualism." *Dr. Faustus* shows the disappointment of such hopes: the
dark and irrational forces were in control, and are fittingly represented in the novel as the demonic. Dr. Faustus is not only Germany in the grip of the Nazis, but modern man in general—and
specifically the artist—insofar as he follows the Dionysian principle alone without its necessary Apollonian counterbalance.
Leverkühn is based, we remember, at least in part on Arnold
Schönberg, type of the artist as uncompromising extremist. In
his earlier essay on Freud (1929), Mann had used Freud's whole
body of work as well as his explicit precepts to argue that, in politics, art, and morality, both Apollonian and Dionysian are necessary, and that to abandon either is to invite disaster.[8]

The most influential recent interpreters of Freud's metapsy-
chology have taken, however, a very different view. Partly in the
name of Nietzsche, they reassert the Dionysiac principle against
Freud himself. The most popular version is that of Norman O.
Brown, who, in *Life Against Death: The Psychoanalytical Meaning of History* (1959) and *Love's Body* (1965), has pictured the
delights of the paradise of polymorphous-perverse sexuality before the tyranny of the genital was established and the future
joys of the liberated Eros. The comparatively austere and unsen-
sational *Eros and Civilization: A Philosophical Inquiry into
Freud*, by Herbert Marcuse, however, is both earlier (1955) and
more significant. Together with Brown, Marcuse has provided

8. Joseph Frank, *The Widening Gyre* (New Brunswick, N. J., 1963),
p. 136.

much of the philosophical basis for the "youth revolt" and the Hippie subculture.

Noting Freud's belief that the pleasure principle and the reality principle are eternally opposed, Marcuse argues that Freud's definition of the reality principle is based on an economics of scarcity. Freud assumes that "the struggle for existence takes place in a world too poor for the satisfaction of human needs without constant restraint, renunciation, delay . . . whatever satisfaction is possible necessitates *work* . . ." (p. 35); the "notion that a non-repressive civilization is impossible is a cornerstone of Freudian theory" (p. 17). But the scarcity which Freud assumes to be an unalterable fact is, says Marcuse, merely the result of a specific organization of society, a rationale of domination. Nietzsche exposed this "gigantic fallacy" on which Western philosophy and morality were built: the transformation of historical into metaphysical conditions. Interpreting Nietzsche in Marxist terms, Marcuse says that the transformation had a twofold function: "to pacify, compensate, and justify the underprivileged of the earth, and to protect those who made and left them underprivileged" (p. 121). Nietzsche, he says, speaks in the name of a reality principle opposite to that of Western civilization; the "traditional form of reason is rejected on the basis of the experience of being-as-end-in-itself—as joy. . . . The struggle against time is waged from this position: the tyranny of becoming over being must be broken if man is to come to himself in a world which is truly his own" (pp. 121–22). This will happen only when the transcendence has been conquered and eternity has become present in the here and now: what Nietzsche sees as the closed circle, the eternal return of the finite exactly as it is, not progress. Eternity will be reclaimed for earth when the life instincts are totally affirmed, when man has an erotic attitude toward being, in which necessity and fulfillment coincide.

Play, Marcuse argues, serving no purpose beyond itself, is entirely subject to the pleasure principle, in contrast to work, which serves ends outside itself. Thus pre-genital sexuality corresponds to play, while genital sex, serving the ends of procreation, is work. Work could be transformed into play if we could reactivate polymorphous eroticism, get rid of domination and sublimation, reject the performance principle, and return to non-repressive culture-heroes such as Orpheus and Narcissus.

Marcuse is particularly suggestive (for our purposes) in describing these mythological figures who are akin to Dionysus, and like him, represent a reality principle other than that dominant in the West. In contrast to Prometheus, hero of the performance principle, or Apollo, "theirs is the image of joy and fulfillment; the voice which does not command but sings; the gesture which offers and receives; the deed which is peace and ends the labor of conquest; the liberation from time which unites man with god, man with nature" (p. 162). "The images of Orpheus and Narcissus reconcile Eros and Thanatos. They recall the experience of a world that is not to be mastered and controlled but to be liberated . . ." (p. 164). In the Orphic and Narcissistic experience, the "opposition between man and nature, subject and object, is overcome. Being is experienced as gratification" (p. 166); the song of Orpheus breaks petrification, moves forests and rocks to partake in joy. "The Orphic-Narcissistic images are those of the Great Refusal: refusal to accept separation from the libidinous object (or subject) . . . Orpheus is the archetype of the poet as *liberator* and *creator:* he establishes a higher order in the world—an order without repression" (p. 170). He is also associated with the introduction of homosexuality, and hence is torn to pieces by the Thracian women; he rejects the normal Eros in the name of a fuller Eros, protesting against the repressive order of procreative sexuality. Like Orpheus, Narcissus lives by an aesthetic reality principle: his life is beauty, his existence contemplation.

As Marcuse points out, these deities play an important role in modern literature, though more on the continent than in England or America. Narcissus is prominent in Gide (*Traité du Narcisse*) and especially in Valéry (*Narcisse Parle, Cantate du Nar-*

cisse, and others throughout Valéry's career), where he is the hero-martyr of the contemplation of the Ideal in oneself, complementing the Young Fate, the Oracle, the Snake, and other members of Valéry's private menagerie. In Rilke, especially in the *Sonnets to Orpheus,* both figures often appear, and sometimes fuse as an image of the poet (I, 9). There is also the related image of the dancer, reconciling, as in Yeats's "Among School Children," labor and play (II, 28).

In English poetry, Dionysian themes are increasingly frequent from Blake on. The bourgeois are shocked and liberal humanism rejected at varying levels of profundity, from Blake's repudiation of everything Newton and Locke began and Sir Joshua Reynolds finished through many forms of Satanism, neo-paganism, and aestheticism to Dowson, Wilde, and the other Decadents of the 1890s; and from them the line is clear to Yeats and Pound.

Writing to Lady Gregory in 1902, Yeats called Nietzsche "a strong enchanter" and remarked, "Nietzsche completes Blake and has the same roots." [9] But by 1903 he is writing to John Quinn,

> I have always felt that the soul has two movements primarily: one to transcend form, and the other to create form. Nietzsche, to whom you have been the first to introduce me, calls these the Dionysian and the Apollonic, respectively. I think I have to some extent got weary of that wild God Dionysus, and I am hoping that the Far-Darter will come in his place (p. 403).

In that he wants to create form rather than transcend it, then, Yeats declares ultimate allegiance to the Apollonian. His affirmation of the self and of life as good are further evidence of the same choice. But Yeats retains a powerful consciousness of the Dionysian in every sense. To take the simplest matters first, the influence of Nietzsche would seem to have merged with that of Walter Pater not only in making Yeats conscious of the Apollo-Dionysus formulation but in reinforcing his natural suspicion of

9. W. B. Yeats, *Letters,* ed. W. A. Wade (London, 1954), p. 379.

abstraction, dislike of the bourgeois and sentimental and popular, and admiration for nobility, aristocracy, and the aesthetic ideals of hardness and intensity. For both, "not the fruit of experience, but experience itself" (in Pater's words) is the goal; and both celebrate Dionysus as against Christ. The influence of Nietzsche probably contributes to the change in Yeats's style from 1903 to 1914, together with Yeats's experience in the theater; as early as 1904 he seeks to rediscover "an art of the theatre that shall be joyful, fantastic, extravagant . . . and altogether reckless," and speaks of "tragic joy" as its goal. Tragedy, says Yeats, "must always be a drowning and breaking of the dykes that separate man from man and . . . it is upon these dykes that comedy keeps house"; tragedy is "the confounder of understanding." [10] His apothegm, "We begin to live when we conceive life as tragedy," flowers out in such late lyrics as "Lapis Lazuli" and the Crazy Jane series in the theme of tragic joy as against conventional morality. The Dionysian concept of truth is seen most clearly in the plays, from the vision of destruction, of revelation where there is nothing, in "The Unicorn from the Stars" (1908), through "The Hour Glass" (1914), in which the Wise Man discovers too late that his rational skepticism was false, to "The Resurrection" (1931), which is a Dionysian interpretation of Christianity. (Other plays and poems deal also with the union of mortal and immortal at a full moon in March marking the Magnus Annus.) The two songs in "The Resurrection," written in 1926, present Christianity as an inferior successor to the Dionysian: "a staring virgin" stands where "holy Dionysus died"; Christianity is a "fabulous, formless darkness," and the "odor of blood when Christ was slain" will make vain the classical virtues.

Yeats's scorn for Paudeen the shopkeeper who fumbles in a greasy till, prudently reckoning the profit and the loss, and remote from saint, hero, or poet, has been described often enough, as has his tendency to repudiate Western civilization. As for so many others, the First World War was the final proof, capped

10. Quoted by Balachandra Rajan, *W. B. Yeats* (London, 1965), pp. 59–60.

off in Yeats's case by the subsequent murderous Irish troubles. Perhaps his most eloquent rendering of this theme is "Nineteen Hundred and Nineteen." Unlike simpler poems where he expresses a perfect willingness to strike a match and burn the "great gazebo" of Western civilization, this poem assimilates all the unpleasant revelations about human nature that have shown us to be "but weasels fighting in a hole" and admits that "we were crack-pated when we dreamed," but turns finally to mock at those who mock at the good, wise, and great. Yeats's feelings about these matters are always mixed: as the end of "the beautiful humane cities" is lamented in "The Resurrection," so Yeats will not give up the humane values entirely, though skeptical of them. "The Second Coming" is the definitive embodiment of his ambivalent feelings about the future, and is ever more appropriate as the twentieth century rounds toward its end: "what rough beast . . . ?" The same ambivalence is present in his attitude toward literary modernism: after seeing Jarry's *Ubu Roi* in 1895, he prophesied: "After us, the Savage God." [11]

Pound's revolt against the era is, superficially at least, very flamboyant; his early poems celebrate the joys of free love in a garret as against those of respectability, sympathize with "the adolescent who are smothered in family," and protest against "all sorts of mortmain." He laments explicitly the victory of Christ over his pagan counterpart, Dionysus:

> Christ follows Dionysus,
> Phallic and ambrosial
> Made way for macerations;
> Caliban casts out Ariel.

Mauberley, from which the stanza above is taken, is a repudiation primarily and specifically of modern Britain; but it also repudiates the whole "botched civilization" of which the Great War was the final fruit. In the *Cantos*, from the second one (in which he is the central figure) on, Dionysus plays an important role. He presides over both metamorphosis and fertility rites, two of the central activities of the poem; both of them are perhaps metaphors ultimately for the process of artistic creation. At any rate, Pound's rendering of the awesome power and mystery of these activities is his nearest approach to religious awareness, and it would not be much of an exaggeration to say that Dionysus is his god. Eliot's Mr. Apollinax, with his "submarine and profound" laughter and his pointed ears, is more than a witty affront to Cambridge propriety; like the mermaids and the undersea imagery of "Prufrock," he represents the world of repressed emotion, the Unconscious. (The name means "son of Apollo," but to Cambridge, no doubt, the difference between the two pagans, Apollo and Dionysus, would be insignificant.) Death by water in Eliot has, of course, a psychological as well as religious meaning; the encounter with the Unconscious is perilous, with no transformation guaranteed, just as drowning may—or may not—be also baptism and metamorphosis. *The Waste Land* is, among many other things, the classic embodiment of the sense of the break-up of civilization, as the "city over the mountains / Cracks and reforms and bursts in the violet air / Falling towers / Jerusalem Athens Alexandria / Vienna London / Unreal," while the hooded hordes swarm and the towers are next seen "upside down in air."

Hart Crane was strongly influenced by Nietzsche, of whom he wrote a prose defense in 1918; in 1921 he praises a friend as a "good Nietzschean." [12] Under this influence, he dedicates himself consciously to the Dionysian. Thus he expounds and demonstrates a Dionysian aesthetic in "Sunday Morning Apples" and describes the end of "For the Marriage of Faustus and Helen" as "Dionysian in its attitude, the creator and the eternal destroyer

12. Hart Crane, *Complete Poems and Selected Letters and Prose* (N. Y., 1966), p. 197; *Letters* (N. Y., 1952), p. 75. This aspect of Crane is discussed by L. S. Dembo, *Conceptions of Reality in Modern American Poetry* (Berkeley and Los Angeles, 1966), p. 139.

dance arm in arm . . ." (*Letters*, p. 121). In "Lachrymae Christi" he explores the Christ-Dionysus link—the association of both with wine, sacrifice, and renewal of vegetation—and ends by celebrating the "unmangled target smile" of a restored Dionysus.

D. H. Lawrence is perhaps the most obviously Dionysian of all the great writers of this century. In *Sons and Lovers* (1913), Walter Morel has some Dionysian qualities—his dancing, his sensuality, his gaiety, his ability to descend into the depths; Gertrude's faults are all clearly indicated as products of her bourgeois background, with its puritanism, individualism, self-righteousness, and most of all its possessiveness, which she and Miriam exhibit alike. William dies, literally, of the white collar he wears in fealty to her, and Paul almost does. Both symbolically, in this novel, and explicitly in essays and in poems such as "Snake," Lawrence warns of the disastrous consequences of failure to respect the dark gods. Clifford Chatterley, bourgeois intellectual dead below the waist, is an awful warning.

Lawrence also exhibits to the full the tendency of all the modern arts to show an awareness of the deeper levels of the psyche, in contrast to the older belief in the primacy of the conscious will. (The same kind of awareness may be seen in Conrad and Ford, of course, and full-blown in Joyce, Woolf, and others.) *Women in Love* must be the most richly and transparently psychological novel ever written; everything in it is charged with psychic significance, and one feels that this results not from theory or even intention, but simply because the novel exists on this visionary level of psychic reality, its world constituting a psychological goldfish bowl. In it victims seek their murderers, all sickness is psychosomatic, there are no accidents, and all deaths take place in symbolic water or snow. This is, in a sense, a rejection of humanist individualism—or, more accurately, of the humanist conception of the individual—the "old stable ego of the character," as Lawrence calls it. Eliot's "escape from personality" may be seen as a parallel phenomenon. As Stead points out, the escape "is made, not away from the self, but deeper into the self, 'below the levels of consciousness.'" Thus the "escape" is actually an inclusion of deeper levels of the personality extending to the archetypal and collective; and Stead shows how small a role Eliot gives to the conscious will in the process of writing poetry.[13]

BEYOND CIVILIZATION

"The middle road is the only one that does not lead to Rome," said Arnold Schönberg (Opus 28), and his fictional counterpart, Adrian Leverkühn, in Mann's *Dr. Faustus*, seems to live by this belief. In *The Magic Mountain*, the dialectical play of opposites was intended to reveal the necessity for a higher synthesis: all the characters were to be reconciled and transfigured by Hans Castorp, who represents the precarious balancing point of the "human" and is lord of counterpositions. But the "human" has been eliminated from *Dr. Faustus* except as helpless onlooker, and "the symbolic structure is thus controlled by the fusion of extremes without mediation," as Joseph Frank puts it (*The Widening Gyre*, p. 142). When the Devil in that novel says "the artist is the brother of the criminal and the madman" and laughs at the Goethean ideal of sane and sound greatness, "What was once merely a Nietzschean paradox has become diabolism and the spirit's self-betrayal."

Much of what we shall have to say in this section is implicit in the rejection of bourgeois humanism that we have just been discussing; but it seems worthwhile to indicate briefly some of the philosophical and religious consequences of this rejection. The concern of modern artists is characteristically apocalyptic and eschatological, even when they are atheistic and anti-clerical: they have little interest in keeping the ship afloat, seeing that life goes on in the City; instead they are obsessively concerned with the ultimate questions, the Last Things: Death, Judgment, Heaven, Hell—or secular equivalents for the last three. They tend to

13. C. K. Stead, *The New Poetic* (N. Y., 1966), p. 131.

feel not only that the era that began with the Renaissance is ending, but that the whole human enterprise is likely to end at any
moment, or to continue only in some fearfully inhuman mode
(again, the classic text is Yeats's "Second Coming"). This catastrophism (one of the themes explored in Kermode's *Sense of an
Ending*) begins with the hopes and fears arising toward the end
of the last century (when, as the early scientific romances of
H. G. Wells show so clearly, many people foresaw not only *fin de
siècle* but *fin du globe*) and has since been fed by the emotions
and apprehensions associated with the fact that the present century will mark the end of the second milliennium A.D. The First
World War was, for many, the anticipated catastrophe; and the
feeling was widespread in the 1920s that not only an era, but history, had ended. (The release of energy in the 1920s certainly
came partly from this feeling, even if it sometimes appeared to be
a dance of death.) With the end of World War II, the atomic
bomb gave a new focus to apocalyptic fears, since it made possible an end of all things with unprecedented speed and thorough-
ness. But it seems unlikely that this has made much real difference
to the imaginative apprehension of the human condition; no one
could regard civilization as more precarious than did the early
moderns, and death for the individual is always certain. The new
technology merely provided more efficient means.

The moderns were led by their overwhelming sense of crisis to
an attitude that must be called religious, in the sense of intensely
personal concern with some form of salvation. It may also be
called existential in the large sense of recognizing that this is a
matter in which detachment is impossible and the subject is necessarily involved. As Paul Tillich says,

> The decisive event which underlies the search for meaning and
> the despair of it in the twentieth century is the loss of God in
> the nineteenth century. . . . This is felt both as a loss and as a
> liberation. It drives one either to nihilism or to the courage which
> takes nonbeing into itself. . . . On this basis Existentialism, that is

the great art, literature, and philosophy of the twentieth century, reveals the courage to face things as they are and to express the anxiety of meaninglessness.[14]

The moderns, at the same time they gave a new seriousness to art, were thus constantly moving beyond it, determined to prevent any use of their art as escape. Truth, honesty, were matters far more important than art; and hence the barriers between art and life were constantly being called in question. For example, the development of *collage* at about the same time (1912) abstraction in painting reached its first full flower; or the parallel and simultaneous exhibition of both tendencies in Joyce's *Ulysses*, in which a separate world of art is created but some material from life is deliberately left unassimilated.

Truth, however, was conceived of in a new way, as psychological rather than objective (to use very rough terms). According to Trilling, Matthew Arnold thought of himself as asking the question Goethe had taught modern Europe to ask: "But is it true? Is it true for *me?*" Pater, in the Preface to *The Renaissance* (1873), said, "Beauty, like all other qualities presented to human experience, is relative; and the definition of it becomes unmeaning and useless in proportion to its abstractness." In all realms, a new recognition of subjectivity, an awareness of the complex and inescapable relation between inner and outer, observer and observed, is apparent. In physics, Planck's quantum theory, Einstein's special theory of relativity, and Heisenberg's indeterminacy principle all demonstrate the inseparability of subject and object. In painting, the parallel development is very obvious indeed, from the Impressionists through Cézanne to Cubism; and in theology and religion, the movement loosely called Existentialist moves in a similar direction, though it does not attract much attention until after the Second World War, when Kierkegaard, Heidegger, Buber, et al. were rediscovered through Sartre. The most thor-

14. Paul Tillich, "The Courage to Be," 1952, in *The Modern Tradition*, p. 945.

ough exploration, however, was made in the developing practice of psychoanalysis. As Freud kept insisting (but without making any impression on his opponents or, to this day, on the general public), psychoanalysis is not a system of abstract and objective truth, but is involved with the emotional dynamics of transference, resistance, and the like, so that it cannot be understood or judged apart from the specific analytical situation. In short—although Freud would not have liked the comparison—there is a profound sense in which psychoanalysis, like religion, must be believed and experienced before it can be known. As Thomas Mann observed, this is the "most profound and mysterious point of contact" between the worlds of Freud and Schopenhauer: Schopenhauer's idea that "precisely as in a dream it is our own will that unconsciously appears as inexorable objective destiny, everything in it proceeding out of ourselves and each of us being the secret theatre-manager of our own dreams, so also in reality . . . our fate, may be the product of our inmost selves, of our wills, and we are actually ourselves bringing about what seems to be happening to us." This is, Mann suggests, an astonishing anticipation of analytical conceptions. "For . . . I see in the mystery of the unity of the ego and the world, of being and happening, in the perception of the apparently objective and accidental as a matter of the soul's own contriving, the innermost core of psychoanalytic theory." [15]

In literature the same tendencies—the rejection of civilization in favor of the eschatological and the conception of truth as psychological and subjective—are very plain indeed. "Massive hostility to civilization" is Trilling's definition of the essence of modernism in literature, as we saw in the last chapter; and we have mentioned some of the more striking examples of primitivism and apocalyptism, from *Heart of Darkness* (1899) to *Women in Love* (1916; pub. 1920), which Lawrence originally thought of calling *The Latter Days* or *Dies Irae* and worried about because it was "so end of the world." A few words more about the no-

15. Ibid., p. 672 ("Freud and the Future," 1936).

tion of truth as psychological will be sufficient.[16] Baudelaire, among the Fathers, asks, "What is the modern conception of Art?" and answers, "To create a suggestive magic including at the same time object and subject, the world outside the artist and the artist himself." [17] We have quoted Stead's observation (anticipated and reinforced by such Jungian commentators as Elizabeth Drew and Maud Bodkin) that the impersonality of Eliot's poetry consists chiefly in drawing its images from the deep and ultimately collective unconscious. The stress on impersonality in Eliot's criticism may well derive partly from the unconsciously felt need to counterbalance this quality in the poetry. And his critical arguments themselves implicitly recognize subjectivity in the most fundamental way—for example, in the notion of past and present as forming a simultaneous order and the image of the "existing monuments" shifting and changing whenever a new one is introduced. The idea of history in which everything is simultaneously present resembles the theory of Cubist painting, and those moving monuments have a surrealist flavor, like early De Chirico. Similarly, the enormous elaboration of "point of view" and "method of narration" in the Impressionist novel from Henry James on is an attempt to recognize, be honest about, and make effective use of, subjectivity. The subjectivity of the open or naked poetry of the latter 1950s and the 1960s needs no pointing out; it is nothing if not personal, and much of it is plainly written in the faith that madness and disease are instruments of knowledge.

BEYOND ART

As the Dionysian impulse drives beyond liberal humanism and then beyond civilization, so it drives finally beyond art. Truth is

16. *Symbolic* would be a better word, and is used by such modern exponents of the philosophical tradition of Kant and Cassirer as Susanne Langer and Philip Wheelright. I avoid it because it overlaps confusingly with the literary use.

17. Quoted in W. H. Auden, *The Enchafèd Flood* (N. Y., 1950), p. 61.

seen as a higher value than Apollonian illusion, and life itself as more important than the Apollonian problems of form in art. In all the arts, however, modernism first manifests itself as an intensified aestheticism: because of external and historical pressures, the arts become purer, more specialized, dissociated from their traditional functions. This is clearest in painting, where the function of representation of the external world was completely taken over, for all useful purposes, by photography. Baudelaire denounced the painters of 1859 for attempting to rival photography:

> Each day art further diminishes its self-respect by bowing down before external reality; each day the painter becomes more and more given to painting not what he dreams but what he sees. . . . Could you find an honest observer to declare that the invasion of photography and the great industrial madness of our times have no part at all in this deplorable result? [18]

Baudelaire's conception was prophetic, for the development of painting was, of course, steadily away from literal representation, from the Impressionists and Cézanne through the Cubists to abstraction in which mimesis was completely abandoned. "Art is a harmony parallel to Nature," said Cézanne; [19] and the notion of art as creating another nature, a heterocosm, rather than imitating that which already exists, is at least as important in painting as in literature, and much easier to recognize. An intense aestheticism, a concentration upon problems of form and technique, was involved in this development from the Impressionists through the early Cubism of Picasso and Braque to the abstractions of Kandinsky. The goal of this early development was, in a sense, aesthetic discontinuity.

Economic factors, as well as technological ones such as the development of photography, play an important part in the history

18. *The Mirror of Art*, p. 231 (Letter II, "The Modern Public and Photography").
19. Haftmann, *Painting in the Twentieth Century*, I, 32.

of the arts in the late nineteenth and early twentieth centuries. As populations increase, the level of literacy rises, and education becomes more widespread, the size of the potential audience becomes far greater and the economic stakes correspondingly higher: in short, it becomes possible to make really large amounts of money from the arts. Naturally, a split or dissociation develops between two kinds of art: on the one hand, art as business, designed to please the largest possible public and make the maximum amount of money; on the other, art as pure art, without regard for any audience except for an occasional note of scorn and defiance of the larger public. The aesthetes of the nineties are the most extreme examples of the latter type; as Yeats said of his friends of the Rhymers Club, they "kept the Muse's sterner laws," however disorderly their lives. But the mirror image of the *Yellow Book* in which the aesthetes—Beardsley, Wilde, Dowson, Lionel Johnson, Yeats—appeared was the yellow journalism that arose at about the same time, the fruit of the new literacy resulting from the introduction of free compulsory education in 1870. By the early 1900s such expert literary entrepreneurs had appeared on the scene as Arnold Bennett and Henry Newbolt, whose books of verse sold as much as 70,000 copies. Writers of this kind, as well as yellow journalists, became efficient in giving the enlarged public just what it wanted, reflecting back its prejudices and beliefs in a simple and flattering manner. A very little acquaintance with them (as Stead demonstrates in *The New Poetic*) makes one realize fully why Yeats felt such abhorrence for "opinion" and "rhetoric" in poetry, and why he, Pound, and many other moderns felt a reverential bond with the "aesthetes."

In painting and music, there are technological reasons for specialization. As we have seen, the development of photography completely eliminates the need for literal representation in painting, and the improvement of techniques for reproducing paintings has made at least a minimal acquaintance with them far more widespread than ever before. In music, the pianola and the phonograph, with radio and television, take over the function of providing entertainment formerly performed by live musicians; it seems likely also that, by exaggerating the elements of mechanical repetitiveness and simple melody, they tended to discredit these elements in serious music. In literature, there is no exact parallel, though similarly the function of providing entertainment and escape is taken over, to an increasing extent, by other media such as movies, radio, and finally television. But the satisfaction of these needs through prose fiction remains a large and profitable enterprise; what happens is that commercial motives tend increasingly to dominate it, so that (with occasional happy exceptions) the producing of best-sellers becomes an industry having nothing to do with serious literature.

All the arts, then, lose their utilitarian functions, which are taken over by the mass media of communication and entertainment. The serious arts are driven in upon themselves and develop their proper natures under pressure; hence they become specialized, pure, advanced, extreme, austere. As they become more serious, intense, and uncompromising, they become more and more uninviting and incomprehensible to the public at large. The gap between the serious arts and the popular arts becomes wider and wider, until there is a reaction—like the massive one of the 1950s. Actually, this statement is an oversimplification, because the gap is never impassable and everyone—serious artist, popular artists, audiences—is unhappy with it; the gap widens and narrows in smaller movements within the larger ones, and is always being crossed from both sides. Nevertheless, in a large way one may say that the trend of the early modern arts was in this direction: precisely the opposite direction from the late-Victorian fusion and confusion of the arts that Irving Babbitt attacked in *The New Laocoön* (1910), as exemplified by Pre-Raphaelite "literary" paintings, by the tone poems and program music of Strauss and Debussy, by the "musical" writings of Amy Lowell and Vachel Lindsay, by Wagner's music-drama, and by the musical verse of some of the *Symbolistes*. The modern arts, emerging at about the time of Babbitt's book, are characterized instead by economy, objectivity, extremism; the uncompromising rejection of popular attractions; an unceasing exploitation of the medium and exploration of technique. Each of the modern arts strives to realize its own nature, having detached itself from utilitarian functions and other impurities; at the same time each art strives to transcend its former limits.

The early modern arts, as we have seen, turn away from the mimetic tradition. Music is regarded by some painters and poets as a model of the non-mimetic, of purity and detachment; it is only in this very different sense that the modern arts can be said to strive toward the condition of music. Mimesis is, of course, not completely abandoned; but it is seen to be—like Aristotelian logic, Euclidian geometry, and Newtonian physics—partial and inadequate, needing to be complemented by other views of reality. It is not that representation in painting or rational structure in poetry are discarded, but that various kinds of abstraction in painting and rhetorical discontinuity in poetry are explored.

Let us look specifically at literature, and particularly at verse, to see how these tendencies we have been discussing are manifested. The most obvious innovations in early modern poetry are free verse and rhetorical discontinuity, often found together. Perhaps the chief motive in the use of the former is the desire to break with the dominant forms of English verse since the Renaissance and to transcend the former limits of the art; in the use of the latter, there is the determination to distinguish poetry sharply from prose, the medium of rhetoric and opinion, and to gain intensity through ellipsis and economy. Neither technique is entirely an innovation, Wordsworth's Lucy poems, for example, being excellent examples of the "structure of simple juxtaposition and occasional stark confrontation," the alogical bringing together without explanation or rhetorical accommodation of disparate images.[20] No one any longer would identify modernism with free verse, and I have argued in the last chapter that rhetori-

20. Cleanth Brooks, "A Retrospective Introduction" to the new edition of *Modern Poetry and the Tradition* (N. Y., 1965), p. xiv. Brooks agrees with Auden that this kind of structure was "the real novelty in Romantic poetry. . . ."

cal discontinuity is almost as unsatisfactory: both are characteristic of the modern only spasmodically, and then only in degree, not kind. Similarly, the notion of art as a second nature, of the imagination as lamp rather than mirror, of the poem as heterocosm rather than imitation goes back at least to Blake and can be regarded as characteristic of modernism only in the large sense that modernism can be said to begin then.[21]

Perhaps the largest generalization that can be made is that there are two primary impulses in modern literature, both always present but one or the other dominating. The first is the drive toward aestheticism, toward the purification of form, its refinement and exploration, the development of those features that are most distinctive. The illusion becomes more convincing and self-sufficient; there is a tendency for the art-world to become separate and independent from life. This is countered by the opposing impulse, to break through art, destroy any possibility of escape to illusion, to insist that the immediate experience, the heightening of life is the important thing. Both elements co-exist from the beginning: *Ulysses* is a world of art, but with elements of raw and deliberately unassimilated reality, like the *collage* materials—old newspapers, bits of wood and string—used in so many early modern paintings. *Trouvage* and Raw Materialism recur in painting, as do neo-naturalism and anti-experimentalism in the novel and drama. In a general way, one may say that the first impulse—the formal and experimental, aimed at the perfecting of the art—dominated the early modern movement, especially in the two decades following 1909; the second impulse—toward "life," "reality," naturalism, against form and illusion—dominated the movement beginning in the latter 1950s, in the novel, drama, and poetry. In drama, where the temptation to escape into the well-made world of the play is perhaps strongest, Brecht early developed his built-in alienation effect to prevent this. More recently, the Theater of Involvement has operated in a different

21. See M. H. Abrams, *The Mirror and the Lamp* (N. Y., 1953), and the work of Northrop Frye as discussed below in Chapter Seven.

way toward the same end, pulling the audience into the world of the play (sometimes physically) but trying to keep the distinction clear between Truth and Illusion. An extreme awareness of art as illusion, fiction, in some sense a trick and a lie, has been apparent in the novel, where the neo-naturalistic and anti-experimental trend that was dominant after World War II has been succeeded by what one critic calls "fabulators": [22] writers like Joseph Heller, John Barth, and Vladimir Nabokov, who absorb the element of illusion and trickery into their works and make sophisticated play with it. This awareness operates in many ways and on many levels, from Beckett's anti-novels with their dogged persistence in getting at the bare truth ("He went to the window. It was midnight. It was raining. It was not midnight. It was not raining.") to the dazzling manipulation of point of view, the deliberate tricking of the reader and then revealing the trick, in Nabokov and Barth, to the more comic versions of Heller. (An element of comedy, however sad, is of course present in all of them; all may be called anti-novelists of the Absurd.) Auden, prescient here as so often, defined the theme early in *The Sea and the Mirror* (1944); Mann, in his last novel, *Confessions of Felix Krull, Confidence Man* (1954), gave to this theme, as he had to so many others, perhaps its most profound expression.

The drive toward form and then through it, to art and then beyond it and back to reality, truth, immediate experience; and the incorporation of this whole process into art—these are central to modernism. We examined briefly in the last chapter Frank Kermode's thesis that allegiance to the Romantic Image, both as privileged mode of cognition and as agent of the poet's alienation, is the hallmark of modernism, and found it not entirely satisfactory. In a recent essay on Eliot, Kermode suggests a broader definition that takes into account the matters we have been discuss-

---

22. Robert Scholes, *The Fabulators* (N. Y., 1967). The theme is explored by W. H. Auden in *The Dyer's Hand* (N. Y., 1962), E. H. Gombrich, *Art and Illusion* (N. Y., 1960), and Frank Kermode in *The Sense of an Ending* and *Continuities*, both N. Y., 1968.

ing. Considering *The Waste Land* as primary example of the modern work, Kermode proposes the word *decreation* (which Wallace Stevens took from Simone Weil) as a "useful instrument for the discrimination of modernisms." (Stevens said, "Modern reality is a reality of decreation, in which our revelations are not the revelations of belief, but the precious portents of our own powers.") Decreation is not destruction, but a creative act of renunciation: "God could create only by hiding himself. Otherwise there would be nothing but himself," said Simone Weil. For men, decreation "implies the deliberate repudiation (not simply the destruction) of the naturally human and so naturally false 'set' of the world: 'we participate in the creation of the world by decreating ourselves' " (Kermode, quoting Weil). The modern poets of the great early years, Kermode suggests,

> also desired to create a world by decreating the self in suffering; to purge what, in being merely natural and human, was also false. It is a point often made, though in different language, by Eliot. This is what Stevens called clearing the world of "its stiff and stubborn, man-locked set." In another way it is what attracted Hulme and Eliot to Worringer, who related societies purged of the messily human to a radical abstract art (*Continuities*, p. 75).[23]

Works like *The Waste Land, Mauberley,* and some poems by Stevens and Lowell, says Kermode, are "a new kind of creation, harsh, medicinal, denying the consolations of predictable form but revealing to us the forces of our world. . . ." This decreative poetry is to be sharply distinguished from "destructive" poetry, which is merely anarchic or programmatically negative.

Another attempt to define the modern attitude toward form, its break with the Western Renaissance tradition and its tension between the drive toward art and the drive beyond it or against it, is that of Joseph Frank in *The Widening Gyre* (1963). What

23. Eliot was not attracted to Worringer and apparently did not like abstract art, according to Sir Herbert Read in *T. S. Eliot,* ed. Allen Tate (N. Y., 1966).

T. E. Hulme called Classicism, Frank argues, may be more accurately described as Spatial Form, the literary equivalent of the non-naturalistic style defined by the art historian Wilhelm Worringer. Worringer (whose influence was acknowledged by Hulme) maintained that there has been throughout history a continual alternation of naturalistic and non-naturalistic styles; that these are simply two permanent polarities, and neither should be considered a norm. In non-naturalistic periods—primitive, Egyptian, Byzantine, Romanesque—the artist "abandons the projection of space entirely and returns to the plane, reduces organic nature to linear-geometric forms, and frequently eliminates all traces of organicism in favor of pure lines, forms, and colors" (p. 51). All these periods exhibit a feeling of disharmony and disequilibrium with the cosmos; men fear nature, and hence do not want to represent it, or they reject the world of nature for that of the spirit. Hence in their art there is no modeling, no illusion of space; instead, there are linear-geometric patterns and the dominance of the plane. Though Worringer says nothing about modern art, his description obviously applies to modern culture, and his book (*Abstraktion und Einfühlung*, 1908) was taken as prophecy and justification of the new developments. According to Worringer, it is space or depth which gives objects a time-value because it places them in the real world in which events occur. "Now time is the very condition of that flux and change from which, as we have seen, man wishes to escape when he is in a relation of disequilibrium with the cosmos; hence non-naturalistic styles shun the dimensions of depth and prefer the plane" (p. 55). Hence the plastic arts are most spatial when they do not represent the dimension of space; in non-naturalistic styles, "the inherent spatiality of the plastic arts is accentuated by the effort to remove all traces of time-value." Spatial form in literature is thus the complement to developments in the plastic arts. Pound's definition of the Image as "that which presents an intellectual and emotional complex in an instant of time" is a description of spatial form, whose impact is instantaneous and not discursive. In order to include more than one image in a poem, however, it is necessary to "undermine the inherent consecutiveness of language, frustrating the reader's normal expectation of a sequence and forcing him to perceive the elements of the poem as juxtaposed in space rather than unrolling in time" (p. 10). This is what Eliot does in *The Waste Land* and Pound in the *Cantos*, Frank says; syntactical sequence is given up for a structure depending on the perception of relationships between disconnected word-groups, which must be juxtaposed and perceived simultaneously.

Frank relates spatial form to the preoccupation with myth characteristic of modern literature.

> Just as the dimension of depth has vanished from the sphere of visual creation, so the dimension of historical depth has vanished from the content of the major works of modern literature. Past and present are apprehended spatially, locked in a timeless unity that, while it may accentuate surface differences, eliminates any feeling of sequence by the very act of juxtaposition (p. 59).

The time world of history is transmuted into the timeless world of myth, for which historical time does not exist, but only eternal prototypes. This timeless world finds appropriate aesthetic expression in spatial form.

Eliot has testified on several occasions to the formal as well as substantive importance of myth in modern literature. In his introduction to *In Parenthesis* (1937), by David Jones, Eliot suggests that Jones has in common with Joyce, Pound, and himself three characteristics: first, the use of language in a new way; second, a break with logical order; and third, the use of myth and allusion on several levels. This comment is of special interest, both as a capsule definition of modernism by one who should know and as an indication of the importance of the new use of myth. In 1923, reviewing *Ulysses*, Eliot had celebrated Joyce as the discoverer of the "mythical method." The problem for the modern artist, Eliot then observed, is how to deal with the present. He must deal with it, for there is no use being "classical" by ignoring "nine-tenths of the material which lies at hand, and selecting only mummified stuff from a museum." [24] Joyce's discovery, Eliot says, is a "way of controlling, of ordering, of giving a shape and a significance to the immense panorama of futility and anarchy which is contemporary history"; it has the importance of scientific discoveries like Einstein's, and is "a step toward making the modern world possible for art. . . ." "Instead of narrative method, we may now use the mythical method," which Eliot defines as "manipulating a continuous parallel between contemporaneity and antiquity." There can be little doubt that Eliot himself had learned much about the method from Joyce; as we shall see in the next chapter, *The Waste Land* resembles *Ulysses* in several fundamental respects, as well as in many curious small points.

In the review we have been discussing, Eliot noted that the mythical method was "a method already adumbrated by Mr. Yeats, and of the need for which I believe Mr. Yeats to have been the first contemporary to be conscious. . . ." He adds that psychology, "ethnology, and *The Golden Bough* have concurred to make possible what was impossible even a few years ago." Frazer's *Golden Bough* (Eliot is clearly thinking of the expanded edition in twelve volumes, not complete until 1915) was the first full demonstration of both the immense variety and the recurrent patterns of myth (including ritual, folklore, and related beliefs and practices), with the relation between human and plant reproduction—e.g. vegetation myths and fertility rituals—as a central theme. Frazer's point of view was that of a conventional late-Victorian positivist, however; he regarded religion as essentially an addiction to magic, and myth as an expression of the primitive mind, truth being the exclusive property of the mature scientific mind. Malinowski and others took myth more seriously, showing its tremendous importance in primitive societies and suggesting its universal significance. Freud demonstrated the universality of myth and its fundamental relation to the individual Unconscious, which expresses it directly or in disguise; and Jung carried this

24. "Ulysses, Order, and Myth," in *The Modern Tradition*, pp. 679–81.

kind of analysis further and generalized it with his theories of the archetypes and the collective Unconscious. Myths, according to Jung, "are first and foremost psychic phenomena that reveal the nature of the soul"; all the "mythologized processes of nature . . . are symbolic expressions of the inner, unconscious drama of the psyche which becomes accessible to man's consciousness by way of projection. . . ." [25] The archetypes are "structural elements of the human psyche in general"; predispositions of the psyche, un-filled outlines given content by overt myth, fantasies, and the like. "An archetypal content expresses itself, first and foremost, in metaphors. . . ." This mythical material vexes the intellect be-cause it refuses to fit into any formula, and so there is a constant effort to banish it; but "we can never legitimately cut loose from our archetypal foundations unless we are prepared to pay the price of a neurosis. . . ." The myths and archetypes, Jung insists, must be reinterpreted to "connect the life of the past that still ex-ists in us with the life of the present, which threatens to slip away from it." This parallels Mann's concept, based on Freud, of the "lived myth," of life as "a steady mythical identification, a procession in the footsteps of others, a sacred repetition. Yet this world of man is reborn through us; we remake it at every turn. It is at once passively experienced and actively created, at once his-torical and prophetic, timely and timeless." [26] The most obvious fictional embodiment is Mann's Joseph novels; but Ellmann and Feidelson suggest that Joyce's *Ulysses* is closer in spirit to this conception of myth than to Eliot's, to "lived myth" than to a "classical" effort to find an external source of meaning. At any rate, both Eliot's "mythical method" and the "lived myth" find in myth a source of meaning larger and deeper than the rational, and both provide, through myth, an escape from the dilemma we examined in the first chapter: a mode of continuity with the past.

It is thus appropriate that a mythical figure, Dionysus, should be our primary symbol for modernism, which is characterized by

25. *The Modern Tradition,* p. 643.
26. Ibid., p. 620.

its recognition of the importance of myth and finds through it a central means of continuity with the past. In the next chapter we proceed to the necessary complement of Dionysus, the archetype of the City.

CHAPTER THREE

THE
NATURE OF MODERNISM:
THE CITY

WHEN WALTER PATER observed that Greek tragedy began when Dionysus entered the City, he expressed memorably (and independently) the theme of Nietzsche's *Birth of Tragedy*.[1] The word *city* derives from *civitas*, city-state, which is properly an aggregation of *cives*, citizens; *civilization* has the same derivation. The City, then, even in its etymology, is internal as well as external: the city is a society of individuals who subscribe to an ideal of rational order. The physical city is merely a reflection of this ideal, and actual societies and institutions are imperfect embodiments of it. Both for the individual and for the society, the principle of order is, being based on reason, Apollonian, as contrasted to Dionysian community based on lower or higher faculties. Greek tragedy, according to both Nietzsche and Pater, developed in the tension between Apollo and Dionysus.

In a different sense, modernism may be said to have begun when Dionysus entered the City, meaning by it this time the literal and physical city which dominates the modern environment

1. "A Study of Dionysus," in *Greek Studies* (London, 1911), pp. 39–40.

and is both cause and symptom of our characteristic maladies. This city is the literal environment and scene, and hence a part of the subject, of most modern literature; it is the background which produces the typical modern man and the stage upon which he acts.

In earlier times, *Civitas Terrena*, the Earthly City, was seen as striving toward a Heavenly City, *Civitas Dei;* not expecting to embody on earth its perfection, but not without hope of achieving the Good Society. For the moderns, however, the City is seen as falling (things fall apart; falling towers) or as fallen (towers upside down in air; *la tour abolie*) and therefore moving in the other direction, toward the Infernal City—hence bathed in an infernal light, or revealing beneath its mundane outlines those of the City of Dis.[2] Dante and Baudelaire are the poets whose infernal visions haunt the modern writer; or else images of snow, desert, and the sea—the opposite of the City. But enough of such preliminary generalizations; let us proceed to consider these matters in more detail.

THE CITY WITHIN

While Nietzsche joyfully celebrated his revivified Dionysiac principle, he was emphatic in asserting that the Apollonian must be retained. Art, he said, "owes its continuous evolution to the Apollonian-Dionysiac duality, even as the propagation of the species depends on the duality of the sexes, their constant conflicts and periodic acts of reconciliation."[3] Their marriage produced Greek tragedy. Without Apollo, the Greeks would have been reduced by Dionysus to the condition of the barbarians, who indulged their lust and cruelty. "What kept Greece safe was the proud, imposing image of Apollo, who in holding up the head of

2. Ideal cities do sometimes appear: Yeats's Byzantium, Eliot's Elizabethan London, Pound's Ecbatan. But these tend to be highly personal visions, with little sense of community or society.
3. *The Modern Tradition*, p. 548.

the Gorgon to those brutal and grotesque Dionysiac forces subdued them." But the Apollonian Greek, seeing a votary of Dionysus, would realize with a shudder "that all this was not so alien
to him after all, that his Apollonian consciousness was but a thin
veil hiding from him the whole Dionysiac realm."

Freud, too, while making his revelation of the Dionysiac scope
and power of the irrational, mysterious forces of the Unconscious, affirmed the importance of retaining and strengthening the
Apollonian principle. Thomas Mann pointed out, in his essay
"Freud and the Future" (1936), the profound resemblances in
this and other respects between Nietzsche and Freud. Freud
shares Nietzsche's love of truth, his "psychological agony" of
self-knowledge, self-crucifixion; and he carries to vastly greater
lengths Nietzsche's theme of disease as an instrument of knowledge. Observing in the Nazi Third Reich the "moral devastation
which is produced by the worship of the unconscious, the systematic glorification of the primitive and irrational," Mann
pointed out how remote this was from Freud's ideal. Freud, like
Nietzsche, he argues, points toward a "humanism of the future,"
standing in a different relation to the powers of the lower world,
the unconscious and the id: "a relation bolder, freer, blither, pro-
ductive of a riper art than any possible in our neurotic, fear-rid-
den, hate-ridden world." [4] For the "analytic revelation is a revolutionary force," and Freud regarded it as reclamation work, like
the draining of the Zuider Zee.

As we have seen, the great early modern writers all tended to
feel that they were witnessing the end of an era, that the values
that had governed Western civilization for the past four centuries
were doomed. But, though this sense of cataclysmic change, of
collapsing and disintegrating civilization, is profoundly important
in their work, it does not mean that they abandon the vision of
man in society, the image of the City. In contrast to the Romantics a century earlier—or some of them, and some of the French
Symbolists—they do not retreat, after early Utopian and revolu-

4. Ibid., p. 585.

tionary dreams, into the individual consciousness; even Wallace Stevens, superficially so much like Mallarmé, keeps the city dump in view ("Man on the Dump"). Their apocalyptic visions are far from paradisal, but they do not completely abandon hope of the collective human enterprise. As Harry Levin points out, the pioneers all belong to a particular historical moment: born early enough to participate in the values of the older civilization, and yet late enough to identify themselves primarily with the new, they feel themselves not oppressed by the *fin de siècle* but stimulated by the sense of belonging to the new century.

We have already mentioned Lionel Trilling's thesis that the central characteristic of modern literature is the "bitter line of hostility to civilization" that runs through it. But it is typically only the new civilization—or certain aspects of it—that the moderns oppose, while they profess allegiance both to the vanishing old order and to the idea of civilized society. (There are, of course, exceptions.) Man's fate is envisioned, however gloomily, as a social one, not merely individual. Though the great moderns are far more concerned with the deeper and more mysterious communion of Dionysus, they do not give up the Apollonian idea of order; and hence they exhibit the fruitful tension between the two principles that Nietzsche described. Those who abandon it are the catastrophists, anarchists, or jokers, from Dada to Beat, who will be discussed in Chapter Seven.

THE CITY IN POETRY

Of the city as physical fact, dominating the modern scene, it is unnecessary to say much; there will be few readers of this book who are not intimately acquainted with it. The urbanization of our culture, in England, Europe, and perhaps most spectacularly in the United States, has been the major sociological phenomenon of the last century. Twenty million people in the United States moved into the cities between 1945 and 1968; in the latter year 70 per cent of the population lived in cities, on 1 per cent of the land. The City is both massive fact and universally recognizable symbol of modernity, and it both constitutes and symbolizes the modern predicament: the mass man, anonymous and rootless, cut off from his past and from the nexus of human relations in which he formerly existed, anxious and insecure, enslaved by the mass media but left by the disappearance of God with a dreadful freedom of spiritual choice, is the typical citizen of Megalopolis, where he enjoys lethal and paralyzing traffic, physical decay and political corruption, racial and economic tension, crime, rioting, and police brutality. This is the lurid picture we are accustomed to; and even for those who have never heard of Dante or Baudelaire, it is the most natural of metaphors to speak of this scene of cruelty, ugliness, inhumanity, and despair as Hell. It is no wonder that, for the great modern writers, the line between literal and symbolic City is similarly tenuous.

In the Augustan period, from Dryden to Johnson, there had been some excellent urban poetry, chiefly satirical or parodic, and usually in "imitation" of a Roman model—for example, the "City pastoral" or "town eclogue" of Swift and Gay, or the epistles and dialogues imitating Horace done by Prior and Pope, and Johnson's "London," done in imitation of Juvenal. But English poetry since the mid-eighteenth century offered few examples of successful rendering of the City. There were occasional brilliant exceptions: Blake's visionary "London," Wordsworth's Westminster Bridge sonnet with its astonished recognition that the City is after all alive, James Thomson's overwrought "City of Dreadful Night," Henley's vividly realistic "In Hospital" and "London Voluntaries"; but in general the poets regarded the city as something alien, and they were not interested in writing about it. Perplexed by the "strange disease of modern life / With its sick hurry, its divided aims," they sought healing and consolation in Nature; and from Arnold through Housman they escape into a pastoral landscape where they adopt a dignified Stoic posture. London is present in Yeats's "Lake Isle of Innisfree" only insofar as its "pavements grey" provide an implicit contrast and motive for escape, and Yeats's poem was the model for innumerable genteel pastorals confessing a yearning to fly urban complexities for country simplicities.

There was little in the English poetic tradition, then, to help a modern poet to learn how to deal with what must be the great modern subject. Even Yeats, with all his varied excellences, had little to offer here, for the City appears only peripherally in his work. In the early verse, as we have just seen, it appears as that London from which he wishes to escape to the lake isle of Innisfree or the land of heart's desire; in the middle period as that Dublin, contemptible but real, with which he has to deal as playwright and theatrical manager, and which can, surprisingly, be the site of heroism (as in "Easter 1916"); in the later period as Byzantium, itself a pastoral symbol, an aesthete's paradise (among other things), but essentially an individual rather than a social or communal ideal, and hence not really a City. Yeats's hatred of the literal city is mitigated only when he thinks of the idealized eighteenth-century Dublin of Swift and Burke or (as we saw in the last chapter) when he sees the "beautiful humane cities" as threatened by Dionysiac forces.

Ezra Pound's achievement, against this background, was a considerable one, for he did confront the modern City and deal with it seriously and critically. His attitude is as different from that of the Futurists, who accepted all the appurtenances of urban mechanization with adulation, as from that of the genteel pastoralists who rejected it all with an equally uncritical completeness. From 1909 on, and especially from *Ripostes* (1912) to *Mauberley* (1920), Pound wrote admirably sharp and often witty observations of life in the metropolis of London. He learned something from the French, from Baudelaire to Samain and Laforgue, but far more from the poets of Augustan Rome, who seem often to be in his mind. Pound does, in fact, a kind of "two-plane" writing in which the Roman poets' treatment of their city serves as a continuing allusion, sometimes as model and sometimes as object of parody, and with innumerable shades of irony in between.

(This is, of course, very much what the English Augustans did in the "imitation"; and Pound, in spite of his general dislike of this period of English literature, surely was aware of the genre.) Thus Pound puts Martial's epigrams in modern terms; he parodies Horace's theme of pastoral retirement by longing for the urban peace and security of a little tobacco shop where he can exchange a friendly word with the passing whores. "Homage to Sextus Propertius" (1917) is his most extended and complex work in this mode, rendering imperial London in terms of imperial Rome. In other poems he observes with aesthetic detachment both "les Millwin" and the arty students of the Slade; he contrasts the vitality of the children of the very poor to the emotional anaemia of the over-cultivated lady; he draws a lovingly malicious picture of one type of London *salonnière* ("Portrait d'une Femme"). Returning to New York, he observes "a million people surly with traffic," but nevertheless calls the city a "maid with no breasts" and offers to immortalize her. This kind of romantic personification of city as woman is, however, rare in Pound; usually he is both subtle and detached. His most famous short poem, "In a Station of the Metro," fuses the urban image of faces in a crowd with the contrasting natural image of petals on a wet, black, bough. The City is portrayed as decadent in *Mauberley*, where it is very specifically postwar London, as Pound bids farewell to it, and in the *Cantos*, where other cities, too (but none with the special animus directed at London), represent the "old bitch gone in the teeth" that is Western civilization. On the other hand, there are glimpses of ideal Cities as the *Cantos* go on, "the city of Dioce whose terraces are stars," as there are the values of Confucius, of John Adams and the early Republic, and of many odder people; and there are even a few kind words for the English.

The great master of the City theme among the modern poets, however, is Eliot. We know with unusual exactness, from his own statements, how he began to write and which poets influenced his early work. It was Baudelaire who first showed him that the experiences of an adolescent in an industrial city could be the material for poetry, and that the sordid aspects of the modern metropolis might be fused with the phantasmagoric.[5] The immediate stimulus to the writing of the earliest characteristic poems was the reading of Laforgue, from whom Eliot took a manner and an attitude; but from the beginning the City that appears in these poems is, like Baudelaire's, at least half a projection of inner psychic states. In Eliot's poems of 1909–11 the urban consciousness is rendered with a profundity, wit, and power unmatched since Baudelaire. The "Preludes" present "such a vision of the street / As the street hardly understands" (especially IV, beginning, "His soul stretched tight across the skies," and ending, "The conscience of a blackened street / Impatient to assume the world"); the "Rhapsody on a Windy Night" fuses inner and outer subtly and inextricably. The peculiar desolation of urban life is given vivid expression: "The worlds revolve like ancient women / Gathering fuel in vacant lots." Occasionally the city is distinctively Boston ("The Boston Evening Transcript") or Cambridge, where Mr. Apollinax visits Professor Channing-Cheetah; usually it is any metropolis. "Portrait of a Lady" and "Prufrock" both portray individuals in relation to an urban society; in both, inner and outer fuse to create a double portrait of both an individual and a society. Winding streets, lonely men in shirtsleeves leaning out of windows, and the like characterize both the speaker and the city.

Other early poems seem to be experiments in various ways of dealing with the City. "Burbank with a Baedeker . . ." evokes Venice largely through literary allusion; "Lune de Miel" is based on a satirical contrast between Ravenna with its Byzantine mosaics of the ascetic St. Apollinaire and the miserable honeymooners in the heat and bedbugs with their thoroughly physical concerns. "A Cooking Egg" is terribly British in its theme of the loss of the "penny world" of the nursery and very specifically Londonian, especially in the last stanza, and "Le Spectateur" a marvelously grotesque little satire on one aspect of London life—conservative

5. See full discussion, with references, in the next chapter.

journalism—with an added edge and detachment given by the French medium. "Mélange Adultère de Tout" is a kind of self-parody, burlesquing the cosmopolitanism and exoticism—the exaggerated topographical sense—of such poems as the foregoing, presenting the poet as completely eclectic chameleon. "Dans le Restaurant" is very Parisian, being, among other things, a satire on the French waiter's attitude to l'amour.

The Waste Land is, of course, Eliot's greatest City poem. Almost certainly, the basic formal influence on The Waste Land was that of Joyce's Ulysses. We will have to return to the topic of Joyce and the City, which would constitute too large a digression at this point; here we are concerned only with indicating briefly what Eliot learned from him. This was, as Eliot indirectly acknowledged in his review of 1923, the "mythical method" which is fundamental to the poem, the manipulation of a continuous parallel between the present and the past, or "two-plane" writing, as Joyce called it in conversation.[6] As Ellmann shows, Joyce made sure that Eliot saw each new episode of Ulysses as it was finished (most of it was published serially in 1918–19), and of its powerful impact on him there is plenty of evidence: Eliot wrote to Joyce in May, 1921, "I wish, for my own sake, that I had not read it." [7] As several critics have suggested, there are numerous other resemblances between the poem and the novel, and it seems likely that most of them indicate borrowings, presumably unconscious, by Eliot. Thus the "Oxen of the Sun" episode might have suggested both the title ("Agendath is a waste land, a home of screechowls. . . .") and, at the end, the theme of infertility and chaos as typical of the modern world. "Circe," and other episodes, might have suggested the notion of the City as Inferno, and of fantasy merging with the sordid details of low life. The early episode "Hades" contains the themes of burial of the dead,

6. Richard Ellmann, James Joyce (N. Y., 1959), p. 541.
7. Ibid., p. 542. In the following summary I am indebted to Hugh Kenner, Dublin's Joyce (Bloomington, 1956), p. 210, and W. Y. Tindall, A Reader's Guide to James Joyce (N. Y., 1959), p. 160, as well as to Ellmann.

(fusing with the descent to the underworld) and death by water, references to Tiresias and the dog, and the method of allusion and quotation that the poem carries further. Stephen's meditations on the theme of metamorphosis and death by water are similar: seachange. "Those are pearls"; but Stephen is hydrophobe, and is rescued by Bloom from spiritual drowning. It is "in connection with drowning, physical dissolution into circumambient matter . . . that the theme of eternal recurrence (the Wheel of Mme. Sosotris' pack), the metempsychosis which puzzled Molly Bloom, achieves its sharpest definition: . . . 'A seachange this . . . Seadeath, mildest of all deaths known to man. Old Father Ocean. . . .' " [8] Many more details might be cited, but it seems best to conclude with two larger points. The first is that, in addition to the "mythical method," or perhaps as a concomitant to it, Eliot probably learned from *Ulysses* how to achieve spatial form. As Harry Levin puts it, speaking of *Finnegans Wake,* but in words that apply equally to *The Waste Land,* Joyce's lifelong endeavor was "to escape from the nightmare of history, to conceive the totality of human experience on a simultaneous plane, to synchronize past, present, and future in the timelessness of a millennium. Time is spatialized, a mere auxiliary to the other three dimensions. Space is curved, boundless and finite, the same anew." [9] Finally, Eliot must have learned, from *Dubliners* as well as *Ulysses,* how to use the City as locus of this spatialized form and "two-plane" writing (which Eliot multiplies to at least three, and often more, planes), how to make realistic details resonate and suggest metaphors and allusions (as paralysis, living death, madness, frustration, and spiritual corruption are suggested in *Dubliners*), and how to make one city a microcosm of all cities and of all life, as Dublin is in *Ulysses.*

In 1921 Pound, reviewing Cocteau's *Poésies 1917–20,* said that

8. Kenner, *Dublin's Joyce,* p. 212. See also Stuart Gilbert, *James Joyce's "Ulysses"* (N. Y., 1930), on the relation of the drowned Phoenician sailor to Stephen and Bloom.
9. Harry Levin, *James Joyce* (N. Y., 1960), p. 198.

Cocteau wrote poetry of the city intellect: "The life of a village is narrative; you have not been there three weeks before you know that in the revolution et cetera, and when M. le Comte et cetera, and so forth. In a city the visual impressions succeed each other, overlap, overcross, they are 'cinematographic.' . . ." [10] Howarth suggests that Eliot took a cue from this for the form of *The Waste Land*, and that Pound also had it in mind in helping him to cut and rearrange the poem. Howarth also suggests that Stravinsky's *Sacre* may have influenced the form of the poem; Eliot saw it performed by the Russian Ballet in the summer of 1921, and defended it in a London letter to *The Dial*. Its music, he said, metamorphosed the "rhythm of the steppes" into "the scream of the motor horn, the rattle of machinery, the grind of wheels, the beating of iron and steel, the roar of the underground railway, and the other barbaric cries of modern life" (pp. 234–35). It brought home, he said, the continuity of the human predicament: primitive man on the dolorous steppes, modern man in the city with its despairing noises, the essential problem unchanging.

The most perceptive comment on the City image in *The Waste Land* is Frank Kermode's. Eliot, he argues, in a "weirdly pure sense," is an imperialist:

> This imperialistic Eliot is the poet of the *urbs aeterna*, of the transmitted but corrupted dignity of Rome. Hence his veneration not only for Baudelaire . . . but for Virgil. . . . The other side of this city is the Babylon of Apocalypse, and when the *imperium* is threadbare and the end approaches of that which Virgil called endless, this is the city we see. It is the *Blick ins Chaos*. . . .

> In another mood, complementary to this of Babylon, Eliot still imagined the Empire as without end, and Virgil, its prophet, became the central Classic. . . . In him originated the imperial tradition. To ignore the "consciousness of Rome" as Virgil crys-

10. Quoted by Herbert Howarth, *Notes on Some Figures Behind T. S. Eliot* (London, 1965), p. 236.

tallized it is simply to be provincial. . . . The European destiny, as prophesied by Virgil, was imperial; the Empire became the secular body of the Church. The fact that it split is reflected in *The Waste Land*, where the hooded Eastern hordes swarm over their plains, and the towers of the City fall. And as the dignity of empire was split among the nations, the task of the chosen, which is to defeat the proud and be merciful to the subject, was increasingly identified with Babylonian motives of profit—a situation in which Kipling's relevance is obvious. . . . Thus does the poet-historian redeem the time. His is a period of waiting such as occurs before the apocalypse of collapsing cities. But behind the temporal disaster of Babylon he knows that the timeless pattern of the eternal city must survive (*Continuities*, pp. 73–74).

Of the intimate presence of the physical city of London in the poem it is unnecessary to speak: the crowd in the first section, at once specifically localized and supernatural, fusing with the crowds of Dante and Baudelaire, "ou le spectre en plein jour raccroche le passant"; not two-plane, but multi-level, going Joyce more than one better. Then the vivid pub scene, the Thames-daughters who "expect nothing"; the passage about St. Magnus Martyr and the fishermen's restaurant, and so on: the poem is permeated by the physical presence of the city of London, both contemporary and Elizabethan, and by the City as symbol of order, civilization, all that is the opposite of the Waste Land. In this latter sense it is, of course, collapsing—"Jerusalem Athens Alexandria / falling towers" and "London Bridge is falling down"; only fragments to be shored against ruins.

Finally, we must cite the famous patrol of the air-raid warden in *Little Gidding*, where the dialogue with the ghost of a long-dead master takes place. The burning city looks like the Inferno, they agree; and this passage marks the high point of the fusion of the natural and the supernatural Cities in Eliot: for the ghost is not just the past, but a specific representative of poetic tradition; and the vision of the City as Inferno could hardly go further.

Perhaps the two most intensely local passages in the *Four*

Quartets are the descent into the Underground in *Burnt Norton* and this dead patrol of the air-raid warden in *Little Gidding*. Both are visionary, but in quite different ways: the first proceeds by literal and realistic description of an everyday urban scene, which only gradually takes on an additional meaning: the descent into the subway of people with "strained, time-ridden faces," "eructation of unhealthy souls / Into the faded air, the torpid," becomes the Dark Night of the Soul, the journey of deprivation, of abstention from motion. Vacancy, meaninglessness, darkness and deprivation are carried to their utmost limits in the hope that the Negative Way will prepare the soul for God. In *Little Gidding*, however, the scene is supernatural and visionary to begin with: illumination and active suffering are provided by the flames, and there is no low-keyed realism but the highest intensity of vision and adjuration to active purgation, to enter the flames and "move in measure like a dancer."

To pursue the theme of the City among other modern poets would require a separate book: Williams, Cummings, Stevens, Hart Crane come immediately to mind as exhibiting versions of great interest. For reasons of space, we will have to restrict ourselves to two poets: W. H. Auden, who uses the City symbol explicitly, extensively, and in a manner quite different from Eliot's, and Robert Lowell, whose treatment is different from those of any of the poets mentioned.

The City has been a prominent feature of Auden's moralized landscape from the beginning. In the early poetry it is a natural symbol for civilization, order, collective responsibility as opposed to escapist and isolationist islands. Thus "Paysage Moralisé" concludes with the exhortation that we "rebuild our cities, not dream of islands"—islands "where love was innocent, being far from cities" in our unreal and sentimental imaginings. When Auden took up residence in New York in 1939, he chose to live his myth almost like Yeats in his tower with its winding stair. "New Year Letter" is based upon a parallel between two types of *civitas*, art and society: "To set in order: that's the task / Both Eros and Apollo ask." (In the elegy on Freud, Eros is called "builder of cities.") In "New Year Letter," the only existing order is that of art—the "*civitas* of sound" produced by a passacaglia of Buxtehude; but this exists inside the order represented by Elizabeth Mayer's New Year's Eve party: a small group of civilized persons, cosmopolitan, mostly exiles, existing precariously in the huge anonymous city and coming together briefly to form a temporary order of art and civilization. At the end of the poem, after much inconclusive exploration of the problem of relating internal and external ideas of order (though concluding firmly that art "cannot be / A midwife to society / For art is a *fait accompli*"), the poet looks out at the "ironic points of light" in the darkened city and imagines them to represent scattered individuals who participate in the same internal order of art and civilization, and he prays that he will in response "show an affirming flame." In *For the Time Being, The Age of Anxiety*, and numerous shorter poems of the 1940s, the City image is a fusion of ancient Rome and the modern city, suggesting a parallel between our own naturalistic civilization and that of decadent Rome: both cultures reject, in the name of reason, the Absurd of Christianity, which alone can give meaning to history as well as to individual life. "The Fall of Rome" portrays our secular culture in terms of the collapsing Roman one; "Under Sirius" presents the ironically-named Fortunatus in Rome in the dog-days of history, uncertain what to wish for, longing for yet fearing the supernatural.

"Memorial for the City" (1949) is Auden's most systematic development of the symbol. The first section contrasts the naturalistic and Christian attitudes toward history and time. The world as it appears to animals or cameras is one in which time is the enemy and human events are without significance; only Nature is "seriously there" because she endures. But human beings, even "now, in this night / Among the ruins of the Post-Vergilian City" know, because of the Christian revelation, that the "crime of life is not time," that we are not to pity ourselves nor to despair. The second section describes man's attempts to build a City. The Middle Ages achieved the Sane City, but it became corrupt; Luther denounced it, pointing out a "grinning gap / No rite could cross," and the City became insecure and divided. In the Renaissance "poets acclaimed the raging herod of the will." Later, reason and science (based upon the false belief that Nature "had no soul") brought civility and prosperity; the French Revolution aimed at the Rational City, based on natural goodness, seeking the prelapsarian man. In spite of all disasters, the same goal of the Glittering and Conscious City has been pursued ever since. The third section returns to the present: the end result of this progress is the "abolished City," in which civilization has broken down completely, leaving the barbed wire and ruins of war. The ultimate cause is that this secular ideal falsifies human nature, "the flesh we are but never would believe." The last section, "Let Our Weakness speak," personifies human weakness. This weakness, the despair of logicians and statesmen, is the irreducible core of individuality which protects man while it infuriates the social planners, the Apollonians ("As for Metropolis, that too-great city; her delusions are not mine").

The symbol of the City dominates the volume *Nones*, in which the shorter poem we have been discussing appeared, and it is extremely important in the next volume, *The Shield of Achilles*. The title poem contrasts to the "Marble well-governed cities" of Homer's world the modern featureless plain on which an "unintelligible multitude" is ordered about by a faceless voice citing statistics, victims are tortured and executed by "bored officials," and a juvenile delinquent loiters "who'd never heard / Of any world where promises were kept, / Or one could weep because another wept." It is a grim picture of the complete breakdown of the ideal of community and civilized society, the most extreme contrast of ancient and modern. But Auden does not usually take so glum a view of the modern predicament; he does not give up hope or abandon the ideal, however improbable it appears. The first section of "Memorial for the City" ends:

As we bury our dead
We know without knowing there is reason for what we bear,
That our hurt is not a desertion, that we are to pity
Neither ourselves nor our city;
Whoever the searchlights catch, whatever the loudspeakers blare,
We are not to despair.

In "Winds" (*Bucolics*) he takes a much lighter tone: weather "Is what nasty people are / Nasty about and the nice / Show a common joy in observing: / When I seek an image / For our Authentic City, / . . . I see old men in hall-ways / Tapping their barometers, / Or a lawn over which / The first thing after breakfast, / A paterfamilias / Hurries to inspect his rain-gauge." And in "Sext" (*Horae Canonicae*) he describes the human capacity for vocation, for ignoring the appetitive goddesses and "forgetting themselves in a function." Without those "nameless heroes" who first took this step, we humans would be "Feral still, unhousetrained, still / wandering through forests without / a consonant to our names, / slaves of Dame Kind, lacking / all notion of a city" (but also, being still animals, incapable of sin: "and at this noon, for this death, / there would be no agents").

In his critical prose Auden has extensively discussed the City and related symbols. Thus in *The Enchafèd Flood* (1950) he observes that the Romantics abandon the image of the Just City because they no longer believe in its possibility, and symbolize modern civilization as a desert, level and mechanized, which destroys individuality. "Urban society is, like the desert, a place without limits. The city walls of tradition, mythos and cultus have crumbled." "The images of the Just City, of the civilised landscape protected by the Madonna . . . and of the rose garden or island of the blessed, are lacking in Romantic literature because the Romantic writers no longer believe in their existence. What exists is the Trivial Unhappy Unjust City, the desert of the average from which the only escape is to the wild, lonely, but still vital sea" (pp. 25–26). Auden argues that we "live in a new

age . . . in which the heroic image is not the nomad wandering
through the desert or over the ocean, but the less exciting figure
of the builder, who renews the ruined walls of the city." Our
temptations are different from those of the Romantics: "We are
less likely to be tempted by solitude into Promethean pride: we
are far more likely to become cowards in the face of the tyrant
who would compel us to lie in the service of the False City"
(p. 153).

More recently, the section of *The Dyer's Hand* called "The
Poet and the City" presented Auden's latest reflections on the relation between art and society. In the relation of the poet to the
city, one of the most damaging modern developments has been
the emergence of a passive, uncommitted, abstract "public," or
crowd, created by the growth of populations and the development of mass media. The "appearance of the Public and the mass
media which cater to it have destroyed naïve popular art." The
sophisticated "highbrow" artist survives, because his audience is
too small to interest the mass media; but the "audience of the
popular artist is the majority and this the mass media must steal
from him if they are not to go bankrupt." This they do by offering not popular art, but entertainment, to be consumed and replaced. "This is bad for everyone; the majority lose all genuine
taste of their own, and the minority become cultural snobs."

> The characteristic style of "Modern" poetry is an intimate tone
> of voice, the speech of one person addressing one person, not a
> large audience; whenever a modern poet raises his voice he sounds
> phony. And its characteristic hero is neither the "Great Man" nor
> the romantic rebel, both doers of extraordinary deeds, but the
> man or woman in any walk of life who, despite all the impersonal
> pressures of modern society, manages to acquire and preserve a
> face of his own (p. 84).

The analogy between the order of art and the order of society
that Auden explored in "New Year Letter" and elsewhere he reduces to an even sharper contrast. The good poem is analogue to

Utopia or Eden, not to a historical society: a "poetic city would always contain exactly the same number of inhabitants doing exactly the same jobs forever"; a society which was really like a good poem would be a "nightmare of horror," and a poem which was really like a political democracy would be "formless, windy, banal, and utterly boring." On the other hand, in our age "the mere making of a work of art is itself a political act." The existence of functioning artists reminds "the Management of something managers need to be reminded of, namely, that the managed are people with faces, not anonymous numbers, that Homo Laborans is also Homo Ludens."

Although Auden has thus rigorously distinguished between the realms of poetry and politics, he has never become indifferent toward the collective human enterprise nor despaired of it. The ideal of civility and community dominates his latest volume, *About the House,* with its sequence called "Thanksgiving for a Habitat." These poems celebrate the House, and in that obvious sense the ideal has become very much more personal, the symbol shrunk from civil to domestic. Since "New Year Letter," as we have seen, Auden has conceived of the City as embodied in scattered individuals who participate in civility, and not embodied in any actual society.

"On Installing an American Kitchen in Lower Austria" is retitled "Grub First, Then Ethics" and incorporated into the cycle. Celebrating the art of cookery (which Auden has called in prose "one art in which we probably excel all other societies that ever existed . . . the one art which Man the Laborer regards as sacred"), the poem offers a humorous and minimal defense of our civilization. The last stanza puts explicitly the image of the City as composed of scattered individuals—and their houses:

> the houses of our City
> are real enough but they lie
> haphazardly scattered over the earth,
> and her vagabond forum

is any space where two of us happen to meet
   who can spot a citizen
without papers. So too, can her foes. Where the
   power lies remains to be seen,
the force, though, is clearly with them: perhaps only
   by falling can She become
Her own vision, but we have sworn under four eyes
   to keep Her up—all we ask for,
should the night come when comets blaze and meres break,
   is a good dinner, that we
may march in high fettle, left foot first,
   to hold her Thermopylae.

The House poems continue this notion, for the House is more
than personal: it is an outpost and repository of civilization. The
poems regard it characteristically through long perspectives of
history, archaeology, geology, and biology, counterpointing such
formal themes with the easily personal and humorous.

In the context of Auden's work, one would not expect *The
Bassarids* (1966), the libretto based on Euripides that Auden and
Chester Kallman wrote for Hans Werner Henze's opera, to be a
simple act of homage to Dionysus. It is, if anything, closer to
being the reverse, for the awesome and appalling victory of
Dionysus in it suggests a lesson in the horrors produced by the
Dionysiac forces when not checked by Apollonian ideals of civility. This kind of application would make the opera a counterbalance to Auden's earlier poems stressing the inadequacy of Apollonian classicism. Fundamentally, however, *The Bassarids* remains
ambiguous in the same way as *The Bacchae*, of which E. R.
Dodds well says—against both those who interpret it as a rationalist exposé of religion and those who take it as Euripides's pali-
node, his final surrender to the mysteries—that its purpose is not
to prove anything, but to enlarge our sensibilities and our understanding of experience.

To sum up, there are, it seems to me, two kinds of meaning in
the opera, both faithful to Euripides but going beyond him in im-

plication. The first is psychological. Dionysus, like Aphrodite in the *Hippolytus*, presides over the force that "through the green fuse drives the flower," in realms larger than human nature. As Dodds puts the theme of *The Bacchae*, "We ignore at our peril the demand of the human spirit for Dionysiac experience," which, if repressed, becomes destructive. Auden suggests an analogy with Mozart's *Magic Flute*. Pentheus's "attempt completely to suppress his instincts instead of integrating them with his rationality brings about his downfall. One might say that a similar fate would have befallen Sarastro, had there not been a Tamino and a Pamina to marry and so reconcile Day to Night." [11]

The foregoing kind of significance is embodied chiefly in the character of Pentheus, the arrogant individual who rejects the Dionysian completely. There is, however, a complementary meaning of the same sort, though collective rather than individual, suggesting the tyranny of the irrational and emotional—the triumph of the demonic—that results from the complete victory of Dionysus. This is clearest in the final scene of the opera, which projects the theme into the future and shows the consequences of Dionysus's victory. (Henze describes his music for this as a requiem, a *dies irae, lacrimosa der Götter*.) Semele and Dionysus are replaced by "two enormous primitive fertility idols of an African or South Seas type: fetish masks etc. The male is daubed with red paint." The Bassarids kneel and adore them, as does Tiresias. Finally the Child (mute) "smashes her doll at the foot of the tomb and jumps up and down with joy," thus repeating in little Agave's murder of Pentheus.

11. Program note for the Salzburg premiere. In *Secondary Worlds* (N. Y., 1968), pp. 109-10, Auden develops this analogy more fully: "Today we know only too well that it is possible for whole communities to become demonically possessed as it is for individuals to go off their heads. Further, what the psychologists have taught us about repression and its damaging, sometimes fatal effects, makes us look at Sarastro with a more critical eye. Like Pentheus when confronted by the cult of Dionysus, Sarastro's only idea of how to deal with the Queen of the Night is to use force, magical in his case, and banish her to the underworld."

The second kind of meaning is religious. This works chiefly by negative implication: what is lacking in the Dionysiac religion shows why it was necessary for Christ to come, why Christianity is unique. Dionysus is beyond our good and evil, and human morality is irrelevant to him; his victory brings nothing but suffering to the humans involved. Agave, the central and only fully sympathetic character, suffers most; Pentheus suffers a dreadful and ironic fate—to become, as ritual victim, the god he denies—but may not fully understand it. Agave says to his corpse, "We both did what neither would: The strong gods are not good." William Arrowsmith suggests that the latter part of *The Bacchae* reveals the discovery of compassion,[12] and this may be said more emphatically of the opera. Dionysus has no compassion whatever; he cares nothing about human beings. When Beroe pleads with him to spare Pentheus because he is a good man, Dionysus says: "What is his goodness to me? I have no need of his worship. I have no need of time." And he refuses to spare him. Cadmus, at the end, says, "An Immortal God ought to forgive, not be angry Forever like ignorant men." Dionysus's last words in his epiphany are, "Down slaves, Kneel and adore." The contrast with Christianity in all these respects is sufficiently striking and needs no discussion; Dionysus neither suffers nor forgives, and he is not related to human morality.

The City plays a very different role in the poetry of Robert Lowell. There is no use of it as an abstract concept or conscious symbol, but rather a close-up sense of immersion in the life of a highly specific City as it is and has been, with a bitter sense of contrast between these realities and the professed ideals of civilization. Lowell's powerful historical sense makes the past City as real to him as the present, and his social awareness and responsibility make him feel personally involved in the deficiencies of the existing society. The literal city for Lowell is usually Boston, and the fact that his New England ancestors did set out to found

12. Introduction to his translation in *The Complete Greek Tragedies*, ed. David Grene and Richmond Lattimore (Chicago, 1959), IV, 540-41.

New Jerusalem or Salem in a new land lends a special acerbity to the bitterly ironic contrast Lowell likes to indicate between their millenarian professions and the actual modern city. It is not, however, that the Puritan ancestors were pure and their modern descendants corrupt; as many commentators have observed, Lowell seems to have Weber and Tawney on the relation between Protestantism and Capitalism in his bones, and no one ever painted a less sentimental and more toughly realistic picture of the Puritans. (Perhaps "Children of Light" is the most brilliant short version.) It is hardly too much to say that this critique of the American (not only New England) ideal of the City and of its issuance in fact is the central theme of his poetry, reaching its fullest flowering in the dramatic trilogy, *The Old Glory.*

Lowell's Catholic allegiance, in his earlier poetry, gives him a firm standpoint from which to criticize both modern civilization in general and specifically its New England Protestant corruptions; later, as in "Beyond the Alps," he stresses the corruption of the Catholic tradition itself. The image of Rome, naturally, represents this standpoint in both cases. But let us end these generalizations and look at a few poems. The early sonnet, "Concord," puts the matter simply: the modern, and specifically American, and more specifically New England, predicament of lacking an adequate religion and tradition:

> Ten thousand Fords are idle here in search
> Of a tradition. Over these dry sticks—
> The Minute Man, the Irish Catholics,
> The ruined bridge and Walden's fished-out perch—
> The belfry of the Unitarian Church
> Rings out the hanging Jesus. Crucifix,
> How can your whited spindling arms tranfix
> Mammon's unbridled industry. . . !

In the companion sonnet, "Salem," the actual town is implicitly contrasted to the Biblical vision and to the earlier whaling village whose fishermen did great deeds against Leviathan; the modern town is sick, and "Charon's raft / Dumps its damned goods into the harbor-bed." "As a Plane Tree by the Water" is a powerful evocation of modern Boston, with the superimposed images of Babel and of Babylon, and of the modern city as literally in the power of the devil. Boston is a "planned Babel," but worse, for "our money talks / And multiplies the darkness . . ."; the loudest voice is that of money. The devil's domination is shown by the flies of Beelzebub: "Flies, flies are on the plane tree, on the streets." The devil, with his "golden tongue / Enchants the masons of the Babel Tower / To raise tomorrow's city to the sun / That never sets upon these hell-fire streets / Of Boston. . . ." Across the Atlantic the miracle of Bernadette takes place at Lourdes; but in Boston there is no revelation: "Our Lady of Babylon, go by, go by. . . ." "Dea Roma" describes "How many roads and sewers led to Rome"; but, with all its corruptions and cruelties, "your fisherman / Walks on the waters of a draining Rome / To bank his catch in the Celestial City." "Where the Rainbow Ends" is an ironic apocalypse of Boston, city of coldness, greed, and apostasy. "The wild ingrafted olive and the root / Are withered"; only the bridge called the "Pepperpot, ironic rainbow, spans Charles River. . . ." But, though "Every dove is sold" and "In Boston serpents whistle at the cold," the "dove of Jesus" miraculously brings an olive branch to the altar, even in this exile. *Life Studies* is, of course, deeply imbued with a sense of place, even to different neighborhoods of Boston; but there is little symbolic overtone. "Inauguration Day: January 1953" is a fine evocation of New York in winter—paralyzed by cold and snow, in the midst of the Cold War—with Grant's Tomb as its spiritual center: "Cyclonic zero of the word, / God of our armies, who interred / Cold Harbor's blue immortals, Grant!" The poem ironically celebrates Eisenhower as his spiritual successor, "and the Republic summons Ike, the mausoleum in her heart." "Beyond the Alps," as we have said, gives a disillusioned view of the Pope and the Catholic tradition; as the poet travels from Rome to Paris, "Much against my will / I left the City of God where it belongs," and he recalls "There the skirt-mad Mussolini unfurled / The eagle of Caesar . . ." and reflects that the same Roman crowds have just rejoiced at the Pope's proclamation of the Virgin's bodily assumption. "God herded his people to the *coup de grace*—." But the poet can no longer believe— "Our mountain-climbing train had come to earth"—and is left with only reason, Minerva, to guide: "pure mind and murder," as he goes on to Paris, "our black classic." Boston appears symbolically in only one poem, "Colonel Shaw and the Massachusetts 54th," where the dedication of Colonel Shaw and his Negro infantry is contrasted to the forgetful, commercialized modern world. The poem is a marvelously vivid rendering of the modern city: instead of the old Aquarium, there are now parking-spaces "like civic / sandpiles in the heart of Boston"; the Statehouse is braced against the excavation for a garage, as it faces St. Gaudens's relief of Colonel Shaw and his Negro infantry, who, according to the epigraph, "relinquunt omnia servare rem publicam." Their monument "sticks like a fishbone" in the throat of the frivolous and irresponsible modern City, for the uncompromising Shaw is "out of bounds now," and there are "no statues for the last war here." "Space is nearer," but on the television the "drained faces of Negro children rise like balloons," the Negroes still submerged like fish in the old aquarium. Now "giant finned cars nose forward like fish; / a savage servility / slides by on grease."

This poem, renamed, became the title poem of *For the Union Dead* (1965). We must postpone discussion of this volume and of its successor, *Near the Ocean* (1967), until Chapter VII, noting at this point only that in them the City theme becomes central.

THE CITY IN FICTION

Our concern is not really with the whole topic of fictional treatment of the City, which would require discussion of many novelists from Balzac to Kafka, at the least, but with the introduction of the City as principal subject of fiction in English and with the handling of this new subject in a manner distinctively modern. The writer who accomplished both these feats at one blow was James Joyce. Joyce, in so many respects "old father, old artificer" of literary modernism, established in *Dubliners* and brought to fullest development in *Ulysses* both the central image of the City and the special method by which it is rendered by following writers, poets as well as novelists. This method is, of course, the "mythical" one discussed in our last chapter, providing both through continuous parallel with a dominant myth and through multiple and many-layered allusion a means of apprehending past and present simultaneously. The method is, as we have suggested, in one sense a solution to the problem of discontinuity, since it is a bridge across the chasm, a way of uniting the two sides and making sense of them. From another point of view, it requires a faith in the possibility of continuity to begin with, for if human nature or the human predicament have changed fundamentally the juxtaposition of past and present could produce only comic or satirical effects. Joyce plainly has this enabling faith: though the exact boundaries between comic, satirical, and serious parallels may be hard to define in *Ulysses*, it can hardly be maintained that there are no serious ones. In spite of his apostasy, his anti-clerical strain, his strong naturalistic inclinations and his skeptical cast of mind, Joyce has, as Eliot remarked, the "most orthodox sensibility" of any modern writer. His characters are seen in traditional ethical and spiritual dimensions, in a well-rounded context of family and social relations, duties, and responsibilities. Eliot, in *After Strange Gods,* goes on to draw a contrast with Lawrence, whose characters are so incomplete by comparison: they seem, for instance, never to have heard of moral obligations. Joyce's characters seek love of various kinds, not the one kind celebrated in Lawrence, and communion; they rarely find them. But Joyce thinks of life as not a matter of the isolated individual, or two individuals, but as something fundamentally social; and for this reason, throughout his work, the central image is that of the City.

At the same time, Joyce was intensely aware of the "great chasm between yesterday and today," as his master Ibsen expressed it. This appears most explicitly in the early version of the *Portrait* discarded by Joyce and published posthumously. In *Stephen Hero*, written 1904–6, Stephen is consciously "modern." This appears in his discussion with Cranly, where he says ". . . you think me fantastical simply because I am modern," and Cranly replies, "You're always talking about 'modern.'" Have you any idea of the age of the earth? You 'say you're emancipated' but, in my opinion, you haven't got beyond the first book of Genesis yet. There is no such thing as 'modern' or 'ancient': it's all the same." [13] Stephen insists, however, that the "modern spirit is vivisective": "The ancient method investigated law with the lantern of justice, morality with the lantern of revelation, art with the lantern of tradition. But all these lanterns have magical properties: they transform and disfigure. The modern method examines its territory by the light of day."

The same motif has appeared earlier in Stephen's interview with the President of the U.C.D., in which the President says that Stephen's essay for the Debating Society represents "the sum-total of modern unrest and modern freethinking" and will fill the minds of the audience with "all the garbage of modern society" (p. 91). Stephen defends Ibsen by arguing that his view of modern society is ironical, and objects to the President's grouping him with Zola. He describes himself as an admirer of "the classical temper" in art, and expounds his Thomistic theory to defend Ibsen, noting that in Aquinas "I hear no mention of instruction or elevation."

Stephen uses the word most illuminatingly in describing his own "love-verses." In his expressions of love, he says, "he found himself compelled to use what he called the feudal terminology and as he could not use it with the same faith and purpose as animated the feudal poets themselves he was compelled to express his love a little ironically. This suggestion of relativity, he said,

13. *Stephen Hero* (N. Y., 1963), p. 185.

mingling itself with so immune a passion is a modern note: we
cannot swear or expect eternal fealty because we recognize too
accurately the limits of every human energy. It is not possible for
the modern lover to think the universe an assistant at his love-af-
fair and modern love, losing somewhat of its fierceness, gains also
somewhat in amiableness." But Cranly will not hear of this because "he had in his own mind reduced past and present to a level
of studious ignobility" (p. 174).

Pound discovered Joyce's work through Yeats in 1913; after
the initial correspondence about poetry, Joyce sent Pound *Dubliners* and the first chapter of the *Portrait*, and Pound began his
long and successful campaign to get Joyce published and help
him find an audience. As Forrest Read puts it, "Joyce appeared to
Pound as the great new urban writer, a great synthetic expresser
of the modern consciousness," for in *Dubliners* (written 1905) he
had "made the city a formal principle for the first time in modern
English literature." [14]

To discuss Joyce's treatment of the City would require another
book. The point we need to keep in mind is that Joyce renders
both its horror and its potential glory, its necessity as an ideal and
its sordid and painful actuality, with unprecedented fullness and
power. No writer has ever been more fully aware of all the defects of the modern City, from literal Dublin in 1904 to the generalized image of modern society. Joyce presents it in every tone
from the most savage satire and bitter irony to light and even
gentle comedy. The "Circe" episode of *Ulysses* is, as Pound said
in a letter when it was first published, "a new Inferno in full
sail"; it established for modern literature the image of the City as
Hell and the mode of hallucination, of blending fantasy and sor-
dor in representing it. In both *Dubliners* and *Ulysses* there are recurrent minor parallels with Dante that recall the image to the
reader's mind. The images of paralysis, madness, sterility and
frustration, and finally of coldness and death that dominate *Dubliners* need not be recapitulated here, nor the varied panoply of

14. Introduction to *Pound/Joyce* (N. Y., 1966), p. 8.

effects produced by the parallel with the *Odyssey* in *Ulysses;* it is these latter that are responsible for most of the comedy and lighter tones. "The Lotus Eaters," for example, is a very penetrating and amusing anatomy of modern escape, through dreams, drugs, the fantasy world of advertising and that of popular fiction, and the like. But Joyce does not expect the City to change very much: it is true that in one sense, as Kenner says, he regards Dublin as "an immense blasphemy against the New Jerusalem of the faith of Christ"; [15] but it is also true that the millenarian hot-gospeller the Reverend Alexander J. Dowie, with his pamphlet about the Second Coming, is a figure of bitter comedy: "Are you a god or a dog-gone clod? . . ." One of the funniest and profoundest passages in the book is that in the "Circe" episode when Bloom imagines himself as the Savior, Prophet, Reformer who is going to usher in the millennium, for the parody is both of religious millenarianism and of the secular hopes of "enlightened," progressive moderns like Bloom. Thus Bloom says: "My beloved subjects, a new era is about to dawn . . . ye shall ere long enter into the golden city which is to be, the new Bloomusalem in the Nova Hibernia of the future." His program is a marvelous confusion of the religious and secular, Alexander J. Dowie and H. G. Wells, so to speak: "I stand for the reform of municipal morals and the plain ten commandments. New worlds for old. Union of all, jew, moslem and gentile. . . . Saloon motor hearses. Compulsory manual labor for all. . . . Tuberculosis, lunacy, war and mendicancy must now cease. . . ." [16]

Even *Finnegans Wake*, in its complex and indirect manner, pays homage to the ideal of the City. The first builder of the City of Man was Cain, who fuses with Lucifer and the building of Pandemonium. Finnegan himself is, of course, a master builder, Daedalus as bricklayer; he is emphatically a citizen, immersed in a society. Dublin represents all cities and all civilizations, through all the transmutations of history; and if the vision is one of disas-

15. Kenner, *Dublin's Joyce*, p. 234.
16. *Ulysses* (Modern Library edition, N. Y., 1961), pp. 484–85, 489.

ter, of the bankruptcy of civilization, it is also one of cyclical return: what falls shall rise again. The view is cosmic, apocalyptic;
as Levin says, "Street life and Homeric legend are scrupulously
differentiated throughout *Ulysses*. The locus for *Finnegans Wake*
is that point in infinity where such parallels meet." But the view,
if valedictory, is still of the city and not of the isolated individual; to quote Levin again: in *Finnegans Wake* "Joyce is finally
taking his leave of the monumental ruins of the city of man, and
attaching his hope to the matriarchal continuity of the years, the
seasons, and the months." [17]

David Jones, in the preface to *In Parenthesis* (1937), has acknowledged his great debt to Joyce and has taken occasion to
protest against the common representation of Joyce as a negative
or nihilistic writer. Jones argues that Joyce is, in his way, a sacra-
mentalist; that far from destroying, he charges words with the
absolute maximum of meaning: every character and event, as well
as every word, gains immensely in significance and interest. This
is creation, not destruction, Jones affirms. Certainly there is much
in *Finnegans Wake* to bear him out. The book neatly exemplifies
most of the definitions of modernism we have been suggesting: it
breaks with liberal humanism and with rationality as previously
understood in order to reveal a different and more complex view
of reality; it is discontinuous rhetorically and in many other
ways; it is a massive revelation of the night world of dreams and
the unconscious; it takes truth to be centrally mythical; it is
apocalyptic and eschatological. But yet the City is also affirmed:
Finnegan is always a builder, and the City remains as ideal, per-
petually destroyed and rebuilt; the book, perhaps the most
learned ever written, is at once a parody and a celebration of the
Gutenberg Galaxy (it is, of course, McLuhan's Holy Book), a
book to end all books, quite literally. Since it asserts that everything is valuable and that nothing is, everything makes sense and
nothing does, its ultimate assertion is that rationality is not adequate, that the Dionysian realm of the unconscious and collective

17. Levin, *James Joyce*, pp. 142, 200.

must be the source of meaning. Yet it also affirms the Apollonian as necessary: Shem and Shaun, penman and postman, are certainly, among countless other things, Dionysus and Apollo.

THE MISSING CITY

The great Romantics, as everyone knows, had little interest in the City, literal or symbolic. Instead, they represented modern civilization as a desert, or sometimes as the sea of possibility through which the isolated quester made his way. In general, modern writers who reject the City and are preoccupied with the individual tend to follow the same symbolic pattern, while introducing some new symbols of isolation and desolation. But the great moderns who have an allegiance to the City also render its opposite most powerfully. Eliot's poem is, after all, called *The Waste Land* and not *The City*, and the waste land is not only a place of trial and temptation for the quester but a land desolated by the Fisher King's sterility, cold and unreviving in spring, a desert with no shelter save an ambiguous red rock—in short, a place where there is no City but falling towers, where civilization is only a bundle of fragments. It is Joyce, however, who introduces and first develops what seems to be the basic modern symbol for isolation and absence of community. In *Dubliners*, the dominant symbol in the last story, "The Dead" (but anticipated in many earlier stories) is snow, embodying the qualities of paralysis, death-in-life, insulated coldness, arrested growth, isolation, and unfulfilled potentialities that characterize Dublin specifically and all modern cities by implication.

Perhaps because of the qualities of whiteness, featurelessness, barrenness, and desolation that it shares with it, snow appears to be the modern equivalent of the Romantic symbol of the desert. In fact, since it contains at least potentially the possibility of regeneration and rebirth, it has also much of the significance of the Romantic sea; and thus from its first fully developed use in "The Dead" it is a highly ambiguous symbol. Its primary significance, however, is usually to suggest isolation and those other attributes that are the opposite of the City—the fragmented and insulated ego or consciousness cut off from human contact. Obvious examples are Conrad Aiken's fine story, "Silent Snow, Secret Snow," where the snow becomes the madness walling the boy off from others, or Wallace Stevens's "The Snow Man," where the snow is abstraction, as well as the qualities we have been discussing. Or Frost's "Stopping by Woods on a Snowy Evening," where the snow's seductive beauty and danger are stressed, in addition to isolation and abstraction, until it suggests very powerfully everything that is the opposite of the world in which there are "promises to keep" and sleep (or death) can be indulged in only after "miles to go." Frost's "Design" pictures a white scene that reveals either nothingness or "design of darkness to appall." In Eliot there is the "forgetful snow" at the beginning of *The Waste Land* that kept us warm though barely alive until cruel April stirred us up; and the mountains where you "feel free" are the snow-covered (escapist) mountains of Marie's childhood (where she was afraid to ride on a sled). In "A Song for Simeon" the "snow hills" of the "stubborn season" suggest an obvious equivalence with the old man's resigned yearning for an internal thaw; in the *Quartets* it is the paradoxical union of winter and spring—"Late roses filled with early snow," "Midwinter spring is its own season"—that forms one of the central symbolic patterns: snow reconciled with both rose and fire. *The Waste Land*, we remember, was written in a sanitarium in Lausanne, where Eliot was recovering from a nervous breakdown, and it is curious how frequently the detachment of Switzerland and the remote isolation of the Austrian alps recur in modern literature with symbolic overtones. In Hemingway's *Farewell to Arms*, for instance, the lovers are happiest in their isolated retreat in the Austrian alps; but they are obliged by Catherine's approaching confinement to re-enter the world of obligations and evil which then proceeds to kill Catherine. In Mann's *The Magic Mountain* the sanitarium in the Swiss alps, surrounded by snow, represents (among many other things) an isolation and abstraction so dangerous that life in the Flatlands seems alien, remote, and inconsequential after a time. It is a world of extremes, a "solemn, phantasmagorical world of towering peaks"—"above the zone of shade-trees, also probably of song-birds"; "Home and regular living lay not only far behind, they lay fathoms deep beneath him. . . ." It is in the snow that Hans Castorp has his vision of the reconciliation of the Dionysiac and Apollonian.

The fullest exploitation of the snow symbol, however, is that in Lawrence's *Women in Love*. In the famous conversation in the train, Birkin puts the problem very simply: all the old ideals, social and religious, are dead; the only hope is the relation of a man and a woman in "ultimate marriage":

> "The old ideals are dead as nails—nothing there. It seems to me there remains only this perfect union with a woman—sort of ultimate marriage—and there isn't anything else."
>
> "And you mean if there isn't the woman, there's nothing?" said Gerald.
>
> "Pretty well that—seeing there's no God."
>
> "Then we're hard put to it," said Gerald.[18]

Birkin's "dislike of mankind, of the mass of mankind, amounted almost to an illness," and he says, "I always feel doomed when the train is running into London. I feel such a despair, so hopeless, as if it were the end of the world." Gerald says only, "And does the end of the world frighten you?" When they drive into the city in a taxi, Birkin says, "Don't you feel like one of the damned?" and insists, "It is real death." The apocalyptic vision of the City as Hell, as death-in-life, could hardly be more explicit. To return, however, to the snow symbolism, insofar as it can be discussed without getting involved in the full complexities of this extraordinary novel. The snow-world symbolizes, to begin with, the opposite pole from the African heat-consciousness represented by the fetish of the pregnant woman with the beetle face:

18. *Women in Love* (Modern Library edition, N. Y., N. D.), p. 64.

the mindless knowledge of the senses, knowledge of dissolution and corruption—what Conrad summed up in his "Heart of Darkness." "There remained this way, this awful African process, to be fulfilled. . . . The white races, having the arctic North behind them, the vast abstraction of ice and snow, would fulfil a mystery of ice-destructive knowledge, snow-abstract annihilation" (p. 289). Snow is thus, racially and epistemologically, the polar opposite; but it is equally death-like, because a world of extremes. Ursula, as the novel comes toward its end in the Austrian Alps, hates "the snow, and the unnaturalness of it, the unnatural light it throws on everybody, the ghastly glamour, the unnatural feelings it makes everybody have" (p. 495); she realizes with relief that "this utterly silent, frozen world of the mountaintops was not universal! One might leave it. . . ." Ursula is, of course, of all the characters in the novel the one closest to being a norm. Gerald, the blond Nordic type, master of machines, dies willingly in the snow; Gudrun, corrupted utterly by Loerke, the "modern" artist, loves the snow world. (Loerke maintains aesthetic discontinuity, the absolute separation of art and life, and denies any mimetic significance. He says, "Wissen sie, gnädige Frau, that is a Kunstwerk, a work of art. It is a work of art, it is a picture of nothing, of absolutely nothing. It has nothing to do with anything but itself, it has no relation with the everyday world of this and other, there is no connection between them, absolutely none. . . ." But Ursula replies that the horse "is a picture of your own stock, stupid brutality, and the girl was a girl you loved and tortured and then ignored" [pp. 490–91].)

In general, it may be said that Lawrence is an instructive example of the modern writer who is primarily a Dionysiac type, while Joyce is primarily Apollonian. (But both are great writers —to make an inevitable simplification—because they also exhibit the pull of the opposing pole: the pull of the Dionysiac is powerful indeed for Joyce, who encompasses an enormous amount of chaos, disorder, and anti-art in his artistic order. Lawrence is a lesser artist, as I see it, because the Apollonian power in him is vastly overbalanced by the Dionysiac; and after *Women in Love* he goes beyond art, the triumph of the Dionysiac is almost complete, and the fruitful tension appears only in occasional stories and short novels.) But to return to the contrast, which I think is of interest, though my representation will have to be excessively schematic: Lawrence accepts historical discontinuity as a basic postulate, and this is why he is, as we have seen, almost a Futurist, obsessed with time-consciousness, determined to capture the sense of immediacy in his poems (not interested in creating timeless art-works). *The Rainbow* is, in one sense, an exploration of the break with the past, of how the modern is different. The cutting off of the Brangwen farm by a canal is a symbolic representation of cutting off from the past and of the social transition to the isolated family and then the isolated couple and individual. The novel is, of course, about marriage, as the original title, *The Wedding Ring*, made perhaps too clear; instead of the former sacrament, there is now a relation only. The breakup of former community throws exclusive emphasis on the individual relation; alienation from the soil and the loss of religion leaves sexual passion as the sole remaining form of community and of religion (or substitutes): the Rainbow arch of the perfect marriage is a substitute for the Lord's covenant. At the end there is a vision of the new creation, the "living God, instead of the old hard barrier form of bygone living"; the final sentence is a millenarian vision of a new civilization, changed in heart as in architecture: "She saw in the rainbow the earth's new architecture, the old, brittle corruption of houses and factories swept away. . . ." Ursula is the new woman, with her black hair and her freedom; though Lawrence associates aggressive feminism with sterility, as he does machines—so that the feminist homosexual marries the male homosexual who is a machine-man—there is a relation to feminist ideals. But, though Lawrence is firmly convinced of historical discontinuity, he rejects aesthetic discontinuity passionately, and refuses to separate art from life. Joyce is, of course, the opposite: he rejects historical discontinuity, but affirms aesthetic discontinuity: the art-work is an escape from the nightmare of history, transcending time, independent of the artist, who is detached and remote from it.

It has been remarked, with as much truth as such generalizations can have, that Joyce is primarily a mythic, Lawrence a symbolic writer. (*Primarily* is very far from *exclusively*, of course; nothing could be more powerful than Joyce's use of symbols in his stories, especially "The Dead"; and Lawrence, especially in stories and poems, is often centrally mythic.) In describing Lawrence as symbolic, however, one must note carefully that this symbolism has remarkably little in common with that of the French *Symbolistes*. Lawrence's symbols are a heightening and development of natural significances, a making of reality more transparent, a revelation of something that is already there in the object or event; nothing could be further from the evocation of another reality, a heterocosm. Neither Joyce nor Lawrence is very sanguine about the future of the modern artist: Stephen at the end of the *Portrait* goes forth to a dubious fate as both man and artist (some critics read "forge" in the final sentence as ambiguous, suggesting that as artist he will be a fake; and certainly he does not seem on the way to success in *Ulysses*), and Paul at the end of *Sons and Lovers* goes forth "quickly" (i.e. alive, not dead, we may hopefully read) to meet his ambiguous future in the "humming, glowing town."

CHAPTER FOUR

THE BEGINNING OF MODERNISM IN ENGLISH VERSE (1909-1914)

IN THIS CHAPTER our approach will be primarily in terms of literary history, as we attempt to answer the specific questions of when and where modernism first appears in English verse and what influences seem to be operative. The central figure we must deal with is unquestionably Ezra Pound. It is misleading to call Pound the father of modernism. No one man deserves that title: the present chapter will provide further evidence for what has already been suggested, that modernism emerges simultaneously and independently in a great variety of artists and writers in many different places. But Pound is undeniably the catalyst of literary modernism, the impresario and promoter of it as a conscious movement. His early career is therefore the best point of vantage from which to survey its origins and inauguration.

The story begins in London in 1909, where Pound, having arrived the preceding year after a brief sojourn in Venice, had already established relations with Yeats, Ford Madox Ford, T. E. Hulme and the group dominated by him, and others to be mentioned later. In his specialized study of the period, C. K. Stead observes, "The year 1909 marks perhaps the lowest point of a long decline in the quality of English poetry" (*The New Poetic*, p. 53). The aesthetic movement of the nineties had collapsed with the trial of Wilde and been replaced by the "physical force" school, while the political pendulum had swung to the right. "In April 1909 Swinburne died, and in May, George Meredith. . . . Yeats hearing the news remarked: 'And now I am king of the cats.' In the same year he published his *Collected Poems*, and there were new volumes by Kipling, Noyes, Watson, and Newbolt" (pp. 53–54). As Stead shows, the latter four "public-spirited" versifiers completely dominated the poetic scene, and were much admired by the leading critics, who assured the public that they were continuing the central tradition of English poetry. Looking back on this time, T. S. Eliot says, "In the first decade of the century the situation was unusual. I cannot think of a single living poet, in either England or America, then at the height of his powers, whose work was capable of pointing the way to a young poet conscious of the desire for a new idiom." [1] Yeats, Eliot comments, was a late developer, and "when he emerged as a great modern poet, about 1917, we had already reached a point such that he appeared not as a precursor but as an elder and venerated contemporary."

Faced with this desolate poetic scene, in which the present and the recent past in English verse offered nothing, the young poet might seek inspiration in several different directions. He might turn to other literary forms in his own language that were farther advanced, more modern, than verse. In English, it is clear to us now (but was not to many at the time), the most advanced genre was the Impressionist novel, as perfected by James, Conrad, and Ford. He might turn to poetry of many earlier ages and languages, from Greek to Chinese; or to contemporary poetry in other languages, such as the French, which had already become modern; or to the exciting new developments (not in England, of course, but on the Continent) in the other arts, especially paint-

1. Eliot, *To Criticize the Critic* (N. Y., 1965), p. 58.

ing. The preceding sentence will serve as an adequate description of the common interests that drew together Pound, Hulme, and the pre- or proto-Imagist group, of whom more in a moment. First, however, let us review some of the chief events in painting and music, to serve as background and point of reference for comparison to the process of modernization in poetry.

The Fauvism of 1905 was a manifestation of a new current of interest, running throughout Europe, in the primitive and magical: at this time Picasso returns to the pre-Roman art of Iberia; Matisse, Derain, Vlaminck are excited about Negro masks; in Dresden, Kirchner studies in the ethnographic department of the museum; in Munich Kandinsky is inspired by the primitive paintings of Bavarian peasants. Like later developments, this one occurred thus simultaneously all over Europe. The relation to the past is shown by the fact that the great Cézanne Memorial Exhibition in 1907 was the inspiration for the development of Cubism in the same year; assimilating the formal lessons of Cézanne, Picasso and Braque simultaneously and independently began what was later called Analytical Cubism. (In the same manner, both independently began to use the technique of *collage* about 1912.) Abstraction similarly was discovered by a number of painters in different places; though Kandinsky (1910) in Munich seems clearly to have a slight priority, Larionov in Moscow and Delaunay and Kupka in Paris all independently worked out the same technique. "The problem had been so well propounded all over Europe that the solution was inevitably arrived at in many places at once." [2] In fact, occasional abstractions had been done before 1910, by Macke, Kubin, and Ciurlionis, for example. But Kandinsky, the great theorist, never held that *all* art should be abstract; he called Henri Rousseau's "magic realism" the "greater reality," as opposed to his own (or Mondrian's) "greater abstraction," and suggested that these were the two extremes between which modern painting lies. The Pittura Metafisica of De Chirico, and most of later Surrealism, obviously belong to the "greater reality" side;

2. Haftmann, *Painting in the Twentieth Century*, I, 135.

Matisse and Synthetic Cubists sought a balance, an interplay of inner and outer, rather than pure expression. (Expressionism itself maintained such a balance, of course, though in Kandinsky and others it tended logically toward pure abstraction.)

In music, there are parallel developments at about the same time. Stravinsky's *Fireworks* dates from 1908, and his first ballet, *The Firebird*, from 1910; the Ballet Russe of Diaghilev, performing in Paris from 1909 on and in London after the following year, was an exciting force bringing together the new arts, and Stravinsky was its major composer. Painters and composers—as well as dancers—from many countries were enlisted in its cosmopolitan productions, among them Picasso, Braque, Debussy, and Ravel. *Petroushka* of 1911 marked Stravinsky's major break with the past; his *Le Sacre du Printemps* (1913) in celebrating barbaric ritual, was a kind of musical Fauvism, and provoked the most riotous excitement since *Hernani*. By 1911, also, Bartok had written *Allegro Barbaro* and the opera *Duke Bluebeard's Castle;* Prokofieff had written his *First Piano Concerto*. The chronological parallel is even closer in the case of Arnold Schönberg, the composer whose role is most like that of Kandinsky in painting: both men were pioneering theorists and uncompromising experimentalists who were daring, intense, and extreme, following rigorously where their theories led, and who exercised a tremendous influence on later artists. Both were living in Munich in 1908; they were friends and colleagues, and strongly influenced each other, for each was interested in the other's medium as well as his own. Kandinsky's *Concerning the Spiritual in Art,* written in 1910 and published 1912, presents the theories the two evolved together, and concerns music almost as much as painting. Atonality in music and abstraction in art were thus closely related. Schönberg was himself a painter, and arrived at his musical convictions partly through intense work with Kandinsky on the theory and practice of painting in 1908; in 1912 Kandinsky published an essay on Schönberg's painting. Kandinsky and Klee, on the other hand, regarded the painting of abstractions as equivalent to musical composition; hence the frequent title, "Improvisations." Schönberg had established a reputation as a lush post-Wagnerian Impressionist in the late Romantic mode, but his work in traditional tonality ends with the last movement of the Second Quartet, Opus 10, written 1908, which begins with a soprano singing "I feel the air of other planets." His first atonal (or, as he preferred to call them, pantonal) compositions were written in the same year: the Piano Pieces, Opus 11, and the song cycle, *The Book of the Hanging Gardens*, Opus 15. With them began the "liberation of the dissonance," continued in *Die Glückliche Hand* (1913), for which he wrote his own libretto, *Pierrot lunaire*, a cycle of twenty-one pieces for Sprechstimme and chamber ensemble (1912), and numerous other pieces. Through his textbook *Theory of Harmony* (1912) and his two most distinguished pupils and disciples, Alban Berg and Anton Webern, he had an enormous influence.

To sum up the chronology briefly: in 1907 Picasso painted his first Cubist work, *Les Demoiselles d'Avignon*, and Braque independently did his first Cubist painting, both under the stimulus of the Cézanne Memorial Exhibition; Matisse christened the movement in the following year. In 1908 Schönberg wrote his first completely atonal composition and Kandinsky began, with his first *Improvisation*, the movement toward completely abstract painting that he completed in 1910; the two collaborated in formulating the theories behind the new art and in experimentation. In the same year, 1908, the art historian Wilhelm Worringer published the book, *Abstraction and Empathy*, that seemed to Kandinsky, Schönberg, and others to provide a basis and justification in historical terms for the new movement. (As we have seen, there were numerous other "modern" productions of varied types in both music and painting in 1908–9, which need not be recapitulated.) By 1909, then, the movement was well under way. The Russian ballet began generating great excitement in Paris and, in 1911, in London. In 1909 Futurism began its brief and raucous career in all the arts. To anticipate slightly, we may cite the literary equivalents. In 1908 Pound published his first volume, *A Lume Spento*, in Venice, and then took up residence in London. Hulme and Pound published poems in 1908 that are in some senses modern; by early 1909 they were acquainted and there was a beginning ferment of ideas. Late in 1908 Ford Madox Ford started the *English Review*. T. S. Eliot, across the Atlantic and in complete unawareness of all this, began at almost precisely the same time to write distinctively modern verse (late 1908 and early 1909; none of it was published until after he had met Pound in 1914). In short, modernism emerges in all the major arts very nearly simultaneously, among artists widely scattered throughout the Western world, most of whom are completely independent of each other.

In painting and in music, the revolutions have an internal logic that makes them seem inevitable. Obviously, they are related to the cataclysmic events taking place in the civilization that surrounds them; yet no reference to such a context is required to explain the revolutions, which may be accounted for in terms of the arts alone. In both music and painting, certain lines of development had been followed to their logical ends, so that nothing could be gained by attempting to pursue them further; and unless the arts were to stagnate, a new direction had to be found. Further, the new directions are technical advances, almost analogical with those in science, in that they take certain elements in the preceding tradition and explore and develop them to produce something genuinely new. It is thus that Schönberg and Bartok develop out of Wagner and that Picasso and Kandinsky develop out of Cézanne; they begin by carrying the tradition further and find that by a technical necessity and intrinsic logic it works itself out and points to a new phase.

In poetry in English, the situation was very different. The chief revolutionaries, Pound and Eliot, have little significant relation to their immediate predecessors. (There are, of course, exceptions to be made to this statement: Pound freely acknowledges his relation to Browning, Lionel Johnson, and others; Eliot has more in common with Tennyson and Kipling than at first appears; Yeats retains important ties with the poets of the nineties. Nevertheless, the generalization holds.) Pound and Eliot thus begin under the stimulus of various foreign literatures (especially Provençal for Pound, French for Eliot) together with that of other literary forms in English (the Impressionist novel, Jacobean drama). If the break with the immediate past is sharper, however, the new art is in poetry much less remote from the whole tradition of the Renaissance era than is the case in painting and music. Poetry is always the most impure and most conservative of the arts, and late Edwardian England (almost wholly unpenetrated by modernism in painting or music) was certainly one of the most conservative of cultural environments. But even so, the years from 1909 to 1914 saw a more profound and radical change than any period of equal length in the whole history of English poetry, and one broadly analogous to the revolutions in other arts. Through the efforts of Ezra Pound, London and Chicago were even linked briefly and uncomfortably together as revolutionary capitals. But these are enough preliminary generalizations; let us now come down to cases and consider just how the new poetry began and how it was related to the other arts. We begin with Pound in London in 1908.

How modern was the poetry that Pound was writing at this point, as represented by *A Lume Spento*, published in Venice earlier in 1908? The volume was described in a London newspaper review as "wild and haunting stuff, absolutely poetic, original, imaginative, passionate and spiritual. Those who do not consider it crazy may well consider it inspired. Coming after the trite and decorous verse of most of our decorous poets, this poet seems like a minstrel of Provence at a decorous suburban musical evening." [3] Another review said that the volume seems at first "mere madness." So the poems that Pound describes in his rather discouraged-sounding preface to the recent reprint as "stale cream puffs" seemed like anything but that to the few readers in

3. Quoted in Eliot, *To Criticize the Critic*, p. 163.

Edwardian London who were aware of them. In "Cino" ("Bah! I have sung of women in five countries / And it is all the same") and "Na Audiart," for example, the style is relatively colloquial, economical, intense, and the rhythm is highly individual. The device of the *persona* is fully developed, and some of the poems are strongly dramatic. The ghosts of Browning, Rossetti, and Swinburne hover over the pages, but rites of exorcism are in progress. As to content, not much in the way of modernism appears beneath the heavy trappings of romantic medievalism; the basis is there, but far from being fully realized. Pound develops very rapidly: in *Personae*, published in April 1909, he keeps the best poems from the earlier book but drops twenty-nine of them, and this volume and *Exultations*, published later in 1909, show a considerable advance, which continues until in 1912 there is a long further step toward modernity in *Ripostes*, with its witty depiction of urban life, Roman and contemporary.

Our next question must be, inevitably, what agents or influences are identifiable that helped to produce this rapid increase in modernity during the years 1908–12? Pound's own testimony as to the primary influence on him in 1908 is unequivocal:

> The revolution of the word began so far as it affected the men who were of my age in London in 1908, with the LONE whimper of Ford Madox Hueffer. His more pliant disciples were Flint, Goldring, and D. H. Lawrence. Hueffer read Flaubert and Maupassant in a way that George Moore did not. Impressionism meant for him something it did not for Mr. Symons. . . .[4]

It was the "importance of good writing as opposed to the opalescent word" that Ford insisted upon, the "art of charging words"; and his texts were the great French novels of the nineteenth century, as specimens of the most highly developed form of literary art in existence. Ford was, of course, the grandson of a famous Pre-Raphaelite painter, and was brought up among artists. The critical terminology worked out by James, Percy Lubbock, and

4. *Polite Essays* (1937), p. 50.

succeeding critics to describe the art of fiction is based on an implicit analogy with painting: point of view, perspective, foreground, scale, and the like. When the novel is described as Impressionist, as in the quotation from Pound above, it suggests primarily an emphasis on fiction as an art, in which technique is important; and secondarily a specific resemblance between this kind of novel and Impressionist painting in that point of view is centrally important in both: the reader or spectator is expected to participate actively and to imagine a single definite point of view.

Ford in 1915 described his doctrine as simply that "the rendering of the material facts of life, without comment and in exact language, is poetry and that poetry is the only important thing in life." [5] His basic lesson for Pound, taught by precept and example, was that writing is an art as rigorous and demanding in technique as is painting. Ford was a prolific but rather undistinguished poet (e.g. *Songs from London*, 1910); his chief influence was as critic and editor, as Pound observed, and through his own example as novelist. *The Good Soldier*, his masterpiece, of which part was published in *Blast*, 1914, and the whole the following year, has been called a Cubist novel, or, in the phrase Ford himself quoted, "the finest French novel in the English language." It embodies Ford's sense of catastrophism, of the breaking up of the older moral and social order, leaving man in a chaotic and meaningless modern world.

Pound has sometimes been misinterpreted as attempting in these retrospective comments to substitute Ford for Hulme as founder of Imagism. His point is, rather, that the importance of the Imagist school has been much exaggerated, and that Ford was the major critical stimulus for writing in general: "Ford knew about WRITING." In 1938 Pound said emphatically, "The critical LIGHT during the years immediately pre-war in London shone not from Hulme but from Ford (Madox etc) in so far as it fell on writing at all. . . . The EVENT of 1909–10 was Ford Madox (Hueffer) Ford's 'English Review,' and no greater condemnation

5. Quoted in Glenn Hughes, *Imagism and the Imagists* (N. Y., 1960), p. 46.

of the utter filth of the whole social system of that time can be dug up than the fact of that review's passing out of his hands. Its list of contributors should prevent critical exaggeration of our Frith Street cenacle without in the least damaging Hulme's record." [6]

In these years Pound was also regularly visiting Henry James, for whose achievement he had a just appreciation; we remember the references in the *Cantos* and Pound's description of *Mauberley* as "an attempt to condense the James novel." [7] The tradition in fiction of which Stendhal was the forerunner and Flaubert the founder, variously described as Symbolist, Naturalist, or, most often, Impressionist (the exact, not the soft or blurred kind, as Pound notes later), reached a kind of fulfillment in James's three great novels just after the turn of the century and in Conrad's *Heart of Darkness* and *Nostromo* (which appeared in 1904, the same year as the last of James's three, *The Golden Bowl*). Eliot, like Pound, was imbued in James and Conrad, and we have already seen the powerful influence that Joyce exerted on him after 1914. In view of the explicit statements by Eliot and Pound, and of the mass of evidence we have glanced at, then, there can be no doubt that the Impressionist novel, from Flaubert on, and especially James, Conrad, Ford, and Joyce, was one of the most important influences making for modernism in English verse. [8]

We have already discussed T. E. Hulme briefly in other contexts. Let us now consider in somewhat more detail his relation to Pound, to Imagism, and to modernism in general. Hulme clearly dominated the "Frith Street cenacle" that Pound began frequenting in 1909, and Hulme's poem "Autumn," which appeared in December 1908 in a pamphlet, *Pour Noel*, has some claim to be considered the first Imagist poem to be published. [9]

6. Quoted in Hugh Kenner, *The Poetry of Ezra Pound* (London, 1951), p. 308.

7. *Letters*, p. 180.

8. Allen Tate, in "Modern and Unmodern," *The Hudson Review*, 1968, reaches essentially this same conclusion.

9. Enid Starkie, *From Gautier to Eliot* (London, 1960), p. 156. She adds

The first mention of Imagism, however, is Pound's, in the prefatory note to the *Complete Poetical Works of T. E. Hulme* (five poems) which Pound printed as an appendix to his *Ripostes*, 1912. Pound here speaks somewhat ambiguously of the " 'School of Images,' which may or may not have existed," but salutes the current group: "As for the future, *Les Imagistes*, the descendants of the forgotten school of 1909, have that in their keeping." As Pound later confessed, the term *Imagist* belongs more to the history of publicity than that of poetry: "The name was invented to launch H. D. and Aldington before either had enough stuff for a volume," he wrote in a letter of 1927 (*Letters*, p. 288), and to Harriet Monroe he wrote that "the whole affair was started, not very seriously, chiefly to get H. D.'s five poems a hearing. It began certainly in Church Walk with H. D., Richard [Aldington] and myself. . . ." [10] Richard Aldington wrote to Herbert Read in 1925: "I don't know what Pound got from Hulme, but I do know that my debt to Hulme = o. I disliked the man and still dislike him though he's dead. Also, I had written what Pound christened 'imagist' poems before I had ever heard of Hulme. The point is that imagism, as written by H. D. and me, was purely our own invention and was not an attempt to put a theory in practice. The school was Ezra's invention." [11]

These statements by Pound and Aldington suggest that both Hulme's importance in the Imagist movement and the importance of the movement itself in literary history have been vastly exaggerated; and the suggestion is confirmed by much other evidence, to which we will return. At this point, however, our concern is with the larger matter of Hulme's role in the emergence of modernism in English verse, and to understand this we need to know what Hulme was preaching to Pound and the other members of his "Frith Street cenacle" in 1909. Hulme's "Lecture on Modern

that Hulme wanted to introduce *vers libre* on the model of Laforgue, who had achieved a posthumous popularity in France at this time.

10. Harriet Monroe, *A Poet's Life* (N. Y., 1938), p. 267.
11. A. Kershaw and F. J. Temple (eds.), *Richard Aldington: An Intimate Portrait* (Carbondale, Ill., 1965), p. 127.

Poetry," first delivered in 1908 or 1909, is preserved only in the revised form in which he delivered it again in 1914; but it seems not to have been changed essentially.[12] Hulme, who thought of himself as primarily a philosopher, goes back to first principles: the modern attitude toward form is different because we no longer believe in absolute truth or lasting perfection of form. "Now the whole trend of the modern spirit is away from that; philosophers no longer believe in absolute truth. We no longer believe in perfection, either in verse or in thought, we frankly acknowledge the relative. . . . In all the arts, we seek for the maximum of individual and personal expression, rather than for the attainment of any absolute beauty." The modern does not deal with heroic action, but with "momentary phases in the poet's mind." Hulme draws an explicit parallel with the Impressionist school in painting: "We can't escape from the spirit of our times. What has found expression in painting as Impressionism will soon find expression in poetry as free verse." And he suggests also a musical analogy:

> Say the poet is moved by a certain landscape, he selects from that certain images which, put into juxtaposition in separate lines, serve to suggest and to evoke the state he feels. To this piling-up and juxtaposition of distinct images in different lines, one can find a fanciful analogy in music. A great revolution in music when, for the melody that is one-dimensional music, was substituted harmony which moves in two. Two visual images form what one may call a visual chord. They unite to suggest an image which is different to both.

He then goes on to argue, "from this standpoint of extreme modernism," that the essential feature of the new poetry is that it is read and not chanted. "This new verse resembles sculpture rather than music; it appeals to the eye rather than to the ear. It has to

12. It was published first by Michael Roberts in 1938, and then included in Samuel Hynes, *Further Speculations by T. E. Hulme* (Minneapolis, 1955). I cite the reprint (Lincoln, Neb., 1962).

mould images, a kind of spiritual clay, into definite shapes. . . . It builds up a plastic image which it hands over to the reader, whereas the old art endeavoured to influence him physically by the hypnotic effect of rhythm" (pp. 71–75).

As Hynes remarks, "Hulme's theories had little immediate effect, largely because they were first delivered to third-rate poets and were not published . . ."; the two exceptions were F. S. Flint and Pound, through whom Hulme's ideas "changed the face of English poetry" (p. xviii). The principal members of the "Frith Street cenacle" to whom Pound read his "Sestina: Altaforte" when he first joined them in April 1909 were, aside from Hulme and Flint, Francis Tancred, Edward Storer, Joseph Campbell, and Florence Farr—an interesting and varied group, but not destined for great poetic achievement. They had in common chiefly a dissatisfaction with the current state of English poetry and an interest in the modern French; aside from this they shared a desire to experiment with forms taken from a wide range of languages and times: Greek, Japanese (*tanka* and *haiku*), Hebrew, Provençal, modern French *vers libre*. Most of them continued to meet with some regularity until the late winter of 1910.

The passages we have quoted above from Hulme's early lecture sound very much indeed like Pound; but since we have only the version revised in 1914, it is impossible to say definitely that this shows Hulme's influence on Pound, for by this time the converse is at least as likely. It is certainly a great mistake to think of Imagism as a single doctrine, originated by Hulme, propagated by Pound, and synonymous with the whole modernist revolution. We have already noted Pound's emphatic denial of this view and his insistence on the primary importance of Ford. The key question is that of Hulme's influence on Pound; for Eliot, and most others, knew Hulme's ideas at first hand only after *Speculations* was published in 1924; therefore Hulme's importance in literary history before that date rests primarily upon his effect on Pound (and, on a much smaller scale, F. S. Flint). As we have seen, Hulme's central interest was philosophy; he wrote only a few

poems. "Hulme stopped writing poetry. . . . His evenings were
diluted with crap like Bergson and it became necessary to use another evening a week if one wanted to discuss our own experiments or other current minor events in verse writing . . . ," said
Pound in 1938.[13] And again, "Mr. Hulme is on the way to
mythological glory; but the Hulme notes, printed after his death
[i.e. *Speculations*, 1924], had little or nothing to do with what
went on in 1910, 1911, or 1912. Mr. Yeats had set an example
(specifically as to the inner form of the lyric or short poem containing an image), this example is obscured for posterity and for
the present 'young'—meaning Mr. Eliot and his juniors—by Mr.
(early) Yeats's so very poetic language." [14]

Pound stresses, in short, the importance of writers like Ford
and Yeats, who could provide models for good writing, as opposed to Hulme, who could offer only doctrines and speculations.
Nevertheless, it is plain enough, after all qualifications have been
made, that Hulme's ideas did play some part in suggesting the
doctrines put forward by Pound and others as Imagist and that
they had some influence in forming the critical convictions of
Pound and Eliot.[15] For Hulme was a special kind of philosopher,
suspicious of abstraction and rationality. He admired and translated Bergson, and followed him in the belief that the "flux of
phenomena" is real but concepts are not, and hence that "by intellect one can construct approximate models" but "by intuition
one can identify oneself with the flux"; [16] the language of intuition, dealing in images, is poetry. In an essay published in 1909,
he attacks abstract philosophers such as Haldane, in contrast to
such a visual philosopher as Nietzsche, and suggests that the "history of philosophy should be written as that of seven or eight
great metaphors . . ."; abstraction is necessary, but dangerous:
"As in social life, it is dangerous to get too far away from barba-

13. Quoted in Kenner, *The Poetry of Ezra Pound*, p. 308.
14. Pound in 1937, quoted in Kenner, p. 58.
15. Kermode, in *Romantic Image*, gives a full and just account of the resemblances among Hulme, Pound, and Eliot in critical doctrine.
16. *Further Speculations*, p. xvii.

rism" (p.11). Poetry "is not a counter language, but a visual concrete one. . . . It always endeavours to arrest you, and to make you continuously see a physical thing, to prevent you gliding through an abstract process. . . . Prose is in fact the museum where the dead images of verse are preserved. Images in verse are not mere decoration, but the very essence of an intuitive language" (p. 10).

Hulme was more interested in painting and sculpture than in literature, and many artists came to his salon, among them the sculptors Epstein and Gaudier-Brzeska and the painter Wyndham Lewis. (We have seen how important the analogy with sculpture was in his conception of poetry, as in Pound's.) Hulme did not write about art, however, until the end of 1913, under the stimulus of a trip to Germany during which he had discovered the work of the aestheticians Volkelt and Lipps and the art historian Wilhelm Worringer. From the first two he borrowed the *Einfühlungästhetik* (which appealed to him because it is based on a non-intellectual motor reaction), and from Worringer the whole framework of his theory of art: the division of art into vital and geometrical, the relating of that division to the society's attitude toward the world, and the view that all art since the Renaissance composes a single vital period. But where Worringer is objective and scholarly, Hulme is a propagandist; as he said, "I start with the conviction that the Renaissance attitude is breaking up and then illustrate it by the change in art and not vice versa. First came the reaction against Renaissance philosophy, and the adoption of the attitude which I said went with the geometrical art." [17] At any rate, as Hynes says, Hulme "understood what ab-

17. Quoted in *Further Speculations*, p. xxiii. In *Speculations*, however, Hulme put it the other way around: "The vital art of Greece and the Renaissance corresponded to a certain attitude of mind and the geometrical has always gone with a different general attitude, of greater intensity than this." Hence "the re-emergence of geometrical art may be the precursor of the re-emergence of the corresponding attitude towards the world and so, of the breakup of the Renaissance humanistic attitude" (p. 78, from a lecture of 1914).

stract art was about, at a time when not many non-artists did, and he tried in his essays to formulate a theory of art that would contain and explain it." (The Post-Impressionist Exhibition had introduced Gaugin, Van Gogh, Cézanne, Matisse, and Picasso to London as recently as December 1910.)

Although Hulme freely acknowledged his debt to Worringer, the importance of Worringer in the whole modern movement has only recently come to be fully appreciated. His achievement was to provide a theoretical justification of abstraction just as the artists themselves were striving toward pure abstraction in their painting. When his *Abstraktion und Einfühlung* was published (Munich, 1908), it had an immediate effect, as stimulus and encouragement, on Kandinsky, Klee, and other pioneering abstract painters, and also on practitioners of other arts, such as the composer Schönberg, who were associated with them.[18] Sir Herbert Read, England's best-known champion of the modern, was a professed disciple of Worringer (whose work he discovered in the process of editing Hulme's *Speculations*); and the most stimulating of recent theoretical discussions of modern literature— Joseph Frank's *The Widening Gyre*—is based on a thesis derived from Worringer. *Abstraktion und Einfühlung* is not superficially exciting: its style is ponderous, its tone academic and objective; modern art is never mentioned, and any application of the argument to it must be made entirely by the reader. Worringer's thesis (to state it in grossly simplified terms) is that the artistic tradition dominant among the Greeks and in Europe since the Renaissance is by no means the only legitimate mode. This dominant Western tradition is characterized by empathy with nature and therefore by naturalistic representation. But art of other times and places—

18. Worringer's book was first privately printed in 1905 as a doctoral dissertation; after it was enthusiastically reviewed in an influential periodical, it was printed by a commercial publisher in 1908; by 1910 a third edition was called for. Though excerpts were translated earlier and published in periodicals, a complete English translation did not appear until 1953. Sir Herbert Read's obituary of Worringer appeared in *Encounter* in 1965.

primitive, that of Northern Europe, and that of the Far East—is based on a different reaction to nature, as something to be hated and feared by man; and therefore it is abstract and non-representational. Abstract art, then, will arise again whenever man feels estranged from the world of nature. Modern artists were quick to make the contemporary application; as Paul Klee put it in 1915, "The more horrifying this world becomes (as it is these days) the more art becomes abstract; while a world at peace produces realistic art." Hulme's career as popularizer of Worringer in 1913–14 (his lecture "Modern Art and Its Philosophy," he acknowledges, "is practically an abstract of Worringer's views") was too brief to have much effect; but his volume of *Speculations* (1924) had an important influence on Eliot and many others. Joseph Frank, in the book mentioned above, suggests that Hulme has had an unfortunate influence in giving the name Classicism to the literary equivalent of Worringer's abstract or non-naturalistic art, since Classicism is a historical rather than an aesthetic term. Frank proposes the term "spatial form" as the literary equivalent of non-naturalism, and he argues that the central modern writers —Eliot, Pound, Proust, Joyce, etc.—move in this direction; that is, they intend their readers to apprehend the work spatially in a moment of time rather than as a sequence.

But let us turn from these large theoretical matters back to Pound and the London (and then Chicago) of 1912. Our concern is not with Imagism as a movement (the story of which has been told many times), but with the kind of relation to the past and to the other arts from which distinctively modern elements emerged both in critical theory and poetic practice. Imagism seems to me important not as embodying a coherent philosophy, but as one aspect of Pound's multiform activities; because of the coincidence of a number of unrelated factors, it was blown up out of all proportion.

Harriet Monroe had been introduced to Pound's poetry by Pound's English publisher, Elkin Mathews, who had praised *Per-*

sonae and *Exultations* as he sold her the volumes in London in 1910.[19] She read the books with delight and admiration, and when she sent her circular to prospective contributors to her prospective magazine in August 1912 she "asked with special emphasis his co-operation." Pound replied enthusiastically, sending her two poems, promising full cooperation, and offering his services in the capacity that Miss Monroe soon formalized by giving him the title of Foreign Editor. The point is both that Pound's poetry was part of the inspiration for the founding of the magazine and that Pound's cooperation and advice were important factors from the very beginning. Miss Monroe, notoriously, was half-hearted in her support of the modern, but usually yielded to Pound's insistences. Pound himself, in the volumes of his that she admired, had not yet fully realized a modern idiom; this appears first in *Ripostes*, for which he was correcting proofs when he answered Miss Monroe's first letter. *Ripostes*, published later in 1912, contained the urban and satirical poems we discussed in Chapter Three, and such mature and perfected work as "Portrait d'une Femme," "The Return," and "The Seafarer." As we have seen, it also contained Hulme's poems as an appendix, with Pound's prefatory note about the " 'School of Images,' which may or may not have existed" and their descendants, *Les Imagistes*, who have the future in their keeping. At about the same time Pound began his publicity campaign for the Imagists in *Poetry* magazine by introducing Richard Aldington in the second issue (November 1912) as "one of the *Imagistes*, a group of ardent Hellenists who are pursuing interesting experiments in *vers libre*. . . ." The third and last of the original Imagists was introduced in the issue of January 1913 (Pound himself had, of course, appeared in the first issue) with a group of poems signed "H. D. *Imagiste*"; there was also a note from Pound saying that the "youngest school here that has the nerve to call itself a school is that of the Imagistes." In March 1913 *Poetry* published an article, "Imagisme," by F. S. Flint, together with Pound's "A Few Don'ts by an Imagiste"—one

19. *A Poet's Life*, p. 223.

of his most stimulating pieces of criticism—then in April 1913 Pound's group of poems, "Contemporania," including "The Garret," "The Garden," "Ortus," "Dance Figure," and "Salutation"; these alarmed Miss Monroe considerably, for they were very consciously modern and provocative. In the summer of 1913, Amy Lowell came to London, with a letter of introduction from Harriet Monroe to Pound, who brought John Gould Fletcher to meet her. But this point, from which proliferate many of the complications of Imagism as a movement—Fletcher being much inclined to suspect plots and stratagems, and Amy Lowell to take over the leadership of any group with which she found herself involved—is perhaps a good one at which to pause and consider the significance of Pound's connection with *Poetry*.

Pound, in his first letter to Miss Monroe, showed himself no rootless expatriate but keenly aware of the patriotic aspect of the *Poetry* enterprise and its continuity with the American past. One of the two poems he sent was "To Whistler—American," occasioned by the London exhibition of Whistler's paintings; his letter called him "our only great artist" and expressed the hope that the magazine might be "an endeavor to carry into our American poetry the same sort of life and intensity which he infused into modern painting." (A postscript added, more rhapsodically, that "our American Risorgimento" which Pound believed "in the end to be inevitable" would "make the Italian Renaissance look like a tempest in a teapot!" The other poem Pound sent (and these two poems of Pound's, by the way, were the only "modern" things in the first issue of *Poetry*) was "Middle-Aged: A Study in an Emotion," which he called in his letter "an over-elaborate post-Browning 'Imagiste' affair" (*Letters*, p. 10). Together, the two poems illustrate neatly Pound's awareness, in spite of exoticisms, of continuity with both American and British poetry; "To Whitman" puts the former most explicitly, and the latter was affirmed by his presence in London, in the simple conviction that Yeats was the greatest living poet and therefore he should sit at his feet.

Throughout his correspondence with Miss Monroe, Pound uses

the analogy of painting and music to argue, or sometimes proclaim, that (1) poetry is an art, and (2) modernity is necessary. He asks, "Can you teach the American poet that poetry *is* an *art*, an art with a technique, with media, an art that must be in constant flux, a constant change of manner, if it is to live?" And he demands her assent to the proposition that verse is "a living medium, on a par with paint, marble, and music" as a condition for their editorial association. When he sent H. D.'s poetry in October, he described it as "*modern* stuff by an American, I say modern, for it is in the laconic speech of the Imagistes, even if the subject is classic." He proceeds to explain what he means: "Objective—no slither; direct—no excessive use of adjectives, no metaphors that won't permit examination. It's straight talk, straight as the Greek!" (*Letters*, p. 11).

Modernity, then, was to consist in taking the art of poetry seriously, as the other arts were being taken by modernists; it was to break with the immediate, or late-Victorian past, but might perfectly well be at the same time Greek. (We remember that Aldington and H. D. were heavily Greek in inspiration both in form and themes; Aldington said that his free verse in "Choricos," in the second issue of *Poetry*, was modeled on a chorus in Euripides.) Pound spells out these matters repeatedly in his correspondence with Miss Monroe. He asks her, "whom do you know who takes the Art of poetry seriously? As seriously that is as a painter takes painting? . . . What, what honestly, would you say to the workmanship of U. S. verse if you found it in a picture exhibit?????" (p. 15). He describes his latest verse as "absolutely the *last* obsequies of the Victorian period" and cites the parallel with painting: "It's not futurism and it's not post-impressionism, but it's work contemporary with those schools. . . ." Hence it will "give you your chance to be modern, . . . to produce as many green bilious attacks throughout the length and breadth of the U. S. A. as there are fungoid members of the American academy" (pp. 23–24). But Pound had little interest in the kind of superficial modernism exhibited by the Midwestern poets—Lindsay,

Masters, Sandburg—who were Miss Monroe's real enthusiasms; he is usually polite about them, but when necessary reveals his conviction that Lindsay is essentially a Futurist (p. 55).

In the history of *Imagisme* contributed to *Poetry* for March 1913 by F. S. Flint, the school's relation to the past is defined very clearly. (It is notable that Flint does not, in this piece, claim to be an *Imagiste* himself; he bases his comments on an interview with "an imagiste" who must be Pound.) Flint says:

> The *imagistes* admitted that they were contemporaries of the Post-impressionists and the Futurists; but they had nothing in common with these schools. They had not published a manifesto. They were not a revolutionary school; their only endeavor was to write in accordance with the best tradition, as they found it in the best writers of all time—in Sappho, Catullus, Villon.

The three rules—direct treatment, economy, rhythm of the musical phrase rather than that of the metronome—were then enunciated, and an esoteric "Doctrine of the Image" hinted at but not defined. Then the effectiveness with which they instruct "approaching poetasters" is described, and their earnestness as contrasted to the usual "poetic dilettantism" of London; even their opponents admit that "they do keep bad poets from writing!" If they are, aesthetically, snobs, they are stricter with themselves than with any outsider. Obviously, the break was only with the immediate past, to return to the "best tradition . . . in the best writers of all time"; the emphasis is on wide knowledge of the past, and the positive prescriptions for directness and economy are really designed to insure a break with the late-Victorian. The only rule that approaches the truly prescriptive is the third, which seems to mean, in practice, *vers libre;* this was the most controversial and shortest-lived part of the program.

Pound added to Flint's history "A Few Don'ts by an Imagiste," which was originally drawn up to be sent out with rejection slips (p. 18), and hence intended as highly practical advice to the aspiring poet. Pound begins, however, with a daringly speculative preface in which, perhaps adumbrating the "Doctrine of the Image" hinted at by Flint, he denies the temporal aspect of poetry, defining an image in terms of spatial form; he then suggests a psychological rationale for Imagism: "An 'Image' is that which presents an intellectual and emotional complex in an instant of time. . . . It is the presentation of such a 'complex' instantaneously which gives that sense of sudden liberation; that sense of freedom from time limits and space limits; that sense of sudden growth, which we experience in the presence of the greatest works of art." [20] Patiently, Pound exhorts the neophyte to remember that poetry is an art: "Don't imagine that the art of poetry is any simpler than the art of music, or that you can please the expert before you have spent at least as much effort on the art of verse as the piano teacher spends on the art of music." He urges him to "fill his mind with the finest cadences he can discover, preferably in a foreign language so that the meaning of the words may be less likely to divert his attention from the movement . . . ," and to "know assonance and alliteration, rhyme immediate and delayed, simple and polyphonic, as a musician would expect to know harmony and counterpoint and all the minutiae of his craft." On the other hand he is not to be descriptive in an attempt to rival the painter; instead, he is to present in a way the painter cannot. Examples recommended are Shakespeare, Dante "as compared with Milton's rhetoric," Wordsworth, and especially Sappho, Catullus, Villon, Heine, Gautier, Chaucer: a reasonably catholic tradition, including seven languages and 2500 years.

With this March 1913 issue of *Poetry* the Imagist movement was well launched; it was the focus of excitement and controversy in the magazine, and for the rest of 1913 *Poetry* remained the exclusive organ of the group. Early in 1914 the movement acquired an English outlet when *The New Freewoman* became

20. Pound, *Literary Essays* (N. Y., 1954), p. 4. Pound clearly means something more by Image than do most of the others, for his favorite example of the successful image is Dante's *Paradiso*. (See *The Modern Tradition*, pp. 147–48.)

The Egoist in January, with Aldington as Assistant Editor, and another sympathetic American periodical when *The Little Review* was founded in March. Late in 1913 Pound also completed the first Imagist anthology, *Des Imagistes*, published in February 1914 as an issue of *The Glebe* and in April as a book: it contained ten poems by Aldington, seven by H. D., six by Pound, five from Flint, and one each by Skipwith Cannéll, Amy Lowell, William Carlos Williams, Joyce, Ford, Allen Upward, and John Cournos, with three additional "documents" (travesties) by Pound, Aldington, and Ford. By this time Pound had become interested, with the sculptor Gaudier-Brzeska and the painter Wyndham Lewis, in a new movement called Vorticism, and the first issue of their magazine, *Blast*, appeared in June 1914. (We will return to Vorticism, and Pound's criticism generally, in a moment; but first let us conclude the history of Imagism as a movement.) It was Amy Lowell, a literary statesman and entrepreneur of great talent and energy, who really established Imagism as a movement, organized it like a political campaign, and brought it before a large public. Miss Lowell had found herself as poet in 1913 with the help of the Imagists both through their criticism and verse as she encountered it in *Poetry* and through their personal help in her visit to London in the summer of 1913. *Sword Blades and Poppy Seeds*, her first successful book of verse and the beginning of her real career as poet, was the result. In the summer of 1914 Miss Lowell returned to London and took over the movement, well equipped to do so by her money, confidence, practical *savoir faire*, and genuine talents. As Hughes remarks, why should the impoverished young poets "hesitate to follow a fairy godmother who promised to bring them fame and if not fortune at least a few shiny dollars?" [21] But as Hughes continues,

> . . . she had been compelled to choose carefully from among the poets. Some she could not get on with. . . ; others were unwilling

21. Glenn Hughes, *Imagism and the Imagists* (N. Y., 1950; originally 1931), p. 36.

to subscribe to a fixed program, the imagist program, and one of
Miss Lowell's contentions was that the group must stick together
for a period of at least three years—must not desert the camp
until the battle had been won. At any rate, the personnel even-
tually was determined, and the six poets who became the official
imagists were: Richard Aldington, H. D., John Gould Fletcher,
F. S. Flint, D. H. Lawrence, and Amy Lowell. In the name of
the group, Miss Lowell signed a contract with Messrs. Houghton,
Mifflin and Company for the publication of three anthologies of
imagist poetry, to be issued separately at yearly intervals. This
contract was fulfilled, and the anthologies appeared in 1915, 1916,
and 1917 (p. 37).

The first of these anthologies, *Some Imagist Poets* (1915), contains a preface, written by Aldington and revised by Miss Lowell,
purporting to express the common principles at which the six
poets arrived independently. "These principles are not new; they
have fallen into desuetude. They are the essentials of all great poetry, indeed of all great literature." The six principles are anything but revolutionary; they are essentially watered-down elabo-
rations of the three set forth in *Poetry* two years before; but like
most products of committees—and all the Imagist volumes were
edited by the six official Imagists in committee—they are such
general and innocuous statements as to have little bite left. In
summary, they called for: (1) "the language of common speech,"
and the exact rather than decorative word; (2) "new rhythms—as
the expression of new moods"; not free verse as the only method
of writing poetry, but as a principle of liberty; (3) "absolute
freedom in the choice of subject," whether modern or old; affirming "the artistic value of modern life," but warning that
"there is nothing so uninspiring nor so old-fashioned as an aero-
plane of the year 1911"; (4) "To present an image. . . . We are
not a school of painters, but we believe that poetry should render
particulars exactly. . . ." This point seems to be included as an
obligatory gesture of piety toward the name Imagist; but it is so
perfunctory as to lead one to suspect that the group did not

really understand Pound's use of the name, which was (as we shall see) quite different from this; (5) "To produce poetry that is hard and clear, never blurred or indefinite; and (6) "most of us believe that concentration is of the very essence of poetry" (Hughes, pp. 39–40).

Whatever its shortcomings, this statement of principles served the function of giving critics and journalists something tangible to discuss; this volume and its successors were published by an influential house and energetically and astutely promoted by Miss Lowell, and hence in the United States the movement became, for the larger public, synonymous with modern poetry, and the object of much lively controversy. In England it was largely ignored; one of the few intelligent reviews the 1915 volume received there was F. M. Ford's. What Ford said was low-keyed, self-deprecatory, and non-controversial; but expressive of so much of what still seems to me to be the truth about the situation that it must be quoted. Ford calls his review "A Jubilee," because it marks the twenty-fifth anniversary of his first review in 1890. He suggests that he is himself the progenitor of Imagism in the sense that he has preached for twenty-five years the doctrine they are now proclaiming, which is, essentially, "that the rendering of the material facts of life, without comment and in exact language, is poetry, and that poetry is the only important thing in life" (Hughes, p. 46). He concludes that only two of the six poets—H. D. and Flint—have "the really exquisite sense of words, . . . and insight that justify a writer in assuming the rather proud title of Imagiste—of issuing, that is to say, that challenge, that they will rouse emotions solely by rendering concrete objects, sounds, and aspects."

Into the American controversy over the volumes we need not go, for the story is well told by Hughes; the attacks by such poets and critics as Conrad Aiken, W. E. Leonard, and J. L. Lowes were lively, entertaining and perhaps fruitful.

The significant point, however, is that the six "official Imagists" included no major talents (except for Lawrence, whose presence, anomalous on many grounds, seems to have been the result of Miss Lowell's persuasiveness and generosity, with a somewhat surprising personal congeniality). Pound's comment on Miss Lowell's takeover was perfectly just:

> In the Imagist book I made it possible for a few poets who were not over-producing to reach an audience. That delicate operation was managed by the most rigorous suppression of what I considered faults.
>
> Obviously such a method and movement are incompatible with effusion, with flooding magazines with all sorts of wish-wash and imitation and the near-good. If I had acceded to A. L.'s proposal to turn "Imagism" into a democratic beer-garden, I should have undone what little good I had managed to do by setting up a critical standard. . . .
>
> A. L. comes over here, gets kudos out of association. She returns and wants to weaken the whole use of the term imagist, by making it mean *any* writing of vers libre. Why, if they want to be vers-librists, why can't they say so? But no, she wants in Lawrence, Fletcher, her own looser work. And the very discrimination, the whole core of significance I've taken twelve years of discipline to get at, she expects me to accord to people who have taken fifteen minutes' survey of my results.[22]

To return, however, to Amygism: by 1917 the last ounce of publicity had been squeezed out of the movement, and the fact that *Some Imagist Poets* (1917) did not sell well [23] confirmed the feeling of the six official Imagists that it was time to stop. Describing the larger currents of the time, Pound said of himself and Eliot that in 1917 "two authors, neither engaged in picking the

22. *Letters*, p. 48. As printed in Harriet Monroe's *A Poet's Life*, the letter continues with excellent criticism of individual poets: Aldington, Fletcher, H. D., William Carlos Williams, Eliot, Masters ("hits rock bottom now and again"), Lindsay ("I wish Lindsay all possible luck but we're not really pulling the same way, though we both pull against entrenched senility. He is really of Marinetti's people"), Sandburg, etc (p. 368).

23. S. Foster Damon, *Amy Lowell* (Boston and N. Y., 1935), p. 408.

other's pocket, decided that the dilution of *vers libre*, Amygism, Lee Masterism, general floppiness had gone too far and that some counter-current must be set going. . . . Remedy prescribed: 'Emaux et Camées' (or the Bay State Hymn Book). Rhyme and regular strophes. Result: Poems in Mr. Eliot's second volume not contained in his first . . . also Hugh Selwyn Mauberley." [24] Pound's observation is largely formal or technical, but it reminds us that none of the major talents of the time had any connection with the later movement. The true work of Imagism, to sum up, was the accomplishment of the original group of 1912–13; what it did was to give a name and focus to the break with the immediate past and to call for a conception of poetry as an art with rigorous technical demands. By 1914, as we shall see, all the luminaries of the new poetic firmament were writing. It is therefore doubtful if the three 1915–17 anthologies had any significant effect on poets, though certainly they reached a comparatively large audience and received much publicity in the United States. To repeat: it is a mistake to speak of Imagism in any of its three forms (Hulmean, Poundian, Lowellian) as the central movement in modern poetry, for, of all the major figures, only Pound has any relation to it, and that is brief and equivocal. Whether a non-discursive poetic, or more generally an aesthetic of spatial form or any mode of what we have called rhetorical discontinuity, is central to modernism in poetry is open to debate; but to equate Imagism with any such poetic is to oversimplify and distort literary history.

Let us return to Pound in 1914, and specifically to Vorticism. Though Vorticism was by no means clearly distinguished from Imagism, three differences seem clear enough: (1) Formulated by a painter, a sculptor, and a poet (Wyndham Lewis, Gaudier-Brzeska, and Pound), Vorticism occupies the common ground among the three arts, and deals explicitly with the resemblances and analogies among them; (2) As the name suggests, Vorticism seeks to go beyond the static and superficial qualities

24. Stead, p. 97, from *The Criterion*, July 1932.

of Imagism and incorporate the ideas of violent motion and apocalyptic change associated with such natural vortices as tornadoes,
whirlpools, and the like; (3) Hence the violent name of the Vorticist organ, *Blast* (of which only two issues were published, in
June 1914 and July 1915), and its extremist attitude, which is
anything but aestheticist (except, perhaps, in ultimate standard):
many aspects of British society are satirized or straightforwardly
denounced (there are lists of people and things to be BLASTed).
But Pound insists that, in spite of the common qualities of motion
and violence, "Vorticism is not Futurism, most emphatically
NOT. We like Cubism and some Expressionism, but the schools
are not our school" (*Letters*, p. 57). Futurism, he says, is mere
accelerated impressionism, a surface art, and a rejection of the
past. "The vorticist has not this curious tic for destroying past
glories. . . . I see no reason why I, and various men who agree
with me, should be expected to call ourselves futurists. We do
not desire to evade comparison with the past". The image, he
says, "is not an idea. It is a radiant node or cluster; it is what I
can, and must perforce, call a VORTEX, from which, and through
which, and into which, ideas are constantly rushing." [25]

In his first extended critical work, *The Spirit of Romance*
(1910), Pound states his creed: "All ages are contemporaneous.
. . . This is especially true of literature, where the real time is independent of the apparent, and where many dead men are our
grandchildren's contemporaries, while many of our contemporaries have been already gathered into Abraham's bosom, or some
more fitting receptacle. What we need is a literary scholarship,
which will weigh Theocritus and Mr. Yeats with one balance.
. . ." The same belief lay behind his poetry, as the title *Personae*
(1909) indicates; from the beginning, Pound is most truly himself
when speaking through the mask of a character remote in time,
place, and poetic tradition. No one has ever believed more passionately in the constant relevance of the past to the present, or
demonstrated his belief more effectively in his writing. He ex-

25. *The Modern Tradition*, p. 150 (from *Blast*, 1914).

plains patiently to the aspiring poetess Iris Barry just how the study of the past can liberate the writer from the tyranny of the present:

> The main thing being to have enmagazined some mass of fine literature which hasn't been mauled over and vulgarized and preached as a virtue by Carlyle, *The Daily Mail* . . . or any other proletariat of "current opinion." This mass of fine literature supposedly saves one from getting swamped in contemporaneousness, and from thinking that things naturally or necessarily must or should be as they are. . . . Also should serve as a model of style, or suggest possibilities of various sorts of perfection or maximum attainment (*Letters,* pp. 86–87).

On the other hand, when Pound urges the importance of modernity, he does so through citing the example of the other arts, which are in advance of poetry in this respect: "I think that only after a long struggle will poetry attain such a degree of development, or, if you will, modernity, that it will vitally concern people who are accustomed, in prose, to Henry James and Anatole France, in music to Debussy," he writes in 1908; and again: "No good poetry is ever written in a manner twenty years old, for to write in such a manner shows conclusively that the writer thinks from books, convention and cliché, and not from life, yet a man feeling the divorce of life and his art may naturally try to resurrect a forgotten mode if he . . . think he sees in it some element lacking in contemporary art which might unite that art again to its sustenance, life." [26] In the famous letter to Harriet Monroe which she published in *Poetry* in 1916, he insists again on modernity of language: "Poetry must be *as well written as prose.* Its language must be a fine language, departing in no way from speech save by a heightened intensity (i.e. simplicity). There must be no book words, no periphrases, no inversions. It must be as simple as De Maupassant's best prose, and as hard as Stendhal's" (*Letters,* pp. 48–49). This emphasis on the prose virtues helps to

26. *Literary Essays,* pp. 9, 11.

balance the emphasis of Pound's criticism on the non-discursive aspects of poetry.

Pound carefully distinguishes the kind of parallel of the arts he has in mind from other sorts. Reviewing Joyce's *Dubliners* in 1914, he describes two schools of Impressionists. The first are those "whose forerunner was Stendhal and whose founder was Flaubert"; they deal in "exact presentation" and "have been perhaps the most beneficial force in modern writing." The second school founded themselves not upon writing but upon Monet's painting, and these "soft" impressionists are, Pound says, a bore: "this mimicking of painting ten or twenty years late, is not in the least the same as the 'literary movement' parallel to the painting movement imitated"; the "spirit of a decade" affects all the arts, but the movements are parallel, not imitative of each other. "The force that leads a poet to leave out a moral reflection may lead a painter to leave out representation. The resultant poem may not suggest the resultant painting" (*Literary Essays*, p. 400).

In his book on Gaudier-Brzeska (1916) Pound defines two basic kinds of poetry: in the first, "music, sheer melody, seems as if it were just bursting into speech"; in the second, "painting or sculpture seems as it were " 'just coming over into speech.' " Neither type is new, but the second has only recently been named Imagist. "Dante is a great poet by reason of this faculty, and Milton is a wind-bag because of his lack of it. The 'image' is the furthest possible remove from rhetoric." At this point Pound is not distinguishing between Imagism and Vorticism, but seems to be using the former term to include both. But he insists that there is no resemblance between Imagism and Symbolism:

> Imagisme is not symbolism. The symbolists dealt in "association," that is, in a sort of allusion, almost of allegory. They degraded the symbol to the status of a word. They made it a form of metonomy. . . . Moreover, one does not want to be called a symbolist, because symbolism has usually been associated with mushy technique. . . . An *image*, in our sense, is real because we know it directly. If it have an age-old traditional meaning . . .

that is not our affair. It is our affair to render the *image* as we perceived or conceived it.

Browning's "Sordello" is one of the finest *masks* ever presented. Dante's "Paradiso" is the most wonderful *image*. By that I do not mean that it is a perseveringly imagistic performance. . . . The form of sphere above sphere, the varying reaches of light, the minutiae of pearls upon foreheads, all these are parts of the Image. The image is the poet's pigment; with that in mind you can go ahead and apply Kandinsky, you can transpose his chapter on the language of form and colour and apply it to the writing of verse (*The Modern Tradition*, pp. 147–48).

(The reference is to Kandinsky's *Uber das Geistige in der Kunst*, from which extracts had been translated in the first issue of *Blast*.) Throughout, Pound suggests a parallel between Imagism (used very broadly here) and abstraction in the graphic arts. As distinguished from Futurism, which is "a sort of accelerated impressionism," Imagism takes its "artistic descent *via* Picasso and Kandinsky, *via* cubism and expressionism."

Citing Whistler, Pater, Kandinsky, he defends abstraction: "It is no more ridiculous that a person should receive or convey an emotion by means of an arrangement of shapes, or planes, or colours, than that they should receive or convey such emotion by an arrangement of musical notes." But he does not dogmatically oppose representation: "The image is the poet's pigment. The painter should use his colour because he sees it or feels it. I don't much care whether he is representative or non-representative. He should *depend*, of course, on the creative, not upon the mimetic or representational part in his work. It is the same in writing poems, the author must use his *image* because he sees it or feels it, *not* because he thinks he can use it to back up some creed . . ." (pp. 151, 146–50). As illustration, Pound describes the composition of his "In a Station of the Metro": when he tried to find words for the original experience, he found the equation "not in speech, but in little splotches of colour. It was just that—a 'pattern,' or hardly a pattern, if by 'pattern' you mean something with a 'repeat' in it. But it was a word, the beginning, for me, of a language in colour." The experience, Pound says, led him to feel that if he were a painter "I might found a new school of painting, of 'non-representative' painting, a painting that would speak only by arrangements in colour. And so, when I came to read Kandinsky's chapter on the language of form and colour, I found little that was new to me." [27]

Pound does not make very much of the relation of poetry to music. His knowledge of music was considerable: as he wrote to Iris Barry in 1916, he had come to London originally "more or less under the wing" of the pianist Kitty R. Heyman, "was even an impresario" and knew "the London mondo musicale" (*Letters*, p. 95) in those days; later he spent some time in Paris with the composer Walter Rummell. Pound composed an opera about Villon, championed Antheil and Dolmetsch, corresponded knowledgeably with Tibor Serly, helped to revive Vivaldi, and engaged in musicological studies of the troubadours, Vivaldi, and early English composers. His insistence on the indispensability of the relation between music and poetry could not be stronger: "Poets who are not interested in music are, or become, bad poets. . . . Poets who will not study music are defective"; "poetry withers and 'dries out' when it leaves music, or at least an imagined music, too far behind it" (*Literary Essays*, p. 437). His practical criticism always stresses sound and cadence, and he repeatedly professes belief in an "absolute rhythm" attainable in poetry.

Pound's attitude to music may be described as essentially neoclassical. He objects to the sensationalism of romantic music and to the passivity induced by it: emotional music, he says, "is like a drug; you must have more drug, and more noise each time"; whereas the "early music starts with the mystery of pattern; if you like, with the vortex of pattern; with something which is, first of all, music, and which is capable of being, after that, many things" (p. 434). Emotional or impressionist music starts with

27. The poem, he suggests, tries "to record the precise instant when a thing outward and objective transforms itself or darts into a thing inward and subjective"; hence there is a kind of super-position of images.

being emotion or impression and then becomes only approximately music; and program music "is merely a weaker, more flabby and descriptive sort of impressionist music." In 1918 Pound hopes that "an awakening to the possibilities, not necessarily of 'Old' music, but of pattern music played upon ancient instruments" under the aegis of Dolmetsch may make music again a part of life, just as he believes "that Lewis and Picasso are capable of revitalizing the instinct of design" (p. 435). Nothing could be further than this attitude from any Romantic confusion of the arts.

In his recent book on Pound, subtitled "Poet as Sculptor," Donald Davie argues that Pound is not, either in theory or in practice, "(as T. S. Eliot perhaps is) a 'post-symboliste' writer, except in the narrowest chronological sense; what he deserves on the contrary is the lame though honorific title 'realist. . . .' " Davie quotes Pound's statement, "Nomina sunt consequentia rerum, and never was that statement of Aquinas more true than in the case of the vorticist movement," and comments: "But in *symboliste* poetry the logic works all the other way—things are the consequences of names"; and cites an example from Eliot. "Words, then, *can* create things—and do so continually in *symboliste* poetry. But Pound, as his appeal to Aquinas shows, is in this matter . . . content to be a traditionalist." In contrast to the *Symbolistes*, Pound regards the external world as real: "to Pound it is the outward that transforms itself into the inward, whereas to the devotee of the objective correlative it is always the inward (the poet's state of mind or state of feeling) that seeks in the outward world something to correspond to itself." [28]

28. Donald Davie, *Ezra Pound: Poet as Sculptor* (N. Y., 1964), p. 66. L. S. Dembo, in *Conceptions of Reality* (above, Chapter Two, note 12), explores the "aesthetic mysticism" shared by Pound and other poets. Taking a different view from Davie, Dembo argues that in Pound the central images are "projections of the imagination about which an essentially narcissistic poetic experience is conjured. The means of conjuration is language, which, rather than expressing a state, actually creates it" (p. 162). Again, "All Pound's love or nature poems are, in a sense, chants for the 'transmutation of metals,' the metal in reality being his own state of mind."

At this point we must resist the temptation to explore these questions about Pound and their later ramifications. Our concern here is with the beginning of modernism in English verse, and our terminal point is 1914. By this time, largely through Pound's instigation, most of the poets who were in any sense modern were in touch with Pound, with each other, and with at least the beginning of an audience. But let us come down to cases.

When Pound first met Eliot in September 1914, he expressed astonished gratification at finding someone who had "actually trained himself *and* modernized himself *on his own*. . . . It is such a comfort to meet a man and not have to tell him to wash his face, wipe his feet, and remember the date (1914) on the calendar" (*Letters*, p. 40). With his customary promptness and energy, Pound set about getting Eliot's poetry published: he browbeat Harriet Monroe into publishing "Prufrock" in *Poetry* magazine in 1915, and himself as editor published poems of Eliot's in *Blast* and the *Catholic Anthology* in the same year. No doubt it was the stimulation provided by these publications (his first except for local periodicals in school and college) and by Pound's encouragement and admiration that was responsible for Eliot's return to the writing of poetry after three years of silence. Eliot himself has defined his indebtedness to Pound exactly:

> I was introduced to *Personae* and *Exultations* in 1910, while still an undergraduate at Harvard. The poems did not then excite me, any more than did the poetry of Yeats: I was too much engrossed in working out the implications of Laforgue. I considered them, however, the only interesting poems by a contemporary that I had found. My indebtedness to Pound is of two kinds: first, in my literary criticism; . . . second, in his criticism of my poetry in our talk, and his indications of desirable territories to explore. This indebtedness extends from 1915 to 1922. . . .[29]

The remarkable thing is that Eliot's process of modernization was not only completely independent of Pound but seems to have

29. Quoted in K. Smidt, *Poetry and Belief in the Works of T. S. Eliot* (N. Y., 1961), p. 21.

had very little in common with Pound's. To put it briefly and roughly, when Pound began writing he was steeped in Browning and early Yeats; his medievalism had much in common with Rossetti's; he edited Lionel Johnson and admired other poets of the nineties. In spite of the many and exotic influences apparent in his work, Pound ascribes the chief role in his modernization to Ford and the tradition in the novel of which he is the latest representative. As the one piety of a notably impious man, Pound always acknowledges these English continuities ("Und überhaupt ich stamm aus Browning. Pourquoi nier son père?" [30]); and he also pays tribute to American predecessors: he praises Whistler for his definition of the role of artist, makes a pact with Whitman; he reveres Henry James and sits at his feet in London. Pound's further step in modernization, apparent in his volumes of 1912, shows a keener and often satirical awareness of the contemporary world. For this stimulus the general ferment of theory in the arts was partly responsible—Hulme and other proto-Imagists, and such figures as Kandinsky and Picasso. Much of the most modern poetry of 1912, however, is based on the Roman satirists and epigrammatists; this is the beginning of the technique that culminates in *Homage to Sextus Propertius* (1917), in which the British empire is paralleled to the Roman, and the *persona* of the private and non-patriotic poet who wants to make love and minor verses rather than war (or patriotic epics) is adopted.

With Eliot, the situation is quite different. His juvenile poems are skillful but perfectly conventional imitations of Keats, Tennyson, Kipling, and the like. The change comes with startling abruptness early in 1909; and we know from Eliot's own account what the primary stimulus was: Arthur Symons's *The Symbolist Movement in France*, which he read in December 1908. From this book he went on to the poets therein discussed and quoted, and he made his "deliberate choice of a poet to mimic": Laforgue, whose *vers libre* he found to resemble the loose blank

je crois que j'étais orienté avant de connaître les poètes français modernes.'
not influenced by the modern French before 1912: "Avec toute modestie,
30. *Letters*, p. 218. In the same letter to René Taupin, Pound says he was

verse of Webster, Tourneur, the later Shakespeare, and their contemporaries. Consciously adopting the ironic manner of Laforgue
and a verse form and style deriving partly from him and partly
from Jacobean drama, Eliot had a starting point that was very
different from anything else in English in 1909. Hence the break
with the immediately preceding English tradition is much sharper
and more obvious in Eliot's case than in Pound's. The break is, of
course, by no means complete: like Pound's *personae*, the early
poems have some affinity with Browning's dramatic monologues;
the themes of isolation and the buried life recall Arnold, whose
presence may always be felt in Eliot's criticism; and sometimes
there are incantatory lyrics reminiscent of Tennyson, Kipling, or
even Swinburne. But Eliot has made the point emphatically that
no poetry being written in English in these years seemed to him
of the slightest interest; and instead of coming to London, as did
Pound, he chose to spend the year 1910–11 in Paris. We have
seen earlier the basic debt Eliot acknowledges to Baudelaire and
Laforgue:

> I think that from Baudelaire I learned first, a precedent for the
> poetical possibilities, never developed by any poet writing in my
> own language, of the more sordid aspects of the modern metrop-
> olis, of the possibility of fusion between the sordidly realistic
> and the phantasmagoric, the possibility of the juxtaposition of the
> matter-of-fact and the fantastic. From him, as from Laforgue, I
> learned that the sort of material that I had, the sort of experience
> that an adolescent had had, in an industrial city in America, could
> be the material for poetry; and that the source of new poetry
> might be found in what had been regarded hitherto as the im-
> possible, the sterile, the intractably unpoetic . . . (*To Criticize
> the Critic*, p. 126).

His year in Paris, at this exciting time when new movements
were stirring, must have helped to complete the process of modernization and to confirm its radical difference in quality from
anything being written in English. Certainly the early poems

show a rapid and complete progress, from the rather derivative "Conversation Galante" of 1909 through the first two "Preludes," the "Portrait of a Lady," 1910, the last two "Preludes," "Rhapsody on a Windy Night," and by 1911 to the complete mastery and individuality of "La Figlia Che Piange" and "Prufrock."

Perhaps the most obvious presences in these early poems, aside from those of Laforgue and the Jacobean dramatists, are those of Dante and Baudelaire. As the former provided a springboard from which to begin, a style and manner with which to get the modern world into poetry, the latter and vastly greater pair suggested a spiritual context for its apprehension. The immense gain in significance added to "Prufrock" by its Dantean epigraph is an early example; in 1951 Eliot remarked that Dante had been the most persistent and deepest influence on his work. Of Eliot's sense of continuity with the past it is impossible to speak briefly, except to observe that there is a fundamental difference from Pound. Though the metaphor in "Tradition and the Individual Talent" (1919) of literary works forming a timeless order is superficially like Pound's notion of a "continuous present" (and Eliot may well be indebted to Pound here, as often in his early criticism), the concept of tradition as suprapersonal, beyond the individual, is alien to Pound, as is, perhaps, any real awareness of history. At any rate, the relevant point here is that Eliot's struggle for continuity, his sense of the relevance and importance of the past, are very much stronger than Pound's and are central to all his work. The break with the immediate past in English verse must be seen in this larger context. As Eliot put it in 1953,

> From time to time there occurs some revolution, or sudden mutation of form and content in literature. Then, some way of writing which has been practised for a generation or more, is found by a few people to be out of date, and no longer to respond to contemporary modes of thought, feeling, and speech. A new kind of writing appears, to be greeted at first with disdain and derision; we hear that the tradition has been flouted, and that chaos has come. After a time it appears that the new way of

writing is not destructive but re-creative. It is not that we have
repudiated the past, as the obstinate enemies—and also the stupid-
est supporters—of any new movement like to believe; but that
we have enlarged our conception of the past and that in the light
of what is new we see the past in a new pattern (*To Criticize the
Critic*, p. 57).

It is unlikely that Eliot was unaware, during his stay in Paris,
of all the excitement about painting; and it may be, as Howarth
suggests, that he learned something from the painters about rendering the metropolitan vision, the urban nightmare. But there is
nothing specific to point to, and we have Herbert Read's testimony to Eliot's lack of interest in or sensitivity to modern
painting.[31] As late as 1915 Eliot had to ask Pound who Kandinsky was! [32] It is therefore unlikely that awareness of the revolution in the other arts had much to do with his modernization as a
poet. Eliot is, of course, a poet of music rather than of painting,
as a glance at his titles makes clear—from Preludes, a Rhapsody, a
Love Song, to Quartets, the musical analogy is plain enough; and
such an early piece as the "Portrait" is permeated by musical allusions. Many critics have commented on his auditory imagination,
the musical structure and images of various poems. The music
Eliot has in mind seems to be mostly traditional, however
(though he praises Stravinsky's *Sacre* and is said to have had Bartok's quartets in mind when writing his own; of course, there are
also the jazz and ragtime rhythms of *Sweeney Agonistes*). In
general, about all one can say of the musical analogy is that it
probably helped—like the implicit Dandy pose—to break with the
tradition of opinion and rhetoric in poetry.

To sum up, it appears that Eliot's early poetry was almost
wholly isolated from the literary milieu in which Pound matured.
Aside from Laforgue, the Jacobean dramatists, and Dante, the
more important influences seem to have been non-literary: the
philosophy of Bradley, on whom he was writing a doctoral dis-

31. Sir Herbert Read in *T. S. Eliot*, ed. Allen Tate (N. Y., 1966), p. 33.
32. Noel Stock (ed.), *Ezra Pound: Perspectives* (Chicago, 1965), p. 111.

sertation in these years, of Bergson, whom he heard lecture in Paris, and of others. In later statements, he made his lack of relation to Hulme, Pound, and Imagism in these early years very clear:

> Whether the name and principles of imagism were Pound's invention or Hulme's, I do not know, and I am not very much interested. Imagism produced a few good poems—notably those of H. D.—but it was quickly absorbed into more comprehensive influences, including Pound's. . . . Pound . . . created a situation in which, for the first time, there was a "modern movement in poetry" in which English and American poets collaborated, knew each other's works, and influenced each other.[33]

This puts with admirable succinctness just what Pound's contribution was as far as the "men of 1914" were concerned. Beyond this date there is no need to go: as Eliot handsomely acknowledged many times, Pound gave him extremely valuable help and stimulation from 1914 through 1922 (*The Waste Land* marking its culmination). When Pound left London in 1920, "the place he might have occupied in the post-war literary scene in London was quietly assumed by Eliot." [34] But that is another story.

In Chapter Three we discussed the other "man of 1914" who was discovered by Pound and made part of the movement in that year, after having modernized himself in complete independence. This was, of course, James Joyce. Though Joyce's affinities are with music rather than with painting, his tastes were traditional and the other arts had nothing to do with his process of modernization. This took place primarily under the moral imperative of Ibsen and the banner of naturalism, though Joyce was a part of the Impressionist tradition in fiction that we have described. (Pound called his kind the "hard" impressionists stemming from Stendhal and Flaubert, as distinct from any soft painterly blur-

33. Quoted in Smidt, *Poetry and Belief in the Works of T. S. Eliot*, pp. 21–22.
34. Sir Herbert Read, op. cit., p. 14.

rings and mergings.) At this point we need only remind ourselves of the importance of 1914 in Joyce's career: in this year he sent *Dubliners* and the *Portrait* to Pound, who promptly and effectively set about getting them published. In the same year Pound included one of Joyce's poems in *Des Imagistes;* it was about this that Pound had originally, at Yeats's suggestion, gotten in touch with Joyce. Finally, in 1914 Joyce began *Ulysses.*

Wyndham Lewis, painter, sculptor, and novelist, was prominent among the "men of 1914." (The intimacy of this group should not be exaggerated; Eliot did not meet Lewis until 1915, nor did either of them meet Joyce until 1921—in both cases through Pound.) Lewis was a Cubo-Futurist until 1914, when he broke with Marinetti. With Pound, he founded Vorticism, which was to succeed both Futurism and Imagism. Aside from Lewis, the sculptor Gaudier-Brzeska was the outstanding talent associated with the movement. Since Vorticism had no discernible influence on poetry, it need not be discussed here. Its periodical, *Blast,* of which only two issues appeared, one in 1914 and the other the next year, published poetry by Pound and Eliot, part of Ford's *The Good Soldier,* excerpts from Kandinsky, and some good satire; but the movement perished quickly. Lewis was an aggressive polemicist, and his ideas are of interest because he was in many respects a genuine neo-classicist (though also a monstrous egoist) at the same time that he was in theory and practice unquestionably modern. Thus he detests Bergson, psychology, the exploration of the Unconscious, the collective; he equates Time with Romanticism (*Time and Western Man,* 1927) and campaigns for abstraction and for spatial form.

Yeats is not usually thought of as one of the "men of 1914," but the title would be justifiable, for this date marks both the end of his process of modernization and the time he was probably closest to Pound and to modernism as a movement. The change from Early to Middle Yeats, as described by most critics, takes place in the first decade of this century; put in its simplest terms, it may be seen in the sharp contrast between the dreamy, wavering, subjective style of *The Wind Among the Reeds* (1899) and the clear, hard, objective style of the volume of 1914, significantly called *Responsibilities*. This style deals with the public world of events and personalities as well as the private world of dreams; a taut, bitter restraint is seen instead of the lush diction and swooning rhythms of the earlier work.

The primary agency of modernization for Yeats was, without much doubt, his experience with the Abbey Theatre from 1900 to 1910 as both playwright and manager. His language became more spare and natural, his rhythms more dramatic and flexible. By the turn of the century Yeats had changed his idea of poetry; in his introduction to the *Oxford Book of Modern Verse* he remarks, with truth at least as regards himself, that "in 1900 everybody got down off his stilts." For whatever complex of reasons, by this time he strives for accuracy, definiteness, simplicity—thus anticipating the ideal of Pound and Hulme. It is typical of Yeats that he carries on this process of modernization in the name of protest against the modern; in 1900 he writes:

> . . . vague forms, pictures, scenes, etc. are rather a modern idea of the poetic and I would not want to call up a modern kind of picture. I avoid every kind of word that seems to me either "poetical" or "modern" and above all I avoid suggesting the ghostly (the vague) idea about a god, for it is a modern conception. All ancient vision was definite and precise (*Letters*, p. 343).

In the second chapter we looked at the impact Nietzsche had upon Yeats soon after this time, his influence presumably reinforced by that of Pater in suggesting to Yeats the aesthetic virtues of hardness, intensity, and tragic joy, and strengthening his repugnance for sentimentality and abstraction. There were, of course, very many other possible agencies of modernization, among them Pound, who had been seeing Yeats regularly since 1909 and criticizing his style, urging him in this direction. On the other hand, Pound never ceased to regard Yeats as a model (even for Imagists, as we have seen) and to pay tribute to him, espe-

cially for his achievement in changing his style. In a review dated
December 1911, Pound said, "Mr. Yeats has once and for all
stripped English poetry of its perdamnable rhetoric. He has
boiled away all that is not poetic—and a good deal that is. . . . He
has made our poetic idiom a thing pliable, a speech without inversions" (*Literary Essays*, pp. 11–12). Yeats himself said that
Pound had helped him "to get back to the definite and concrete,
away from modern abstractions." Whatever influence Pound had
probably was exerted after the major change had taken place, especially during the summers of 1913 and 1914, when he and Yeats
shared a cottage in Sussex and "tried to remake each other." [35]
Reviewing *Responsibilities* in *Poetry* (May 1914), Pound praised
the new "quality of hard light" in the poems, their "greater hardness of outline."

In summary, Yeats's modernization seems to have been chiefly a
process of lonely self-discipline, of pruning and re-making both
his poetry and himself. The process was parallel to and contemporaneous with a widespread movement in the work of other
poets; but awareness of any such poets or movements seems to
have been a negligible factor in comparison to the effect of
Yeats's work as dramatist and man of affairs and to the internal
logic of his own career. Though Yeats was, of course, extremely
sensitive to and interested in painting, his tastes were traditional,
and there is nothing to suggest that awareness of the revolution in
painting played any part in his modernization. Of Yeats's relation
to the past little need be said. No poet was ever more responsibly
aware of the importance of continuity with the past; the astonishing thing about Yeats, who was twenty years older than any of
the other poets we are considering, is that he was able to break
away from it sufficiently to re-make himself in middle age. Aside
from other less explicable qualities, it is Yeats's inclusiveness, the
fact that he is both solidly traditional and unquestionably modern,
that has made him seem to many the supreme poet of the century, and certainly the most influential.

35. Ellmann, *James Joyce*, p. 361.

Finally, let us look briefly at some other poets who emerged in 1914, completely outside any Poundian sphere of possible influence. Robert Frost published his first book, *A Boy's Will*, in London in 1913, and like so many others, he was promptly discovered by Pound. As Ellmann comments, Pound "in a burst of enthusiasm would have refashioned both the man and his verse had not Frost rebelled and fled London" (*James Joyce*, p. 362). Frost's *North of Boston*, published in London, 1914, is usually said to be the first in which his distinctive idiom appears. In general, Frost's verse forms and themes remain like those of the Georgian poets with whom he felt the closest affinity; modernization with him means a sparer and more personal idiom, not any obvious or flamboyant change. He shows little awareness of music or painting, and eschews literary movements, but obviously feels their impact at a distance, as the date of his emergence shows.

Wallace Stevens emerges as a modern poet quite suddenly with the publication of a group of poems in *Trend* in September 1914, and then in 1915 with "Sunday Morning" in *Poetry* and "Peter Quince at the Clavier" in *Others*. His earlier poetry had been very conventional, and the recent volume of letters does not help to explain what brought about the change. His affinity with the French Symbolists is undisguised, and though the letters contain no mention of Pound or other modern poets, surely he must have been aware of them. Stevens was a connoisseur of painting, but his tastes seem not to have been very advanced, and the extent to which modern painting influenced him remains uncertain, though probably considerable. His most interesting comments on modernism in general occur in the last essay in *The Necessary Angel* (1951), "The Relations Between Poetry and Painting." He quotes Picasso, Cézanne, Braque, and Klee, and reveals a profound awareness of the difference between modern and older painting. In our age of disbelief, he argues, "poetry and painting, and the arts in general, are, in their measure, a compensation for what has been lost. Men feel that the imagination is the next greatest power to faith: the reigning prince" (p. 171). In our time, "the search for the supreme truth has been a search in reality or through reality or even a search for some supremely acceptable fiction." The arts create "a new reality, a modern reality"; as we have seen in the passage quoted in our second chapter, this is a "reality of decreation," and its ultimate discovery is "that man's truth is the final resolution of everything." In poetry, however, Stevens is against self-conscious modernism, though convinced of the importance of time-awareness:

> A modern painter is more than likely to be the product of a movement. A modern musician sounds like one the moment you hear him. However that may be, what a modern poet desires, above everything else, is to be nothing more than a poet of the present time. I think it may be said that he considers his function to be this: to find, by means of his own thought and feeling, what seems to him to be the poetry of his own time as differentiated from the poetry of the time of Sir Walter Scott, or the poetry of any other time, and to state it in a manner that effectively discloses it to his readers.[36]

A poet of unquestionable talent and promise whom Pound did not even try to promote, educate, or enlist in the movement was D. H. Lawrence. There seem to have been two reasons for this very unusual situation. In the first place, Lawrence had already been discovered (by F. M. Ford, who published his stories and poems in the *English Review* in 1909) and was plainly mature and modern by 1913, when both *Sons and Lovers* and his first volume of poetry, *Love Poems and Others*, were published. The second reason is more interesting: Pound recognized Lawrence's ability, but simply found his work uncongenial. "Detestable person but needs watching. I think he learned the proper treatment of modern subjects before I did," Pound writes to Harriet Monroe in 1913 (*Letters*, p. 17). Pound may have been influenced by

36. Stevens, *Opus Posthumous* (London, 1959), p. 244. See also Stevens's poem, "Of Modern Poetry" (*Collected Poetry*, p. 239).

the fact that Amy Lowell, when she took over the movement, made Lawrence one of her six official Imagists. But he must also have detected, and found far more objectionable, Lawrence's affinity, both temperamental and doctrinal, with the Futurists. Lawrence read in 1914 the anthology *I Poeti Futuristi* (1912), with Marinetti's manifesto, and was much impressed by it.[37] Like the Futurists, Lawrence is an apostle of historical discontinuity, perfectly willing to discard the past and committed to the future; as we saw in Chapter Three, the vision at the end of *The Rainbow* is a good example. As poet, his aim is immediacy, to capture the shimmer of the fleeting present, not to preserve it, but to experience it more fully. He is not interested in the poem as art object, precious and detached from the flux of experience, outside of time; but in the poem as aid to fuller awareness of the flux, more complete immersion in it. Hence he advocates and frequently uses free verse, and is impatient with problems of form. There may be some relation between the fact that Lawrence was painter as well as writer and the radicalism of his position, though he seems to have made his basic definitions before he can well have known much, if anything, about the revolution in painting. At any rate, the resemblance between his attitude and that of many painters (e.g. practitioners of *collage*) is plain, as is the increasing popularity of the position in the 1950s and 1960s.

William Carlos Williams, like Lawrence, is a temperamental Futurist, who takes historical discontinuity as a basic postulate. Thus he writes to Harriet Monroe in 1913, defending his poems against her criticism: "Now life is above all things else at any moment subversive of life as it was the moment before—always new, irregular. Verse to be alive must have infused into it something of the same order, some tincture of disestablishment, something in the nature of an impalpable revolution, an ethereal reversal let me say. I am speaking of modern verse."[38] Hence his practice of

37. V. de Sola Pinto and W. Roberts (eds.), Lawrence, *Complete Poems* (N. Y., 1964), I, 9.
38. *A Poet's Life*, p. 270.

free verse is, like Lawrence's, a philosophical and moral gesture. We must "invent for ourselves . . . a new prosody based on a present-day world"; [39] "The old concept of the line restricts our lives as well to be measured after the standard and so, unless we become aware of it, our poems rather than freeing, as they should do, throw us back on old modes of behavior." [40] Like Lawrence once more, he was greatly influenced by painting. He says in *I Wanted to Write a Poem:* "You must remember I had a strong inclination all my life to be a painter. Under different circumstances I would rather have been a painter than to bother with these god-damn words. I never actually thought of myself as a poet but I knew I had to be an artist in some way." [41] And he says of his early verse, "I think it was the French painters rather than the writers who influenced us, and their influence was very great." [42] But Williams's affinity to painting is too obvious to need demonstrating; it appears in the titles of poems and volumes, and he wrote numerous essays and comments on painters. Williams was keenly aware of the revolution in painting, keeping up with each successive avant-garde from Cubists to action painters, and was undoubtedly much influenced by them. Undoubtedly, also, Williams was much influenced by Pound, who was his friend in college and kept trying to educate him. Pound included him in *Des Imagistes,* and Miss Monroe had published him in *Poetry* the preceding year, after their argument had concluded amicably. The agencies of Williams's modernization are, then, clear; and no poet has ever been, in certain senses, more extremely "modern"—opposition to fixed forms and to the iamb, commitment to all possible meanings of "freedom," analogies with science (the variable or relativistic foot) and with painting (e.g. "St. Francis Einstein of the Daffodils," 1921), rejection of the past.

39. William Carlos Williams, *Selected Letters,* ed. J. C. Thirlwall (N. Y., 1957, p. 269.
40. Ibid., p. 321.
41. W. C. Williams, *I Wanted to Write a Poem* (Boston, 1958), p. 29.
42. J. M. Brinnin, *William Carlos Williams* (Minneapolis, 1965), p. 14.

He is, in short, a stage beyond Lawrence, and several stages beyond Pound: the only poet of much talent besides Lawrence who can be called a Futurist.

In closing, I wish to anticipate slightly by considering a poet whose work lies somewhat beyond the chronological boundary of 1915, but who allows us to see how the modern movement looked in 1915 to an intelligent young man who was also a promising poet and painter. E. E. Cummings, on graduating from Harvard in 1915, gave an address on the "parallel developments of the New Art in the fields of painting and sculpture, music, and literature." His thesis was, "An insight into the unbroken chain of artistic development during the last half century disproves the theory that modernism is without foundation." In painting, he notes that anyone who takes art seriously accepts Cézanne and Matisse, and goes on to defend Cubism and Futurism, including such figures as Duchamp and Brancusi. In music he praises Schönberg and Stravinsky; he likes Satie's humor, and defends Scriabin's "color music." Amy Lowell and Donald Evans provide a literary parallel to Scriabin, he says, and Gertrude Stein—whom he calls a literary Futurist—carries this "sound painting" to absurdity. But even this kind of absurdity is valuable, he argues, as necessary experimentation from which the future will profit. The New Art, he concludes, was a "courageous and genuine exploration of untrodden ways."

Cummings was a professional painter as well as poet. He always painted more than he wrote, painting during the day and writing at night. He painted no abstractions, preferring flowers and girls and sunsets; but when queried about this by an imaginary interviewer, he insists flatly that "painting is nonrepresentational" and suggests that to think otherwise would be idolatrous. The agencies that led him to modernism are indicated above; he was specifically influenced by Pound's *Ripostes* (1912) and the Imagist credo of 1913, and by Gertrude Stein's *Tender Buttons* (1914). But in spite of his cogent defense of modernism, Cummings always insists that conscious modernism is of no value in itself; that the only valid criterion for any form of art is the degree of its aliveness. He is perceptive enough to see very early the superiority in both poetry and criticism of Eliot to Pound, whom he calls an "extraordinarily useful bore." Reviewing Eliot's 1920 *Poems*, he praises Eliot in contrast to those poets "who are obstinately always 'unconventional' or else 'modern' at the expense of being (what is most difficult) alive." [43]

43. George Firmage (ed.), *E. E. Cummings: A Miscellany* (N. Y., 1958), p. 34.

CHAPTER FIVE

THREE SOUTHERNERS
AS MODERNS

JOHN CROWE RANSOM, Allen Tate, and Robert Penn Warren, who emerged as the most important poets among the group who produced the magazine *The Fugitive* from 1922 to 1925 in Nashville, Tennessee, provide an opportunity for a study in some depth of the impact of modernism. We can trace exactly when and how each discovered modernism and what its effect was. Ransom, Tate, and Warren have been highly influential men of letters—critics, teachers, editors—as well as poets, and each has had a different kind of relation to modernism throughout a long and varied career.

The Fugitives were very different in background from most of the poets we have discussed so far. They were not expatriates nor cosmopolites; they were hardly even urban, having come from small towns to the small provincial city of Nashville. Like Yeats in Ireland, Faulkner in another part of the American South, and other occasional products of poor, defeated, and culturally backward societies, they had a profound sense of the past and of history, a hatred of abstraction, and an awareness of tragedy. While they disclaimed regionalism, proclaiming in the first issue that "Southern Literature has expired" and "*The Fugitive* flees from nothing faster than from the high-caste Brahmins of the Old

South," and felt alienation in time as well as place (Ransom, in the first poem of the first issue, called himself "an alien, miserably at feud / With those my generation. . . ."), the posture they adopted was one of enigmatic flight rather than defiance.

IRONIC DUALIST

Ransom's earliest intellectual recollection, he told J. L. Stewart in 1946, was his conviction

> that modern man is crippled by a dissociation of the reason and sensibility which results in an imbalance whereby the reason, armed with abstract principles which have been spectacularly successful in supplying the material needs of the body, tyrannizes over the sensibility and restricts its innocent, profitless delight in the vividness and variety of the world. With this conviction went a "fury against abstractions" and a desire to restore the sensibility to its proper eminence in man and his society and to enable it to enjoy its harmless indulgences.[1]

Although this belief obviously resembles Yeats's hatred of abstraction as opposed to Unity of Being, and Eliot's theory of the "dissociation of sensibility," it appears to antedate them both. Stewart makes the point emphatically (and presumably on Ransom's authority) that Ransom derived his conviction not from books but "from his own experiences and observations; though modified through the years by his reading in Kant, Hume, Bergson, Freud, and many others, it owed its origin to no other man." R. P. Warren disclosed recently that after he wrote an essay in 1935 defining the theme of Ransom's poetry as dissociation of sensibility, Ransom commented that he thought of man rather as an "oscillating mechanism." [2] In other words, he is skeptical about the historical aspect of Eliot's theory, doubting that man had ever possessed unity; to use the terminology of our first chapter, he

1. John L. Stewart, *The Burden of Time* (Princeton, 1965), p. 14.
2. In *Tri-Quarterly*, Winter 1968.

believes in psychological but not historical dissociation of sensibility (though perhaps *divided* or *fragmented psyche* would be better, to make it clear that this is genealogically distinct from Eliot's notion).[3] At any rate, this conviction (again according to Stewart), lay behind Ransom's decision to change his field of study and teaching from Classics to English.

Ransom's first poem, "Sunset," written in 1916, is characteristic in protesting against an abstraction, though the protest is rather mild and tentative than furious and the abstraction is God. It is, however, most uncharacteristic in being in free verse, against which he was soon to take an increasingly intransigent stand. Looking at the fields at sunset with his sweetheart, the poet says, "It is no man-rival I am afraid of / It is God." And he concludes: "I will try to be as patient as Rover, / And we will be comrades and wait, / Unquestioningly, / Till this lady we love / And her strange eyes / Come home from God."

In form and in the visual emphasis of some lines not quoted, this poem may reflect some acquaintance with Imagist verse. Nowhere else in his early verse does Ransom show even this much awareness of modern poetry: his lines are usually rimed and regular, and the only recent models apparent are Hardy, Frost, perhaps Housman and Robinson. Neither the essential theme nor the tone and style are completely defined in *Poems About God* (pub-

3. "Lamenting the modern dualism of thought and feeling, Eliot thinks he finds it bridged in the older order of English poetry. . . . I confess that I know very little about that; and I must add that, having worked to the best of my very little ability to find the thing Eliot refers to in the seventeenth century poets, and failed, I incline to think there was nothing of the kind there. . . . We must not like some philosophers become the fools of the shining but impractical ideal of 'unity' or of 'fusion.' The aspiration here is for some sort of fusion of two experiences that ordinarily repel one another: the abstracted exercise of reason in hard fact and calculation; and the inclusive experience of literally everything at once. . . . It would seem that from that precise moment when the race discovers that what has seemed to be an undifferentiated unity is really a complex of specialized functions, there can be no undifferentiated unity again; no return" (*The New Criticism*, N. Y., 1941, pp. 183–84).

lished in 1919 on Robert Frost's recommendation), and "Ego,"
published in the first *Fugitive*, April 1922, is not much better. By
the time "Necrological" was published in the second *Fugitive*
(June 1922), however, the process of definition was complete.[4]
Modernity seems not to be the result of any literary influence; he
said much later that "some French ladies" had introduced him to
the work of the French Symbolists in 1919 and that they had remained in the back of his head; but he seems to have been unac-
quainted with any real moderns until Tate introduced him to
them—*after* Ransom had defined his style in "Necrological." It
looks as if the stimulation of the group itself, together with the
Zeitgeist and always-mysterious personal factors, was decisive.

In his editorial in the third *Fugitive* (October 1922), Ransom
says that the group are "in tune with the times in the fact that to
a large degree in their poems they are self-convicted experimentalists." He expresses uneasiness about the American tendency to
"throw off the confinements of meter before they have established conclusively that these are or are not habitable," while
such British poets as Yeats, Bridges, Graves, and Hardy achieve
ease while maintaining the traditional prosody. He admits, however, that some work in non-traditional prosody "seems so perfected that we would not wish it to be otherwise," and he cites as
example Allen Tate's "Horatian Epode," in the same issue. Edito-
rializing on "The Future of Poetry" in the February 1924 issue,
he begins: "The arts generally have had to recognize Modernism
—how should poetry escape?" Refusing to attempt an abstract
definition of modernism, he considers first the Imagists, and remarks that their manifestos were exciting, though their practice
was crude—but instructive. Their first principle was honesty of
theme and accuracy of expression; in short, they "conceived the
first duty of the Moderns as being to disembarrass poetry of its

4. According to Tate, "Necrological" was written "before we had even
thought of a magazine" (Louise Cowan, *The Fugitive Group*, Baton Rouge,
1959, p. 39); this places it before March 1922 and means that it was not
necessarily written after "Ego."

terrible incubus of piety in the full classical sense of that term, and they rendered the service." Their second principle was to make their meters more elastic, and in fact they practically gave up meters altogether. "Their free verse was no form at all, yet it made history." Ransom fears that "we moderns" are so "impatient and destructive" that, in eliminating the element of nonsense, we may make it impossible to write poetry. "Our souls are not, in fact, in the enjoyment of full good health. For no art and no religion is possible until we make allowances, until we manage to keep quiet the *enfant terrible* of logic that plays havoc with the other faculties." And he concludes, "The future of poetry is immense? One is not so sure in these days, since it has felt the fatal irritant of Modernism. Too much is demanded by the critic, attempted by the poet."

Ransom's final statement in *The Fugitive* was made in the issue of June 1925. Defining dualism as man's perception of his difference from nature, Ransom describes various attitudes toward it and various escapes from it. Most nineteenth-century poetry, he says, consists of romantic escape from it. "But the earlier and greater poets (Chaucer, Spenser, Shakespeare, Donne, Milton) . . . turned back to the stubborn fact of dualism with a mellow wisdom which we may call irony." Ransom goes on to praise irony in terms perhaps reminiscent of Richards's *Principles of Literary Criticism* (1924): "Irony may be regarded as the ultimate mode of the great minds—it presupposes the others. . . . Irony is the rarest of the states of mind, because it is the most inclusive; the whole mind has been active in arriving at it, both creation and criticism, both poetry and science." Frost's poetry, he says, is "modern in one of the common senses of modern: its spirit transcends the nineteenth century mind and goes back to further places in the English tradition for its adult affiliations," and he notes that it is "immensely metaphysical."

Ransom's basic impulse is, then, a fury against abstraction, against the predatory and ruthless intellect that would destroy (through its instrument, applied science) or ignore the rich particularity of the world's body; against this he exhibits a protective tenderness for the useless and undefined and helpless: for children, old people, the illogical textural details of poems as against their logical or prose structure: for the preposterously unrealistic Captain Carpenter as against his very efficient opponents. He defends play, enjoyment, contemplation, and the aesthetic experience which is allied to them.

But—and this is a point often ignored or obscured—Ransom is a genuine dualist. One cannot say that he is at bottom a believer in one or the other of the two opposed attitudes. He protests against the abstracting intellect because he believes it to be, as embodied in modern science, a present danger; the danger is that it may win too complete a victory, drying up or denying the pleasures of the innocent sensibility. But Ransom never repudiates logic or science; he would not give a complete victory to emotion, texture, play, innocence, and uselessness even if he could. His very effective polemic against Romanticism is, in fact, based on the charge that the Romantics made precisely this error: they and their modern descendants try to exclude the intellect from poetry and hence fall into sentimentality and other kinds of false simplification. Though his father was a Methodist minister and missionary, Ransom was indoctrinated at an early age in a skeptical and "scientific" point of view toward religion ("I came late into an interest in poetry, after I had been stuffed with the law if not the letter of our modern sciences, and quickly I had the difficulty of finding a poetry which would not deny what we in our strange generation actually are: men who have aged in these pure intellectual disciplines, and cannot play innocent without feeling very foolish." [5] Neither belief in Christianity, in any but a highly paradoxical and symbolic sense, nor any other form of supernaturalism seems ever to have appeared to him thereafter as a possibility. As his prose makes clear, Ransom himself has always remained a thoroughgoing skeptic: beneath the personal charm and the gentle and courteous manner he has been detached, unbelieving, unil-

5. *The World's Body* (N. Y., 1938), p. viii.

lusioned, perhaps inclining rather more to the scientific attitude, or at least increasingly sympathetic toward it. There has been a radical hard-headed skepticism, a kind of bleakness, beneath the "traditional" surface. The irony in Ransom's poetry is profound and unresolved; it is tragic, for its only resolution is in the idea of death.

An early review of Freud may help to substantiate these assertions. In "Freud and Literature" (1924), Ransom says that while it is proper that the doctors should still disagree about psychoanalysis, the poets "find much less difficulty in accepting it as gospel truth." And he goes on to show a full and sympathetic understanding of Freud's literary bearings: "The legends, the mythologies, the demonologies, and the fairy tales of all the races bear witness to the truth of Dr. Freud's startling yet not quite novel theses." Freud, he observes, demonstrates the biological continuity of the life-forms; for "what are our aberrant behaviours but the ways of ghosts that haunt within us?" The Freudian man is "multiple rather than simple . . . in fact a pack of demons, going under the name of John Doe . . ."; and as a modernist he is unaware of this continuity:

> Marvellous is the presumption of that dogmatic modernist Doe—ignorant that he is a cave within whom the fabulous civil war may at any moment go to raging—who thinks that he will take unto himself a little wife, and buy a little home on terms, and devote his eight laborious hours to business, and accomplish a stout and dreamless happiness.[6]

Literature, he is sure, will produce an "enormous accession of evidence for Freudianism when it is studied for that purpose"; Freudian psychology will be the work of whole generations of scholars, like a Gothic cathedral; when it is done, it will be "a complexity and yet a unification of doctrine, perhaps as imposing a structure as the world has seen." Psychoanalysis is, he remarks,

6. *Saturday Review of Literature*, Oct. 4, 1924, pp. 151–52.

the "systematic or scientific application of a technique that poets and artists have generally been aware of"; but even James and Conrad, had they known Freud, might have "found truth and depth even readier to their hands. . . . This we say because we have been convinced in our own experience of how much light psycho-analysis can throw upon the baffling relations of life—and of how much more epic and fascinating it shows the daily business of being human to be." Commenting on *Beyond the Pleasure Principle* and other works of Freud, he says that nothing of his "has ever so teased the poetic imagination as the vast and brilliant speculations" in these volumes. There is, he observes, much evidence in English poetry for a Will to Die; poets celebrate mortality even more than immortality. "Human life may be surveyed at this stage in that spirit which may turn out to be the last and most rational of all the modes of mind—the spirit of tragic irony. To be a tragic ironist is to be aware sharply and grimly, but not too painfully, of the constant involvement of life with death. In that spirit Homer sang, and the makers of the ballads, and Shakespeare. . . ."

I have quoted this at perhaps excessive length because it shows Ransom's rationalism, his hospitality to science, and most of all, of course, because it is such a fine early appreciation of the literary significance of Freud, in both his Dionysian (or demoniac, as Ransom likes to call it) and rational aspects. *Poems About God* are emphatically not about belief in God, but more nearly the opposite; they expound a kind of rational humanism. Ransom's most explicitly religious work is *God Without Thunder* (1930). This is a very unorthodox defense of orthodoxy whose ultimate provocation was the Scopes trial in 1925. Like others in the group, Ransom was deeply offended by the condescension toward the South of Clarence Darrow and the reporters and commentators covering the trial of the biology teacher who had taught Evolution in the Tennessee schools. The argument of the book is, to oversimplify grossly, that religion and poetry are in the same boat, and both are endangered by the science-dominated modern world. In memorable terms that simplify a number of very complex matters, Ransom argues for the common cause of poetry and religion as against science:

> Religion is an order of experience under which we indulge the compound attitude of fear, respect, enjoyment, and love for the external nature in the midst of which we are forced to live. . . . Science is an order of experience in which we mutilate and prey upon nature; we seek our practical objectives at any cost, and always at the cost of not appreciating the setting from which we have to take them. . . . The pleasures of use are self-regarding, intense, and destructive of the object, while the pleasures of enjoyment are unselfish, expansive, and respectful or conservative of the object. . . . The perils of action are nowhere in human experience plainer than in the life of sex. . . . One course is love in the romantic sense, as sanctioned by religion and honored in poetry. The other course is lust, which may be defined as the pure abstract act of sex. *Love is the aesthetic and lust is the science of sex.*[7]

The aesthetic attitude, he continues, citing Kant and Schopenhauer (whom he admires, with Aristotle, as against Plato and Hegel), is marked by desirelessness; it is "the most objective and the most innocent attitude in which we can look upon the world, and it is possible only when we neither desire the world nor pretend to control it. Our pleasure in this attitude probably lies in a feeling of communion or rapport with environment . . ." (p. 173).

The World's Body (1938), still, in my opinion, Ransom's best book of criticism, develops similar themes further in the realm of literary theory. Ransom makes it very clear in the preface that he opposes science only insofar as it claims exclusiveness; remaining a dualist, he sees art and science as "equal and opposite" activities, both producing valid and necessary knowledge of the world; and he makes no more grandiose claim for art than that it is necessary

7. *God Without Thunder* (N. Y., 1930), p. 137.

to counterbalance science. His polemic is directed not against science, but against those kinds of poetry—the romantic and sentimental—that exclude or ignore scientific knowledge and attitudes and escape to a fake innocence. What is needed is "not a pre-scientific poetry but a post-scientific one"; and Ransom calls for poetry which is the "act of an adult mind; and I will add, the act of a fallen mind, since ours too are fallen." Romantic poetry which denies the real world because of failure to deal with it satisfactorily and escapes to a private land of heart's desire is, Ransom observes, really a form of neurotic behavior and describable pathologically. On the other hand, those who deal successfully, as scientists and practical men, with the world tend to lose, in the process of achieving their goals, "the body and solid substance of the world." Poetry can recover this world for us. "Men become poets, or at least they read poets, in order to atone for having been hard practical men and hard theoretical scientists." But the poetry must be of a kind that such men can respect, and hence it must be, not romantic or sentimental or immature or escapist, but modern. "For such moderns as we are the poetry must be modern. It is not as in a state of innocence, to receive the fragrance of the roses on the world's first morning, that our moderns the scarred veterans may enact their poetry, but in the violence of return and regeneration" (p. xi).

Some of the essays cast further light on Ransom's notion of modernism and its relation to dissociation of sensibility. Modern poets, he argues, are Puritans because the age is; the age "craves to perfect the parts of experience separately or in their purity." (Ransom uses the term *Puritan* rather than *Purist* because he wants the "zealous and contriving" overtone; he suggests that *Platonist* would be another name for it.) "It seems that we know little but dualisms, pluralisms, successions, the discharge *seriatim* of quite different functions, in these longitudes" (p. 238). In a "late or 'modern' age, like the present one . . . poetry has had to torture itself, becoming difficult and strange, in order to be poetry at all. . . ." "Apostate, illaureate, and doomed to outlawry the modern poets may be. I have the feeling that modernism is an unfortunate road for them to have taken. But it was an inevitable one" (p. 62). Older poetry, we moderns say, with our historical consciousness and sensitiveness to anachronism, "did very well for those dark ages before the modern mind achieved its own disintegration and perfected its own faculties serially" (p. 70).

"Poems are little dramas, exhibiting actions in complete settings rather than pure or efficient actions" (p. 249). Art "wants us to enjoy life, to taste and reflect as we drink; when we are always tending as abstract appetites to gulp it down; or as abstract intelligences to proceed, by a milder analogue, to the cold fury of 'disinterested' science" (p. 39). Ransom remarks that he was "brought up with a glowing appreciation of the noble characters of scientists"; but both scientists (who produce instrumental knowledge serving animal need) and idealists (Platonists who tend to be philosophers, preachers, and educators) ignore the whole or private character of the individual object, and so make us more or less than human. "Science gratifies a rational or practical impulse and exhibits the minimum of perception. Art gratifies a perceptual impulse and exhibits the minimum of reason" (p. 130). As in his later structure-texture formulations (in *The New Criticism*, 1941, and elsewhere), this emphasizes the resemblance of art to play and to contemplation. But it is important to repeat that Ransom does not wish to purify art by excluding the attitude here called scientific from it, any more than he wishes to exclude structure and make the poem pure texture; the poem exists in a tension, and Ransom stubbornly refuses to reduce the two attitudes or elements to one.

Of the manifestation of these same ideas and attitudes in Ransom's poetry it would be pleasant, but unfortunately superfluous, to speak at much length. *Chills and Fever* (1924) indicates the theme precisely in its title. This obsessive theme is, of course, dualism; and mixed feelings are the basis of the characteristic tone of elegant, self-deprecatory irony. The wonderful beginning of "The Equilibrists"—

> Full of her long white arms and milky skin
> He had a thousand times remembered sin—

is the first of an interlocking series of perfectly balanced dualisms, canceling each other out in logic and tone. The two basic metaphors for the lovers ("Close, but untouching") are astronomical bodies ("spinning, orbited nice"), held serenely in balance by changeless natural forces, and (in the title) acrobats whose feats of balance are difficult and perilous achievements, highly unnatural. The poem brings in enormous ranges of allusion for these basic contraries: fire and ice, body and mind, ascetic Heaven and horribly sensual Hell, honor and love, the *Song of Songs* and *Tristan*, Dante and *Aucassin and Nicolette*, life and death—for the "strict lovers, they are ruined now!" cries the speaker angrily, but they lie "perilous and beautiful." The lady in "Here Lies a Lady," like all of us, died of the "chills and fever" which gave the volume its title—six spells of each, in her case; but the girl in "Parting, Without a Sequel" is both at once: "And all the time she stood there hot as fever / And cold as any icicle." "Vision by Sweetwater" contrasts the vision of pastoral innocence—girls sweet, beautiful, birdlike—with the memory, fished up from the "dark of my mind," of a scream from one of the white throats which made the child suddenly old. "Piazza Piece" contrasts Death, who appears as a "gentleman in a dustcoat," a "grey man among the vines," and the Maiden expecting a different suitor ("I am a lady, young in beauty, waiting / Until my true love comes, and then we kiss"). "Blue Girls" (retitled "The Vanity of the Blue Girls") contrasts beauty and wisdom, youth and age, ignorance and knowledge, innocence and experience: the poet encourages the schoolgirls in their ignorance and thoughtlessness and undertakes to ally himself with them; for the beauty which they both serve fights a losing battle:

> Practise your beauty, blue girls, before it fail;
> And I will cry with my loud lips and publish
> Beauty which all our power shall never establish,
> It is so frail.

At its best and subtlest, the dualistic attitude lies behind the two fine poems about children and death, "Janet Waking" and "Bells for John Whiteside's Daughter." As Tate has remarked recently, Ransom's basic themes are love and death, and he is a great elegiac poet.

Wounded Surgeon

Since Tate became among the Fugitives the recognized champion of the moderns, we should consider how and when he became acquainted with them. In the fall of 1921, his senior year at Vanderbilt, where he was a Classics major, Tate met Warren for the first time. At this time he had read Symons's *The Symbolist Movement in France* (the same book, we remember, that had introduced Yeats and then Eliot to the French Symbolists) and had gone on to Baudelaire; he had read Pound's essays and verse in such little magazines as *Poetry, The Little Review,* and *The Dial,* and was stimulated by the magazines to further reading in the Symbolists. But the advent of real modernism was sudden and dramatic. For reasons of health, Tate had to withdraw from the university early in 1922. Hart Crane saw one of Tate's poems in *The Double Dealer* and wrote to him, remarking that the poem showed that Tate had read Eliot. Tate had not in fact done so, "but I soon did; and my difficulties were enormously increased. Anyhow from Eliot I went on to the other moderns, and I began to connect with the modern world what I had already learned from Baudelaire. . . . I mention this personal history because I believe it was through me that modern poetry made its first impact upon the doctors who gathered fortnightly in Mr. Frank's house." [8] The change in Tate's own verse was quickly apparent, for "Horatian Epode to the Duchess of Malfi," his first fully successful and fully modern poem, appeared in the October 1922 *Fugitive.* When Tate returned to Nashville in February 1923 (*The Waste Land* having in the meantime appeared in *The Dial* in Oc-

8. Tate, "*The Fugitive* 1922–1925: A Personal Recollection Twenty Years After," *Princeton University Library Chronicle,* III, 81.

tober 1922), he "began an impertinent campaign in Eliot's behalf in the South."

His campaign started with the editorial, "Whose Ox?," in the December, 1922, issue. Noting that modern painting has broken with the "tyranny of representation" (he cites Duncan Grant and Picasso, and Clive Bell's criticism), Tate speculates on the poetic analogy: a poetry that does not represent but remakes the material world. He argues not that this should be the only kind of poetry but that such a poetry might be legitimate. As we have seen, he cites *The Waste Land* as evidence of the "necessity, in special cases, of an aberrant versification," and assumes that all will grant the authenticity of Eliot's "impersonal and increasingly abstract art. . . ." Ransom disagreed on both counts, saying that *The Waste Land* "seems to bring to a head all the specifically modern errors," and there was a brief sharp controversy, which there is no point in recapitulating here. In the April 1924 issue of *The Fugitive*, Tate wrote an important editorial on the whole issue of modernism, called "One Escape from the Dilemma." Agreeing with Ransom that "free verse has failed," Tate insists nevertheless that "a few writers" in the medium are important—and obviously he has Eliot in mind primarily. The fundamental question at issue, however, concerns the nature of poetry and its difference from prose; and here Tate defines his differences from Ransom sharply. Ransom, he says, believes that the content of poetry is identical with that of prose; "and the assumption implied here that poetry, like prose, is exclusively concerned with the rational exposition, rather than with the pure presentation, of intuitions or ideas, ignores the actuality of a radical difference between a vocabulary of exposition and an idiom flexible enough to accommodate a presentation of the entire fantasy of sensation." The true and necessary modernism, he argues, which begins with Baudelaire, is deeper than free verse; because there is no "common-to-all truth," "the Modern poet might tell you that his only possible themes are the manifold projections and tangents of his own perception." Hence his diction and poetic idiom must be different;

no longer close to speech but embracing "the entire range of consciousness"—and he cites Cummings and Crane. Tate suggests that Baudelaire's theory of correspondences is the "backbone of modern poetic diction and the character which distinguishes it from both the English tradition and free verse. . . ." "It is not direct continuity from the immediate past of English poetry. It is development out of the whole of it under French direction. . . ." In a fine counter-attack, Tate asserts that the true decadents are not the moderns—e.g. Cummings or Crane—but "our Woodberrys, whose lazy vision and vicarious sentiment in 1910 were but ill-disguised in the pretentious frumpery of chaste meters."

Tate is a profound and subtle critic, and to summarize his essays is to distort them, for their chief value is not in the ideas which can be abstracted from them. Nevertheless, we must try to state briefly what his mature position (as represented in the collections *On the Limits of Poetry*, 1948, and *The Forlorn Demon*, 1953) is on the matters with which we are concerned.

In the preface to *Reason in Madness* (1941), Tate remarked that all his essays seemed to be on one theme: "a deep illness of the modern mind," and he used for the gathering darkness the Yeatsian phrase "the mad abstract dark." It is a justifiable simplification to say that all Tate's critical writing deals with some aspect of this theme and that he, acknowledging himself to be infected, is always concerned with the diagnosis and cure of this deep illness. The illness itself Tate describes variously, but all its manifestations may be brought under the rubric of dissociation of sensibility. Like Ransom, Tate is more certain of the psychological fact that the phenomenon exists at present than he is of any historical theory of how it came to be; but he has far more interest than Ransom in exploring the question of its existence in the past—not so much for aetiological explanation as to illuminate the present. Thus Poe is a recurrent example for Tate of anticipation of the modern disintegration of personality, as are Donne and Emily Dickinson; and he follows Maritain in citing Descartes as a key figure historically.

Like everyone else, Tate uses *modernism* in several senses, but perhaps two main ones are distinguishable. (1) Modernism in reference to culture in general. This is the final fruit of dissociation: lacking unity, being fragmented into different compartments, self-conscious, tending to Narcissism and solipsism, modern man is provincial because cut off from his past (historical discontinuity). He is dominated by Positivism and other forms of abstraction so that he over-develops one part of his fragmented psyche at the expense of the rest. (2) Modernism in poetry. Tate regularly argues that this is, if not exactly good, at least inevitable and necessary. Of course, Tate argues differently in different contexts, sometimes defending the modern poets against incompetent or perverted critics and audiences which have lost the ability to read, and sometimes using the poets' defects and failures as evidence of the things that are wrong with modern society. Further, he makes the obvious but often-forgotten point that there is no "great lump of modernist verse in which no distinctions are possible," but many kinds and many qualities. Good modern poetry, however, serves a kind of therapeutic function in helping to counter the distortions of modernism in the bad sense for the reader who approaches it properly. The good modern poet is unable to accommodate the innocent reader who lives in the past, who "likes to see in poetry, if not the conscious ideas, then the sensibility of a previous age." Nor can he accommodate the social reader (modern version of the former moralistic one) who looks for ideas for the future to live by. (Since the poet has "no large scheme of imaginative reference in which he has confidence," he must "attach some irony to his use of 'ideas.'") The poet, "and it is he who is the critical reader—is aware of the present, any present, now or past or future. For by experiencing the past along with the present he makes present the past, and masters it, and he is at the centre of the experience out of which the future must come" (*On the Limits of Poetry*, p. xvi).

A difficulty arises in reconciling the analysis of dissociation of sensibility with the defense of modernism in poetry, and in defining the relation of modern to romantic poetry. (The difficulty remains not from any failure to perceive it but because of Tate's fundamental conviction that candor and fidelity to particular insights are more important than theoretical consistency.) Romanticism he sees as the separation of emotion from intellect, so that "for the first time in Western art, we had the belief that poetry is chiefly or even wholly an emotional experience"—though he exempts Keats from most of the force of this, while Shelley is the horrible example. The "Romantic movement taught the reader to look for inherently poetical objects, and to respond to them 'emotionally' in certain prescribed ways, these ways being indicated by the 'truths' interjected at intervals among the poetical objects" (p. 214). In contrast, "modern poets offer no inherently poetical objects, and they fail to instruct the reader in the ways he must feel about the objects. . . ." In defending modern poetry against its detractors, then, he contrasts it with the romantic; and he argues emphatically that Yeats, greatest of the moderns, is not romantic: "If one of the historic marks of romanticism is the division between sensibility and intellect, Yeats's career may be seen as unromantic . . . because he closed the gap." Yeats, he believes, is "nearer the center of our main traditions of sensibility and thought than the poetry of Eliot or of Pound" (p. 224). On the other hand, Hart Crane was "one of the great masters of the romantic movement," and his career "will be written by future critics as a chapter in the neo-symbolist movement." Crane's sensibility is solipsistic, narcissistic; "he falls back upon the intensity of consciousness, rather than the clarity, for his center of vision. And that is romanticism" (p. 235).

Tate sometimes suggests that dissociation of sensibility leads to the two extremes of scientism and symbolism, and these two extremes constitute modernism in the bad sense: or, in Tate's example, one half of the modern mind is pragmatic and functional, and looking at a horse sees only horsepower in the abstract; the other half sees the horse as just a locus of unpredictable and immeasurable qualities. In contrast to both these half-religions is the older religion of the whole horse, which is able to contemplate images; and although the South never had a fitting religion, and was corrupted by the twin drives of Protestantism and Capitalism, the South still retained the older habit of mind: "The Southerners were capable of using their horses . . . but they could also contemplate them as absolute and inviolable objects. . . ." Hence they "retained a certain status as *images*, and images are only to be contemplated, and perhaps the act of contemplation after long exercise initiates a habit of restraint, and the setting up of absolute standards which are less formulas for action than an interior discipline of the mind. There is doubtless from the viewpoint of abstract history not much difference between a centaur, since we speak of horses, and a Christ, since we speak of historicity" (p. 317).

The same thesis is put in explicitly religious terms in *The Forlorn Demon*, where Tate calls the modern or protestant abstracting mind "angelic" because it tries to achieve direct knowledge of essences without going through the senses: "I call that human imagination angelic which tries to disintegrate or to circumvent the image in the illusory pursuit of essence" (p. 31).

It is easy enough to find inconsistencies in Tate's statements on modernism, but they usually go back to the basic distinction made above. Thus, when he is using poetry as a basis for diagnosing the ailments of modern culture, he stresses its evidence of dissociation of sensibility, the "splitting off of information from understanding, this modern divorce of action from intelligence," of the locked-in sensibility, the lack of connection between sensibility and ideas, of Narcissism and solipsism, the inhuman abstraction of the modern mind; Crane, trying to confute Eliot, simply demonstrated his point that the integrity of the individual consciousness has broken down. The "message" of modern art "is that social man is living, without religion, morality, or art . . . in a mere system of money references through which neither artist nor plutocrat can perform as an entire person" (*On the Limits of Poetry*, p. 276).

On the other hand, the modern writer cannot, and should not, escape modernism; specifically, he argues (against a temporary position of Ransom's), the Southern writer need not stay in the South. "But the arts everywhere spring from a mysterious union of indigenous materials and foreign influences: there is no great art or literature that does not bear the marks of this fusion. So I cannot assume, as Mr. Ransom seems to do, that exposure to the world of modernism (Petrarchism was modernism in the England of 1540) was of itself a demoralizing experience." And he concludes with the shrewd question, "what shall we say of Mr. Ransom's own distinguished and very modern poetry?" Poetry exists in a tension, he argues in a famous definition:

> The metaphysical poet as a rationalist begins at or near the extensive or denoting end of the line; the romantic or Symbolist poet at the other, intensive end; and each by a straining feat of the imagination tries to push his meanings as far as he can towards the opposite end, so as to occupy the entire scale. . . . It would be a hard task to choose between the two strategies, the Symbolist and the metaphysical; both at their best are great, and both are incomplete (p. 86).

But poetry also flourishes best, he argues sometimes, in a historical tension, when a traditional society is breaking up, when there is a special tension between abstraction and sensation. Donne's was one such age, or more broadly, 1580–1660; another was the period in New England from which emerged Hawthorne and Emily Dickinson, and the present century, Tate sometimes implies but never states, is perhaps such another—especially in "backward," formerly traditional societies like Ireland and the American South. Only in such a "perfect literary situation" is the fusion of sensibility and thought possible; "like Donne, she *perceives abstraction* and *thinks sensation*." The situation is far from perfect for the society, of course, and also for the poet as person; in "Miss Dickinson, as in Donne, we may detect a singularly morbid concern, not for religious truth, but for personal revelation. The modern world is self-exploitation. It is egoism grown irresponsible in religion and decadent in morals. In religion it is blasphemy; in society it means usually . . . that the spiritual community is breaking up" (p. 208).

As we have seen, Tate defends in some of his early writings the radical break with prose structure and logic in such poets as Eliot and Hart Crane. His particular opponent in these discussions was Ransom, who would admit illogic into poetry only as half of a frankly dualistic system, consisting of logical structure on the one hand and irrational and playful texture on the other; and who disapproved specifically and strongly of *The Waste Land*. Tate argues, as we have seen, for pure presentation of the entire range of consciousness as a legitimate aim, and he sometimes uses the analogy of non-figurative modern painting. Form "is meaning and nothing but meaning: scheme of reference, supporting symbolism that ceases to support as soon as it is recognized as merely that" (p. 240). Hence the modern poet lacks form, and Tate praises J. P. Bishop's search for "a central source of form," and his uniting of the influences of "Yeats for form, Eliot for the experiment in language." Bishop, he observes, perfected Symbolist poetry in English "perhaps more than any other writer," and he analyzes some of his effects of painting achieved in poetry. But "There is no satisfactory substitute in poetry for the form-symbol," and Bishop was well aware of the problem; he wrote, " 'I am trying to make more and more *statements*, without giving up all that we have gained since Rimbaud.' The difficulty could not be more neatly put. . . . The statement is form, the fixed point of reference; 'all that we have gained since Rimbaud' is the enrichment of language that we have gained to offset our weakness in form" (p. 246).

Though Tate thus defends rhetorical discontinuity in principle, we have seen that he considers the Symbolist strategy to be one-sided, and that he is aware of the tendency of some modern poets to use violent and experimental language as substitute for the other kind of form which comes from a center of belief, of vision; in both he argues that the greatest poetry is that of the center. He emphatically rejects, in *The Forlorn Demon*, the Symbolist notion that language itself can be or create a reality: Poe's diction, with all its faults, "is never that idolatrous dissolution of language from the grammar of a possible world, which results from the belief that language itself can be reality, or by incantation can create a reality: a superstition that comes down in French from Lautréamont, Rimbaud, and Mallarmé to the Surrealists, and in English to Hart Crane, Wallace Stevens, and Dylan Thomas" (p. 61). On the other hand, we have noticed his shrewd suggestion of the Puritan iconoclastic zeal behind the attack on images, symbols, on other modes of knowledge besides abstraction, and his labeling of this as angelism. But Tate, with characteristic scrupulousness, notes that the sensibility of modern Catholic poets is just as angelic as anyone else's (*The Forlorn Demon*, p. 38).

While there is no space for adequate discussion of Tate's poetry, we must look briefly at its picture of the modern world and at the relation of Tate's own practice to his critical precept. In Tate's verse, even more obviously than in Eliot's, there are powerful forces of order to create a fruitful tension against the forces of disorder. Thus most of Tate's poems are in regular and traditional meters: sonnets, blank verse, quatrains, and various intricate stanza forms strictly followed; epodes, odes modeled on "Lycidas" and on Drayton's "Ode to the Virginian Voyagers." There is no shying away from the conventional iambic pentameter, though much of Tate's best work is done in trimeter (e.g. "Seasons of the Soul") or tetrameter—his use of both these latter forms clearly owing much to Yeats's example. The long poem on which he has been at work for the past two decades, and of which three parts have been published so far, is in terza rima, the strictest and most demanding of all forms in English.

Against this ordered formal background there plays the audacious and elliptical language of the poems, passionate, violent, sometimes obscure. Anthony Hecht puts it well: Tate's "poetry seems to me beautifully composed, and yet just barely composed. The stone seems always about to cry out of the wall, and the beam out of the timber to answer it, and the broken bone to come hideously through at the collar." [9]

Tate's obsessive theme, as he put it himself, is "man suffering from unbelief." In one sense, this is very personal, since the man is often clearly the poet himself; in another, it is general, for the poet is a representative modern, and the theme defines the modern world, "from all salvation weaned," oppressed by the approach of mortality, seen usually at twilight and in autumn. Undoubtedly, the pervading metaphor of the modern world as Hell owes much to Dante, to Baudelaire, and to Eliot's fusion of the two; but it is also deeply felt and personal.

Like Eliot again, he sees modern man—in a metaphor that is sometimes an alternative to the vision of Hell and sometimes a variant of it—as the living dead. Sometimes, as in "The Oath," this is a relatively simple contrast of past and present: to the question, "Who are the living and the dead?" the implied answer is that the dead are more living than the moderns who are physically alive but spiritually dead. "To the Lacedemonians" presents a similar contrast: the old Confederate veteran cannot understand the moderns, who "expect too much, do too little. . . ." But he is aware of his own defects—"Yet I, hollow head, do see but little; / Old man: no memory: aimless distractions"—and of those of his cause, with its "Vain / chivalry of the personal will!" Joining both metaphors, he sees the distinction between North and South as meaningless in the face of the living death of modernism, which is Hell: "All are born Yankees of the race of men / And this, too, now the country of the damned." The moderns are dehumanized, obsessed with movement and power, "the streets hard with motion / And the hard eyes that look one way"; forgetting that "There is no civilization without death; / There is now the wind for breath." They are "Eyeless with eyesight only, the

9. In the "Homage to Allen Tate" issue of *The Sewanee Review*, LXVII (1959), p. 569.

modern power" and finally "Damned souls, running the way of sand / Into the destination of the wind!"

The Second World War was for Tate a confirmation of his worst forebodings about the modern world, symbolized for him especially in the mindless force and almost unlimited speed and power of the United States Air Force—e.g. "Ode to our Young Pro-consuls of the Air" and "Jubilo," which is an ironic version of the Negro slaves' millennial hopes: there will be, for bloodless modern man, only "unspeakable salt land" beyond the Day of Jubilo, and the Day will be brought about by boys who "caress the machines they ride / On the Day of Jubilo."

As the last quotation suggests, the moderns are dead because their world is abstract and meaningless: "In an age of abstract experience, fornication / Is self-expression, adjunct to Christian euphoria, / And whores become delinquents; delinquents, patients; / Patients, wards of society: Whores, by that rule, / Are precious." In such a world, "Where are the heroes with sloops and telescopes / Who got out of bed at four to vex the dawn?" Like Alice, who, kissing her own image, went through the looking-glass, the moderns have followed Narcissism into abstraction—the Cheshire cat makes a wonderful symbol of abstraction—bodiless and bored; the poet (and it is notable that he always addresses the moderns as "we," never "they") laments passionately this loss of the world's body and of God with thunder; like Baudelaire, he prays for consciousness of evil as better than spiritual non-existence:

—We too back to the world shall never pass
Through the shattered door, a dumb shade-harried crowd
Being all infinite, function depth and mass
Without figure, a mathematical shroud

Hurled at the air—blessed without sin!
O God of our flesh, return us to Your wrath,
Let us be evil could we enter in
Your grace, and falter on the stony path!

In the preface to *The Forlorn Demon*, he comments ironically on this:

> The saints tell us that confident expectancy of damnation is a more insidious form of spiritual pride than certainty of salvation. The little we know of hell is perhaps as follows: it promptly *adjusts* and *integrates* its willing victims into a standardized monotony, in which human suffering, its purpose thus denied, begins to sound like the knock of an unoiled piston.

Aside from these ironic ones of Alice through the looking-glass, the Day of Jubilo, the Roman Empire revived, and the like, Tate's most striking and fully developed symbol of the modern world is the winter sea, in the third part of "Seasons of the Soul." Each part of this profound and complex poem deals with one aspect of modern man, a "season" in the sense of stage of life and also of role or type, as symbolized by an element. Thus Part I deals with summer and with the body and its fruit, violence and war; these converge in the specific summer of 1940 and the fall of France. (The poem has gradually become recognized as one of the handful of great longer poems to come out of World War II, with Eliot's *Four Quartets*, Auden's *For the Time Being* and *The Sea and the Mirror*, and Stevens's "Notes Toward a Supreme Fiction.") There is no space here for full discussion; it will have to suffice to say that Part II presents the protagonist in autumn at twilight, "no longer young" and "down a well," a relatively obvious image, by contrast with the public hell of Dante evoked at the end of the preceding section, of the private hell of modern man. This becomes individual and psychological, turning into the hall of the protagonist's childhood home, in which he encounters his father and mother but is unseen by them (thus reliving his childhood sense of isolation and aloneness). The third part brings us to the symbol with which we began, the winter sea. The basic symbolism here is of the sexual preoccupation of modern man, which is an attempt to compensate for his alienation and other losses. Thus the section begins with an invocation to Venus ironically asking her to return into the sea, since "all the sea-gods are dead," and to her "salt maidenhead." But the shark rather than the dove shall "pace our company" in this element, "All night to nudge and tear / The livid wound of love." In the winter sea of the modern world, "What sleek facility / Of sea-conceited scop / To plumb the nether mind!" Many images allude to Dante, the climactic one being that of breaking off a branch of coral, which speaks, like the tree of Dante's suicide (*Inferno*, XIII), saying that he "died / of self-inflicted woe, / Lovers whose stratagem / Led to their suicide." And the protagonist observes that he, "like them, / Was maimed and did not bear / The living wound of love." The fine last section deals with the season of spring, with the religious man, and with the element of fire. Before discussing it, we must take a quick look at time in Tate's poetry generally.

As in "To a Romantic" (1924), addressed to Robert Penn Warren, Tate considers exaltation of the past to be romantic:

> You think the dead arise
> Westward and fabulous:
> The dead are those whose lies
> Were doors to a narrow house.

But dismissal of the past as unreal or insignificant, denial of history, acceptance of temporal discontinuity, he obviously considers to be the great modern error—or tragedy. Thus in "The Meaning of Death" the speaker says, ironically,

> Gentlemen, let's
> Forget the past, its related errors, coarseness
> Of parents, laxities, unrealities of principle.
> Think of tomorrow. . . .

And the poem builds up, as the speaker's ironic advice continues, through a contrast of modern isolation with the communal Eucharist—"Desire to eat secretly, alone, lest / Ritual corrupt our charity"—to the audacious line already quoted, "We are the eyelids of defeated caves."

Denying time, with its alternation of day and night, the moderns are condemned to space alone: "All space, that heaven is a dayless night, / A nightless day driven by perfect lust / For vacancy . . ." ("Last Days of Alice"). The denial of time means the denial of the possibility of meaningful action, as in "The Meaning of Life": "In killing there is more than commentary"; and the end of the poem depicts the modern frustrated longing for such action, equating it with time:

> But there's a kind of lust feeds on itself
> Unspoken to, unspeaking; subterranean
> As a black river full of eyeless fish
> Heavy with spawn; with a passion for time
> Longer than the arteries of a cave.

In the last section of "Seasons of the Soul," to which we may return in conclusion, the modern space-obsession with the corresponding denial of time are suggested: "Back in my native prime / I saw the orient corn / All space but no time, / Reaching for the sun / Of the land where I was born . . ."; and in the next stanza, "In time of bloody war / Who will know the time? / Is it a new spring star / Within the timing chill, / Talking . . . ?" This is spatial form with a vengeance.

TRAGIC MORALIST

Warren was the youngest of the Fugitives. While he was, in a sense, the optimum product of their influence and teaching—"that group was my education," [10] he said in a recent interview—Warren was different from Ransom and Tate in some significant respects of background and attitude; and the differences have become more pronounced in his subsequent career. Unlike them, Warren has been for a long time a professed liberal in politics— "I was a New Dealer and I don't take it back now"—and a very successful practitioner of high-level journalism (e.g. *Segregation* and *Who Speaks for the Negro?*); he has won the Pulitzer Prize

10. John Longley (ed.), *R. P. Warren: A Collection of Critical Essays* (N. Y., 1965), p. 23.

for both fiction and poetry, and has appealed to very large audiences, as his repeated appearances on best-seller lists testify.

Warren's analysis of the human condition bears much resemblance to Ransom's dualism. In both, the notion of the Fall as *culpa felix* is central: the transition from Innocence to Experience is necessary and good, though often tragic; for the world of innocence is illusion or escape. Warren told Stewart, however, that his basic themes of dissociation, the perils of abstract idealism, and the like came from his own experience and observation, not from the influence of Ransom and Tate, though they helped him to refine his ideas (*The Burden of Time*, p. 448). Perhaps it is fair to say, then, that Warren began with his own convictions, was influenced by Ransom and Tate in developing them and giving them literary form and substance, and went on to carry them further in his own way.

As essayist and historian, Warren is occupied centrally with moral concerns. (The word *moral* may be misleading; his conception of life is basically tragic, and hence is at the opposite pole from the kind of moralistic interpretation that justifies the self by attributing evil to others or deals in absolute and external judgments.) Perhaps his best short statement is contained in *The Legacy of the Civil War* (1961), in which that war is interpreted as an image and archetype of tragedy:

> It is the story of a crime of monstrous inhumanity, into which almost innocently men stumbled; of consequences which could not be trammeled up, and of men who entangled themselves more and more vindictively and desperately until the powers of reason were twisted and their very virtues perverted; of a climax drenched with blood but with nobility gleaming ironically, and redeemingly, through the murk; of a conclusion in which, for the participants at least, there is a reconciliation by human recognition (p. 103).

Protesting against the perennial American illusion of innocence and virtue, or moral narcissism, that leads to moral crusades and "our diplomacy of righteousness, with the slogan of uncondi-

tional surrender and universal spiritual rehabilitation—for others,"
Warren appeals for the interpretation of the Civil War as tragedy
rather than as the ground of the Southerners' Great Alibi or the
Northerner's Treasury of Virtue, and pleads for a Lincolnian
ethic rather than the absolutist creed of John Brown.

Warren's literary criticism is similarly moral, and assumes the
same view of life as tragedy. The criticism is not large in scope;
most of it deals with writers for whom Warren feels a particular
affinity, and in writing about them he is plainly writing also
about himself and his own aims and problems, artistic and philosophical. The most obvious example is Conrad; it is hardly paradoxical to say that the best single essay about Warren is Warren's
essay on *Nostromo*, which concludes with the following definition of the kind of writer Warren conceives Conrad to be:

> The philosophical novelist, or poet, is one for whom the docu-
> mentation of the world is constantly striving to rise to the level of
> generalization about values, for whom the image strives to rise
> to symbol, for whom images always fall into a dialectical configu-
> ration, for whom the urgency of experience, no matter how
> vividly and strongly experience may enchant, is the urgency to
> know the meaning of experience. This is not to say that the
> philosophical novelist is schematic and deductive. It is to say
> quite the contrary, that he is willing to go naked into the pit,
> again and again, to make the same old struggle for his truth.[11]

For Conrad, "the very act of composition was a way of knowing,
a way of exploration," he continues; and this, like the whole
definition, applies to Warren himself as well as to Conrad.

This unabashedly moral interpretation of the writing and reading of literature informs all of Warren's criticism. Thus, in the
well known and relatively early "Pure and Impure Poetry," he
puts it succinctly:

> The saint proves his vision by stepping cheerfully into the fires.
> The poet, somewhat less spectacularly, proves his vision by sub-

11. Warren, *Selected Essays* (N. Y., 1958), p. 58.

mitting it to the fires of irony—to the drama of his structure—in the hope that the fires will refine it. In other words, the poet wishes to indicate that his vision has been earned, that it can survive reference to the complexities and contradictions of experience (p. 29).

And in "A Poem of Pure Imagination" he describes the reading of poetry in similarly moral terms:

> . . . insofar as each reader must, as a result of his own history and nature, bring to the poem a different mass of experience, strength of intellect, and intensity of feeling . . . the reader does not interpret the poem but the poem interprets the reader. We may say that the poem is the light and not the thing seen by the light. The poem is the light by which the reader may view and review all the areas of experience with which he is acquainted (p. 213).

It is this view, the polar opposite of aestheticism, since it interprets literature in moral and (in the large and undogmatic sense) religious terms, that underlies the extremely influential textbooks, *Understanding Poetry* and *Understanding Fiction*, that Warren wrote with Cleanth Brooks, and that justifies in them the emphasis on irony and similar devices (ambiguity, paradox, etc.), presented not merely as devices but as indices to awareness of moral complexity, maturity of insight, on the author's part. The metaphor of the author as "earning" his insight, or the central character his illumination, recurs very frequently, as does the metaphorical notion of redemption through "coming to terms" with evil or with the fullness of experience. Sentimental literature arrives at solutions that are too easy, because based on the stock response and a limited, exclusive view of experience; the good writer must convince us that he has "earned" his vision by facing all the complex and unpleasant facts.

That Warren is essentially a tragic novelist needs no demonstration—not, at any rate, since R. B. Heilman's memorable review, "Melpomene as Wallflower," in which he explained the inability of most reviewers to understand *All the King's Men* by their inability to perceive this.[12] In a sense, the archetypal Warren hero is like Oedipus, who discovered his own evil and achieved a kind of transcendance of it; or like Dante, who recognizes the various sinners in himself.[13] That his central subject is the nature of the modern psyche, and that he is hence a psychological novelist, in spite of the violence so prominent in much of his work, is, I think, equally plain. His best fiction is obsessively concerned with some version of what we have called psychological dissociation of sensibility. In *All the King's Men* this is very clearly implied: Humpty Dumpty is not just the precarious greatness of Willie Stark, but the fragmented psyche of modern man, split between the abstract intellect of Adam Stanton and the concrete action of Willie; while most of us lack even their distorted and simplistic kind of unity. As Jack Burden sums it up near the end, "Adam Stanton, whom he came to call the man of idea, and Willie Stark, whom he came to call the man of fact, were doomed to destroy each other, just as each was doomed to try to use the other and to yearn toward and try to become the other, because each was incomplete with the terrible division of their age." [14] Warren describes the novel in his 1953 introduction as an attempt to "compose a highly documented picture of the modern world," closely related to *At Heaven's Gate* and, like it, based on the seventh circle of Dante's *Inferno*, where the violent against Nature are punished. Willie is such a violator: "the politician rises to power because of the faculty of fulfilling vicariously the secret needs of others, and in the process . . . discovers his own emptiness." In "Melpomene as Wallflower" Heilman defines the theme briefly as "the split in modern consciousness." Humpty is Willie and he is also Jack—the man who has broken into parts. Further, there is a "very complex theme of past-and-future, a

12. Heilman's review is reprinted in Longley, *R. P. Warren.*
13. See Warren's interpretation of Dante in *Selected Essays,* pp. 29–30. Dante plays a fundamentally important role in Warren's writing.
14. *All the King's Men* (N. Y., 1953), p. 462.

theme which is really another way of presenting the split in the world. Here the split is defined chronologically; the separation of fact and idea is also man's separation from his roots. . . ." Only after accepting and coming to terms with the past is Jack "prepared to face history, to enter 'the awful responsibility of Time.'" (In the terms we have been using, Jack wants to believe in temporal discontinuity so that he will not have to recognize the reality and importance of the present.) This theme of time, of the relation of past and future in the responsibility of the present, becomes increasingly important in the poetry, as we shall see.

Flood, Warren's latest novel (1964), develops very similar themes, but with a simpler and more explicit symbolism. The title is basically psychological in reference: the flood is that of memory and consciousness. It is also the flood of modernism that threatens to obliterate the past, as the literal TVA flooding will obliterate Fiddlersburg; more generally, as in the poetry, it is the flood of Time or History; in the religious sense, it is the Biblical flood that punished sin and gave the opportunity for a fresh start, hence baptismal and redemptive drowning, death by water and rebirth.

Since the flood will literally obliterate the physical setting of Brad Tolliver's past, it is an excellent dramatic device to set in motion a novel that is about Brad's coming to terms with himself, past and present. Brad, a screen writer, learns that the world is real, in contrast to the Hollywood world of illusion:

" 'Christ,' he said. Then: 'I know that this is not a story conference. I know that this is the real thing. It is L-i-f-e.'

'The only one we've got,' Cal said, very softly" (p. 339). And at the end Brad puts it explicitly: "For, over the years, he had run hither and yon, blaming Fiddlersburg because it was not the world and, therefore, was not real, and blaming the world because it was not Fiddlersburg and, therefore, was not real" (p. 367).

One of the persistent themes of the novel is the nature of memory and of illusion, the difficulty of preserving truth from distortion. Brad, for example, sometimes thinks of the modern world as simply bad, in contrast to the older Fiddlersburg, and of the fantastically vulgar Seven Dwarfs Motel as a satisfactory symbol of it. Thus he proposes ironically to end their movie thus: "As Fiddlersburg, with its wealth of Southern tradition, unassuming charm, homely virtue, and pellagra, sinks forevermore beneath the wave, the Seven Dwarfs Motel will rise in spray, glimmering like a dream" (p. 37).

Longley describes *Flood* as a "powerful and moving Divine Comedy of art, Daedailian man, holy and profane love, damnation and redemption" (p. 169). The subtitle, "A Romance of Our Time," he notes, suggests its pastoral and lyrical quality. And he comments that the novel has a strong sense of "that blessedness which shines through the fabric of undistinguished mortality" (p. 171).

To counterbalance this perhaps excessively theological and Dantean interpretation, we may look at a recent essay by Victor Strandberg. Strandberg emphasizes in *Flood* and in Warren's later poetry the notion of a "mystic osmosis of being." He quotes from Warren's essay, "Knowledge and the Image of Man" (1954): "Man is in the world with continual and intimate interpenetration, and inevitable osmosis of being, which in the end does not deny, but affirms, his identity." Psychologically, this means recognition and acceptance of the darker and more bestial part of the psyche, the Freudian Id or the Jungian Shadow; as Jung said, "None of us stands outside humanity's black collective shadow." The clearest examples in Warren are Jefferson in *Brother to Dragons* and Adam Stanton in *All the King's Men*, who deny that they are brothers to dragons and refuse to concede reality to the monster-self within; but, Strandberg points out, the discovery and acceptance of the beast within the self is a basic pattern in most of Warren's novels and poems. This acceptance of the reality of evil within the self is the first step toward psychic wholeness. On another level, this means acceptance of the real father figure and rejection of substitutes; it also means willingness to accept extinction, sacrificial love. The shadow self is both divine and demonic, in Jungian terms; it contains both original sin and the possibility of redemption. Warren's "osmosis, then, postulates an ethic of community transcending self and family and tribe"; the Warren protagonist must accept osmosis, so that he is absorbed into a collective final identity.[15]

The biological connotations of *osmosis* need to be complemented by the tragic and religious connotations supplied by Warren himself in "Knowledge and the Image of Man." Despite osmosis, "man's process of self-definition means that he distinguishes himself from the world and from other men. He disintegrates his primal instinctive sense of unity, he discovers separateness." But through the pain of self-criticism he may develop an ideal of excellence, with its possibilities of depersonalized communion; and through the pain of isolation he may "envisage the tragic pathos of life, and once he realizes that the tragic experience is universal and a corollary of man's place in nature, he may return to a communion with man and nature." Thus man discovers love and law through his return to his lost unity, but "love through separateness, and law through rebellion." "Man eats of the fruit of the tree of knowledge, and falls. But if he takes another bite, he may get at least a sort of redemption. . . . His unity with nature will not now be that of a drop of water in the ocean; it is, rather, the unity of the lover with the beloved, a unity presupposing separateness. His unity with mankind will not now be the unity of a member of the tribal horde . . . [but] that of a member of sweet society." [16] The communion, then, is not simply biological and mystical, but tragic and religious; and it remains so, even in Warren's latest work.

We turn now, at last, to Warren's poetry, as represented in *Selected Poems: New and Old, 1923–1966*. From the beginning,

15. Victor Strandberg, "Warren's Osmosis," *Criticism*, X (1958), 23–40.
16. Longley, *R. P. Warren*, p. 242.

Warren has been the most open in texture and personal in tone of
the Fugitive poets; when he began writing poetry again in 1954,
after a ten-year interval during which he wrote none except for
the long "play for verse and voices," *Brother to Dragons* (1953),
these tendencies were much accentuated. Partly in response, no
doubt, to the same pressures that caused a number of other poets
to write "open poetry" or "confessional poetry" at about the
same time, and partly as a result of private and internal developments, Warren's poems have grown steadily more open, more unabashedly personal, more overtly psychological and religious, and
more interdependent. (There is, in most cases, no attempt to
make each poem self-sufficient; the poems come in sequences of
some length, and knowledge not only of the rest of the sequence,
but often of the whole context of Warren's recent poetry, is required in order to apprehend the full meaning of any single
poem.) The themes are similar to those we have looked at in the
novels; and there is, in the latest poetry, the same new sense of
blessedness, joy, redemption as really possible. The titles of the
recent volumes are themselves significant: *Promises: Poems
1954-1956* (1957) begins with a sequence dedicated to his
daughter, born in 1953, and contains a title sequence dedicated to
his son, born in 1955—the same year Warren's father died; the
title indicates both the new hope and promise that the children
bring to their father and the commitment to the future that they
represent. He sees them in perspectives of time and place—"Infant
Boy at Midcentury," "To a Little Girl, One Year Old, in a Ruined
Fortress"—and through them he relives his own childhood. *You,
Emperors and Others: Poems 1957-1960* is about the "you" who
is both the reader and the poet, as well as the "Roman citizen of
no historical importance, under the empire" whose epitaph is
quoted with the first poem, which begins: "Whoever you are,
this poem is clearly about you"—as well as, obviously, about the
Roman emperors of the following pieces and the various figures
from the poet's earlier life. The group "Tale of Time / New
Poems 1960-1966" deals with time and its possibility of redemp-

tion, the title sequence being about the death of the poet's mother almost forty years ago; there are other obsessive images of guilt and fear ranging from the Kentucky of his childhood to Vermont in autumn to recent scenes by the Mediterranean. The new thing is the visionary note of joy in many of the poems, not dissociated from the evil and confusion, but subsuming them. One sequence, "Delight," affirms that something is going to happen, and it may even be good, be delight. The latest volume, *Incarnations: Poems 1966–1968*, develops these themes but avoids any hint of facile optimism: the communion that it celebrates is one of suffering, and maintained with difficulty; the flesh is that of an old convict dying of cancer in a Southern penitentiary and a Negro maid dying in a meaningless accident in New York.

In looking over the whole of the poems from 1923 through 1966, one is struck by the fact that, although the change in style between the early poems (to 1944) and the later (since 1954) seems at first striking and radical, it is actually only a development of tendencies implicit in the early verse and already distinguishing it from that of Ransom and Tate. The themes and subjects of the poems change hardly at all, though tones and attitudes do. The essential and obsessive theme can, I believe, be put very simply: the poet's guilty and ambivalent relation to his parents and to the past for which they stand. To live fully in the present is to accept both future and past as real.

The second earliest poem in the book, "Letter of a Mother," deals with the ambivalent feelings of a boy in a college dormitory upon receiving a letter from his mother; he speaks ironically in a Shakespearean rhetoric—"By now this woman's milk is out of me. / I have a debt of flesh, assuredly"—and describes his skeleton as "mortmain of her womb"; but still "the flesh cries out"—"The mother flesh that cannot summon back / The tired child it would again possess." But the poem ends ominously with the statement that the boy will be possessed by "a womb more tender than her own"—that of death. The finest of the early poems is "The Return: An Elegy," written in 1931 about returning home for his mother's funeral. The form is somewhat like that of Tate's *Ode*, though far looser; the poet's mixed feelings are presented in a kind of reverie as he travels in the Pullman in the rain. ". . . the old bitch is dead / what have I said!" and in a varied refrain, "the old fox is dead / what have I said." As he thinks of retreating backward in time, urging the train wheels, in a deliberately inflated rhetoric, to "Pursue down gleaming hours that are no more," there is the ironic refrain counterpointing Longfellow with a moment of childhood shame:

> turn backward turn backward O time in your flight
> and make me a child again just for tonight
> good lord he's wet the bed come bring a light

And finally he achieves an offering of his sorrow like a "dark and swollen orchid," coming to terms with his ambivalance:

> the old fox is dead
> what is said is said
> heaven rest the hoary head
> what have I said!
> . . . I have only said what the wind said
> honor thy father and mother in the days of thy youth
> for time uncoils like the cottonmouth

"Revelation," another early poem, deals with a boyhood experience in which guilt for wounding his mother produces violent changes in his view of the world like the cosmic catastrophes in history and literature: "Because he had spoken harshly to his mother, / The day became astonishingly bright. . . ." Experience takes on a new intensity and violence, and the boy, it is made clear, partly enjoys these emotional storms; but more importantly, he learns "Something important about love, and about love's grace." For "In separateness only does love learn definition": this is the theme, to recur so often later, of the necessity of the Fall, of the end of innocence. In this poem, as in the famous

"Bearded Oaks" and innumerable later ones, Warren's image for Innocence, for the kind of love that is outside time and history and therefore escapist and womb-like, is of an underwater seascape:

> Rent was the roof like loud paper to admit
> Sun-sulphurous splendor where had been before
> But a submarine glimmer by kindly countenances lit,
> As slow, phosphorescent dignities light the ocean floor.

This theme persists into the latest poetry, broadening out to include his Negro mammy and his grandmother as well. Thus "Tale of Time," the central sequence of the 1960–66 collection, returns once more to the mother's funeral some forty years before and the poet's intensity of grief, pain, and guilt. But the most painful incident was looking at his face in the mirror, thinking of other things, and wondering if he really felt grief. In the second, "The Mad Druggist," he regrets his boyhood lack of attention to his mother's friends, such as the druggist ("for I had not thought they were real"): the druggist, though mad, knew his mother "was too precious to die: / A fact some in the street had not grasped—nor the attending physician, / nor God, nor I." The next poem stresses the point, with its alternative definitions of death, ending: "Death is only the fulfillment of a wish. / *Whose wish?*" The fourth poem takes up the interim between the funeral and midnight, when the private realization comes; ironically echoing Longfellow's "Children's Hour," the poem begins: "Between the clod and the midnight / The time was." In this time, the poet and his father and brother and sister went to see his Negro mammy, now old, sick, and dying. The solution is to "eat the dead," to accept the past, including one's own past self, however unpleasant it may be: "You must eat them completely, bone, blood, flesh, gristle, even / Such hair as can be forced." This once done, "Immortality is not impossible, / Even joy." Throughout this sequence, and many other of the later poems, this image recurs. Sometimes presented in grotesque and even surrealistic terms ("Ballad of a Sweet Dream of Peace," with grandmother and hogs), it blends connotations of primitive cannibalism with those of the Christian Mass or Love Feast: in all these senses, it affirms human communion. To return to the sequence, the next poem, after this image of acceptance, tries to imagine the mother as a child: "What were you thinking, dear Mother?" And the next, "Insomnia," tries to imagine an actual meeting with his dead mother, and then returns again to the image of mother as child and himself now adult, taking her home; finally, the last section of the poem presents images of hope, of joy from pain, through truth ("I must learn to speak it / Slowly, in a whisper"). Both future and past are unpredictable. The last image is of the stars reborn after heat lightning "as the eye / Adjusts to the new dark, / The stars are, again, born. / They are born one by one."

The relation to the father is far less significant. Of the early poems, "Billie Potts" seems archetypal rather than personal—though the distinction is unreal, considering how basic in most of Warren's novels (as well as poems) is the motif of the Trip West, the Return Home, and the re-establishing of relations with the parents. The interpolated passages put the meaning in modern psychological-moral terms, while the story itself is told in language and verse suggesting (but not imitating) the folk-ballad. Billie goes west in search of a new identity, a new name and face, and this is an attempt to escape from Time: "For Time is always the new place, / And no-place, / . . . For Time is motion / For Time is innocence / For Time is West." And it is a fake redemption: the new name and place "have been dipped in the healing flood. / For they have been dipped in the redeeming blood. / For they have been dipped in Time." The Return is the attempt at acceptance of the self and of history: "Weary of innocence and the husks of Time, / You come, back to the homeland of no-Time, / To ask forgiveness and the patrimony of your crime; / And kneel in the untutored night as to demand / What gift—oh, father, father—from that dissevering hand?" The end of the poem

is ominous and powerful, as "the father waits for the son," and
Everyman (or Oedipus) as wanderer returns like Billie "To kneel
in the sacramental silence of evening / At the feet of the old man
/ Who is evil and ignorant and old. . . ."

As we have said, the conjunction of the father's death and the
son's birth in the same year was obviously significant to the poet,
and has a part in the new tone of acceptance of the past and
commitment to the future. The first poem in *Promises* describes a
vision in which the poet returns to his childhood home and sees
the bodies of his parents:

> Then sudden, the ground at my feet was like glass, and I say
> What I saw, saw deep down—with their fleshly habiliments rent
> But their bones in a phosphorus of glory agleam, there they lay
> Side by side, Ruth and Robert. But quickly that light was spent.

And he hears their voices, the mother saying "Child" and the father, "We died only that every promise might be fulfilled." The
father's death is described in the sequence *Mortmain*, a punning
and ironically journalistic title, as the lengthy title of the first
poem makes clear: "After Night Flight Son Reaches Bedside of
Already Unconscious Father, Whose Right Hand Lifts in a Spas-
modic Gesture, As Though Trying to Make Contact: 1955." And
the poem is perfectly explicit. "What could it be that I, / Caught
sudden in gut- or conscience-gnaw, / Saw rising out of the past,
which I / Saw now as twisted bedclothes? Like law / The hand
rose cold from History / To claw at a star in the black
sky. . . ." But the hand sank down, and "all joy and the hope
that strove . . . Were snatched from me, and I could not move,
/ Naked in that black blast of his love." The rest of the sequence
deals with the father's earlier life, as imagined by the poet: cutting crossties and reciting Greek paradigms at sixteen, in 1885;
the next poem moves to 1956, with the poet taking down the father's old grammar, while his son plays in the next room, and
trying to understand. Then he imagines the father in 1880, at

eleven, and though he cannot communicate, the boy grins at him, and the heat moderates with the promise of rain.

"Homage to Emerson, On Night Flight to New York," in the 1966 collection, is another treatment of the Innocence versus Experience theme that bulks so large in the later poetry. "There is / No sin. Not even error," thought Emerson, and at 38,000 feet he is "dead right"—but only in the "womb-gloom" of the DC-8, where the heart "is as abstract as an empty / Coca-Cola bottle." The poem is a kind of complement to *Brother to Dragons*, similarly dedicated to the task of reconciling the doctrines of the great American sages with the facts of American history, of modern life, and of human existence at any time. *Brother to Dragons* forces Jefferson, with his belief in man's natural goodness and perfectibility, to confront the hideous crime committed by his nephew. "RPW" sums up at the end: "The recognition of complicity is the beginning of innocence. / The recognition of necessity is the beginning of freedom. . . ." ". . . we have, Each, experienced what it is to be men. / We have lain on the bed and devised evil in the heart. . . ." And "Fulfillment is only in the degree of recognition / Of the common lot of our kind. And that is the death of vanity, / And that is the beginning of virtue." "The Day Dr. Knox Did It," another sequence in the 1966 collection, confronts once more a shocking incident from the poet's boyhood, the suicide of a neighbor; the last poem in the sequence is a kind of personal confession of the poet's own sins, since he is, like the reader, the perfect image "of this, our age": "have lied, in velleity loved, in weakness / forgiven, who have stolen small objects, committed / adultery, and for a passing pleasure, / as well as for reasons of sanitation, / inflicted death on flies. . . ." Repeating once more the flood image, of escape into fake innocence as substitute for redemption, he says, "there is / no water to wash the world away."

> We are the world, and it is too late
> To pretend we are children at dusk watching fireflies.
> But we must frame more firmly the idea of good.

My small daughter's dog has been killed on the road,
It is night. In the next room she weeps.

Very close to this theme—in fact inseparable from it except for purposes of discussion—is that of Time, of the necessity of accepting the past in order to accept the present as real, of the falsity of escape to either past or future. "Bearded Oaks," justly famous as perhaps Warren's most beautiful lyric, we have already cited for its image of escape from time as submarine and seductive. But "The world is real. It is there." In *Promises* the two perspectives of the 1950s in the long backward vista of American history and of the poet's infant son with his prospect of the future are blended. Thus "Infant Boy at Midcentury" is very topical, full of the feeling of the Eisenhower years, summit conferences, anxiety and compromise: "You enter at the hour when the dog returns to his vomit . . . When posing for pictures, arms linked, the same smile in their eyes, / Good and Evil, to iron out all differences, stage their meeting at summit." But the poet reminds his son that "ours is not the worst of times. Our country's convicted of follies rather than crimes"; private virtue yet remains, as with the Romans, and in spite of all, he urges "Dream perfection. / Dream, son." The great need is for psychic unity: "Might a man but know his Truth, and might / He live so that life, by moon or sun, / In dusk or dawn, would be all one. . . ." "Ballad of a Sweet Dream of Peace" is based on a grotesque, almost surrealistic image of the visionary hogs who eat the ghostly grandmother and by whom we must be eaten. The image of eating is obviously one of a rite of communion, like the one of eating the dead bodies; we must both eat and be eaten by the past, beyond all pride and rationality: "you fool, poor fool, all Time is a dream, and we're all one Flesh, at last / And the hogs know that, and that's why they wait. . . ." The grandmother obeys the mysterious laws of the supernatural, like Tiresias; because she once found "two toads in coitu on the bare black ground" she "is nightly bound / To come forth to the woods to embrace a thorn tree, to try to understand pain, / And then wipes / the blood on her

silken hair, / And cries aloud, 'Oh, we need not despair, / For I
bleed, oh, I bleed, and God lives!' "

The later poems continue the same double perspective, drawing
hope from the prospect of the son's future. Thus the closing
poem of "Notes on a Life to be Lived" portrays the poet sitting
in the shade and watching his son playing in the sunlight:

> I am the dark and tricky one,
> I am watching from my shade.
> Your tousled hair-tips prickle the sunlight.
> I watch you at your sunlit play.
> Teach me, my son, the ways of day.

And the sequence is, like the others, very topical and immediate;
thus in "Dragon-Tree" the last stanza:

> The world drives at you like a locomotive
> In an archaic movie. It whirls off the screen,
> It is on you, the iron. You hear, in that silence, your heart.
> Have you thought that the headlines are only the image of your own
>   heart?

So far, we have been concerned exclusively with the content of
Warren's poetry, and have ignored its form and language. Obviously, his later verse even more than the earlier is an attempt to
strike through the mask, to address the reader directly in complete candor. (The second person is used extensively, the "you"
being sometimes an imagined person—parents, etc.—and sometimes explicitly the reader, sometimes the poet, and sometimes
both the latter.) The forms are loose and unobtrusive; the language
plain and colloquial, not avoiding journalistic cliché, though sometimes openly rhetorical. The aim is an effect of unself-conscious
spontaneity, at the cost of some diffuseness and flatness. But this
open, accessible, low-keyed surface language is counterbalanced
by the dramatic quality of direct address and the effect of repetition and other devices that are openly emotional. On the other

hand, formal qualities are not neglected as much as they seem to be at first glance: some regular forms are employed, and rime and meter never abandoned, though used with freedom. Further, there are two other elements that tend to counter the surface looseness: a heavy though inconspicuous use of allusion, and the use of intricate patterns of repeated images so that all the poems within a given sequence are interdependent, and the poems, though obviously pointing outward, are also self-reflexive and provide a content for each other.

As in the novels, the formal and intellectual elements balance the naturalistic and colloquial—the scheme from Dante or Spenser or Shakespeare counterbalancing the vivid impression of everyday life, of exact colloquial speech—so in the poetry the concealed elements of formality and order exist in tension with the folk elements and the aspect of personal and direct address.

The one massive conclusion that may be drawn from these three histories is this: that modernism makes its impact on these writers not as a new theory that they are persuaded to accept, or conspiracy that they decide to join, or even literary style that they decide to imitate. In every case, the writers testify that the essential datum that is the basis of their modernism—let us call it loosely psychological dissociation of sensibility—is something that they perceived independently in themselves and in the life around them. They deny awareness of any literary influence or even of any influence on each other in this regard, and such facts as are discoverable bear them out. When they do come to know each other, and, through Tate, discover the modern style in poetry, the ground is prepared, and the impact of these powerful stimuli enables each to define his own poetic style.

Dissociation of sensibility, then, is from the beginning and remains the basis diagnosis, for these writers, of what is wrong with the modern world. The whole agrarian movement may be described as a metaphor for Unity of Being, for the undissociated sensibility. Whatever doubt may be cast on dissociation of sensibility in terms of its probable derivation from de Gourmont, its imprecision as a literary term, or its inadequacy as a historical back-projection, there can be no doubt at all that the term points to something real in the modern psyche, and something centrally important.

The chapter shows, also, I think, some of the paradoxes and contradictions in the relation of the various elements of modernism. The Fugitives were, and are, popularly supposed to be escapists from the modern world, or intemperate rejectors of it; but as we have seen, it is rather the deep awareness of it and the coming to terms with it that make Ransom, Tate, and Warren major writers. Each of the three incorporates in himself, as well as perceives in the outside world, the forces of disorder that we have symbolized as Dionysian. Each has a distinctive version of the tension between this and the opposing Apollonian principle: Tate, the most radical in language and structure, is most conservative in prosody and genre; Warren, striving in his later verse for increased intimacy, directness, spontaneity, loosens his rhythms and flattens his language, while retaining regular forms and employing a special private but systematic group of symbols, sometimes surrealistic. Ransom, simplest on the surface, but fundamentally dualistic, produces cosmic and moving ironies through masterful control of language and tone in a deliberately minor art.

CHAPTER SIX

THE NEWER CRITICISM

RAMSOM CALLED HIS STUDY of Richards, Empson, Eliot, and Winters, published in 1941, *The New Criticism*. This title, though presumably intended as a neutral and unpretentious designation, was an extremely unfortunate one. It suggested (and suggests, for it now permanently inhabits the cloudy mythological landscape of literary history) that there was a definite school of critics with a common program, claiming revolutionary novelty, and striving to overthrow and supplant an Old Criticism. But one revolution succeeds another, if the schools are of the same order; the whirligig of time might be expected soon either to bring back the Old Criticism or to bring in a Newer. (I am not, of course, suggesting that Ransom held any such views; I am expounding the connotations of his title, which achieved far wider currency than the book itself.)

W. J. Ong has recently put the case well against any such relativistic or cyclical view of the recent history of criticism.[1] The New Criticism, he argues with bold simplicity, was genuinely new in being the first really adequate criticism ever to exist. In historical terms, the New Criticism is related to larger cultural developments: to the increase of literacy and the spread of education in general, and specifically to the rise of English literature as

1. W. J. Ong, *In the Human Grain* (N. Y., 1967), p. 33.

a university subject and the consequent need to devise effective ways of teaching it. These phenomena called for a pedagogy that would concentrate on reading. The relation of the two motives— to speed up and improve methods of teaching basic literacy, and to develop and refine more adequate techniques for the teaching of poetry at all levels—is very clear in the work of I. A. Richards and his associates. The New Criticism in its pedagogical aspect, then, is a part of this large movement of democratization which involved the expansion of education in general and the growing importance of English literature as a subject. Its discipline was regarded by its proponents as in part a substitute for what was formerly achieved in other ways—by the study of the Classics, for example, and the discipline of translation; or by the *explication de texte* practiced in French schools; or by the kind of cultural environment and training at home that many of the newer students did not have—but in part it was clearly something new, going far beyond what had been accomplished before in any of these ways. The fact that modern poetry was of an unprecedented difficulty and therefore needed to be explained and justified to a general audience made the problem more than purely academic, though the problem was essentially the same in both contexts. The New Criticism was not, then, a denial of earlier criticism or a deviation from its goals, but a fulfillment of them in terms of pressing current needs.

That the New Criticism was brilliantly successful, hardly anyone would deny; the most frequent complaint has been, in fact, that its success led to too complete a domination of the literary scene. There was, of course, some disenchantment with the earlier and more grandiose hopes: teaching how to read, with emphasis either on poetry or semantics (how to detect propaganda) did not prevent World War II nor even improve the quality of politicians; and it soon became apparent that no pedagogical technique can really insure that a student understands a poem, much less qualify him to judge it. But many of its practitioners—such as the three discussed in the last chapter—were spectacularly effective as teachers and editors as well as pure critics, and they had enormous personal influence. The penalty for this effectiveness was that the New Criticism came to be regarded as an orthodoxy, an Establishment.[2] To achieve its objectives, this criticism also had to neglect some valid and important aspects of literature. For all these reasons, it was inevitable that by the mid-1950s there should be a powerful reaction against the New Criticism.

In part, this reaction was Jacobin or abolitionist, aiming to do away with this criticism root and branch and restore matters to the *status quo ante*, to guillotine these aristocrats of the *ancien régime* so that liberty, reason, and the common man may rule. A more responsible and intelligent form of reaction was to maintain continuity with the New Criticism—to assimilate it, learn as much as possible from it, recognize its value fully—and only after this to go on to explore other kinds of perspectives and approaches. Both the critics I intend to discuss at some length in this chapter exhibit the latter and healthier variety of reaction. Their names will surprise no one: insofar as there is ever a consensus on such matters, I suppose it would be agreed that Frank Kermode and Northrop Frye are the two most considerable critics to emerge since World War II.

Frye and Kermode are very different from each other; in most respects, as I shall be arguing shortly, they represent polar opposites. But they share certain qualities in contrast to most of the New Critics. In the first place, neither is himself a poet, and both are professional academics. Neither is American, but they make full use of American historical scholarship as well as criticism. Both have felt Eliot's power to the full and have written brilliantly about him, but the shortest way of stating their essential similarity is to say that they agree in opposing most of what Eliot stands for as poet or critic. Their objections to the Eliotian

2. By the late 1940s the movement had clearly entered a period of consolidation, with René Wellek and Austin Warren's *Theory of Literature* (1949) and Robert Stallman's anthology *Critiques and Essays in Criticism* in the same year.

poetic are, however, diametrically opposite: Kermode distrusts its Romantic-Symbolist affinities, which he thinks lead it to withdraw from the world of rational discourse, science, and politics, and set itself up as occult and superior; Frye protests because it is not Romantic enough and does not set the poet in his rightful Blakean place as prophet of the imagination. Finally, both dislike Eliot's religious and political attitudes as undemocratic.

History and Reason

Of the two modes of protest against the New Criticism, the prior type chronologically is that which describes it as an offense against reason and a repudiation of history (literary and political). Multiform protests on such grounds begin almost as soon as the criticism does—New Critics, in fact, sometimes make them against each other—and continue unabated to the present. To return to the terminology we defined in Chapter One, we may define the charge as that of fostering aesthetic (art/life) discontinuity by detaching the poem from history, and rhetorical discontinuity by encouraging the abandonment in poetry of any equivalent of prose statement or logical structure. These errors lead, according to the critics of the New Critics, to romanticism (in this context a bad thing): to imitative form representing chaos by chaos, to political escapism and irresponsibility, to a flight to religion or occultism as irrational refuge. As we have seen, Ransom pressed such charges vigorously against Eliot, and, more mildly, so did Yeats. Yvor Winters, in many essays and in a series of books beginning with *Primitivism and Decadence* (1937), drew up elaborate indictments on such grounds of Pound, Eliot, Yeats, and many others, even Frost. William Empson has grown increasingly intolerant over the years of what he considers to be religious irrationalism and political reaction, whether in Milton or in his contemporaries; he remarked recently, "If the modern movement is a revolt against reason I have never been in it at all, so I have not left it merely because I am an old buffer." [3] The party of history and reason has been a compo-nent of the New Criticism virtually from the beginning, then; in fact, as I. A. Richards made clear when he banished the "phan-tom aesthetic state" in *Principles of Literary Criticism* (1924), an acceptance of ontological continuity in the sense of believing po-etry to be open to inspection and analysis and continuous with prose in this sense is fundamental to any kind of New Criticism.

Axel's Castle: A Study in the Imaginative Literature of 1870–1930, by Edmund Wilson (1931), was perhaps the most persuasive and influential of all protests of this type. The book is, of course, much more than this; it is not primarily polemical, but a wonderfully perceptive and intelligent presentation and exegesis of six modern writers. Of poets in English, Wilson dealt only with Eliot and Yeats; his thesis was that they, like the other writ-ers he discussed—Joyce, Gertrude Stein, Proust, Valéry, and, for background, Rimbaud and Villiers de l'Isle-Adam—were contin-uators of the French Symbolist tradition. The Symbolist move-ment was a second wave of Romanticism, Wilson argued, carry-ing further its hostility to science and democracy, its contempt of ordinary life ("Live? our servants will do that for us . . . ," says Axel), and its commitment to the occult and irrational. Although the book was not merely written to a thesis, it was very topical and very much of its time: it must have seemed then that the Auden group was emerging in England promptly on cue to an-swer Wilson's call.

Wilson's criticism of Symbolism as escapist seemed based on a quasi-Marxist expectation that the modern poet should accept a "scientific" version of reality and a goal of political action. Thus in his final chapter, "Axel and Rimbaud," he presents what now appears as a false dilemma: for writers who are not able to inter-est themselves in contemporary society "either by studying it sci-entifically, by attempting to reform it or by satirizing it," there are "only two alternative courses to follow—Axel's or Rim-

3. See Empson's preface to John R. Harrison, *The Reactionaries* (N. Y., 1966).

baud's." The first calls for shutting oneself up in one's own private world; the second for leaving "to find the good life in some country where modern manufacturing methods and modern democratic institutions do not present any problems to the artist because they haven't yet arrived," as Lawrence and other primitivists have done. The price paid by those who choose the first course "is usually to succumb to some monstrosity or absurdity" as did Proust, Yeats, Valéry, Eliot, and Joyce. Wilson therefore makes his conclusion explicit:

> I believe therefore that the time is at hand when these writers, who have largely dominated the literary world of the decade 1920–30, though we shall continue to admire them as masters, will no longer serve us as guides (p. 292).

And he goes on to cite the example of Russia, "a country where a central social-political idealism has been able to use and to inspire the artist as well as the engineer," and to hope for further combinations of Symbolism with Naturalism, in the way that *Ulysses* has shown to be possible, and perhaps for a new unification of science and art as Symbolist experiments with language work, "like modern scientific theory, toward a totally new conception of reality" (p. 297).

Any book which treats large questions of evaluation and interpretation with relative brevity, and through a highly selective discussion of a few writers, is likely to distort and oversimplify. (I say this in full and embarrassed awareness that it applies to the present book.) To put Eliot and Joyce in the company of Gertrude Stein, and then to put them together with Proust, Valéry, and Yeats into Axel's castle, which begins to seem a cork-lined Irish ivory tower, is to exaggerate their Symbolist affinities through the effectiveness of a basic metaphor. Because *Axel's Castle* came so early and was so remarkably attractive, readable, and persuasive, its negative thesis gained instant acceptance along with its positive ones. That is, most readers acquired from it, one suspects, the conviction that the leading moderns were Symbolists and politically irresponsible at the same time they were being shown for the first time the great power and fascination of these writers. Such a conviction, imbibed with mother's milk—or critical wet nurse's—is likely to be felt as beyond argument, a *donnée*.

To adopt Wilson's general posture of admiration of the great moderns combined with grave reservations about their political irresponsibility has been so common among liberal intellectuals that it would be preposterous to give examples. Two American critics should be mentioned, however, because of their considerable influence in the last two decades. Lionel Trilling, in the essays collected in *The Liberal Imagination* (1950) and subsequent volumes, has practiced a larger kind of cultural criticism, sometimes psychological and historical as well as philosophical, that is perhaps the best and most responsible expression of this attitude. His criticism is always double-edged, and constitutes a critique of the point of view of the liberal urban intellectual at the same time that it expresses it. (His models are Matthew Arnold and E. M. Forster, on whom he has written excellent books.) To state with impossible simplicity the tension basic to his work, Trilling finds the rational-humanitarian-optimistic view of life congenial but insufficient; he seems to believe ultimately and reluctantly in a Nietzschean-Freudian tragic interpretation of life and art. Leslie Fiedler, the other critic, is perplexed by no such tensions or self-doubts, but is essentially a polemicist. His essays, first collected in *An End to Innocence* (1955), are more directly concerned with political and cultural criticism than Trilling's. Though he has campaigned effectively to rehabilitate Whitman and Hart Crane and has done some brilliant mythic-archetypal criticism, Fiedler seems to be fundamentally more of a rationalist than Trilling.

In England, there has been a particularly strong protest against rhetorical discontinuity as manifested in poetry or defended in criticism. One reason, perhaps, is the stubborn British tradition of empiricism and common sense; a more specific one is the fact that Dylan Thomas and, under his uncaring shadow, various Apocalyptic, Surrealistic, and neo-Romantic movements dominated the

British poetic scene during the postwar decade. The so-called
"Movement" represented by Robert Conquest's anthology *New
Lines* (1956) therefore stressed the virtues of prose and reason,
common sense, strict form, and wit. Donald Davie, one of the
New Lines poets (and now, appropriately, Yvor Winters' successor at Stanford), wrote a brief but very influential study at about
the same time: *Articulate Energy: An Enquiry into the Syntax
of English Poetry* (1955). Davie's thesis is that all modern poets
assume "that syntax in poetry is wholly different from syntax as
understood by logicians and grammarians . . . ," and that they
derive this assumption from the French Symbolists (p. 148). He
finds Symbolism to be a widespread error, infecting aestheticians
like Cassirer and Susanne Langer as well as critics like Northrop
Frye, and he argues against them all that "in trying to remove the
human smell from poetry, they are only doing harm. For poetry
to be great, it must reek of the human, as Wordsworth's poetry
does" (p.165).

Frank Kermode, the most important of these critics who reassert the claims of history and reason, is emphatically not a representative of any school. He avoids controversy and is suspicious
of concern about critical method. His great virtue (aside from intelligence, perceptiveness, wide knowledge, and a lucid and witty
style—all these go without saying) is his willingness to do any
homework necessary to the full understanding of the work he is
dealing with and then to submit himself to the work patiently
and with full imaginative sympathy before trying to judge it. He
is also willing to go into the arena, giving his time and energies to
reviewing many kinds of books in many periodicals; in a time
when first-rate reviewing seems to be increasingly rare, he deserves much credit for setting an example. No critic was ever less
dogmatic or pretentious; and yet he does not shirk the most difficult issues or avoid responsibility for taking a position on them.

We have already discussed, in Chapter One, Kermode's brilliant and influential *Romantic Image* (1957). In the preface,
Kermode describes his purpose as being to examine the assump-

tion that the image is the "primary pigment" of poetry (the phrase is Pound's) and "that the poet who uses it is by that very fact differentiated from other men, and seriously at odds with the society in which he has to live." These assumptions, he comments, may be thoroughly Romantic, "but they are none the less fundamental to much twentieth century thinking about poetry; and this remains true for critics and poets who are militantly anti-Romantic." We have given some reasons for questioning Kermode's assumption that these assumptions are in fact basic and that they derive through the Imagists from the Symbolists. Let us proceed now to consider the most striking historical thesis of the book, that Eliot's theory of dissociation of sensibility is a mere back-projection into history of Symbolist doctrine. As a historical theory, Eliot's formulation (involving Milton, Dryden, and the English Civil War) was a highly debatable oversimplification, as Eliot himself later conceded. But to deny that there were changes which are related somehow to characteristic modern predicaments seems an even more rash simplification. There is, in short, a great deal of evidence that the phenomena Eliot described and attempted to explain were real, and not hallucinatory back-projections. In literary studies, the theory has been enormously stimulating, giving fresh vigor and interest to the interpretation of seventeenth- and eighteenth-century poetry; Milton's reputation was temporarily damaged, but the ardor with which he has been defended has certainly restored the balance, and the controversy has put him and many other poets in a fresh perspective. The theory, then, is no mere delusion of Eliot's, but a hypothesis attempting to account for something real.

As to the psychological aspect of dissociation of sensibility, or the theory as a perception about modern life, the evidence of its reality is all too plentiful. The fragmentation of the modern psyche is described not only by the great psychiatrists but by most of the major writers; in addition to those covered in the last chapter, one thinks of Lawrence, Yeats, Valéry, and Kafka as conspicuous examples of writers preoccupied by the theme and uninfluenced by Eliot. Surely Kermode might have said more plausibly that the historical theory was a back-projection from this genuine perception than from any literary doctrine, Symbolist or not; to explain it all in terms of literary influence is to commit more heinously the fault Eliot confessed to when he said that the original theory attempted to explain in purely literary terms things much broader than literature alone. Dissociation is not something Eliot invented, or a delusion into which he was led by the Symbolists; it is something he perceived in himself and in the life around him. The relation to the past is debatable; it is possible to argue, with Ransom, that modern man is no more fragmented than his ancestors, that dissociation is the perennial human condition; but it is not possible to deny the reality of the perception that modern man is dissociated.

C. K. Stead, in *The New Poetic* (1964), provides an implicit corrective to Kermode in several respects. In contrast to Kermode's argument that the historical theory of dissociation of sensibility is a back-projection from the Symbolist and Imagist mystique of the Image, Stead suggests that the relation was the other way around: the doctrine of the Image was a response to the perception of psychological dissociation of sensibility:

> The emphasis both Hulme and Pound put on "art," on the technique of poetry and the process by which a poem crystallized out of experience, was a means of escape from an alternation of sentiment and morals in verse. Pound's most important definition—"An 'Image' is that which presents an intellectual and emotional complex in an instant of time"—is only another attempt to define the ideal of poetic fusion perceived in Yeats's phrase 'blood, imagination, intellect, running together,' and in Eliot's definition of the 'undissociated sensibility' (p. 99).

By a careful presentation of the whole literary context of the times, including the bad popular poets, Stead reminds us of the sway exercised by rhetoric and opinion. The doctrine of the Image, seen in this context, was a necessary reaction against the "forces of discursive mediocrity." "Yeats and Eliot have employed quite different techniques, but in each case the principal effort has been to avoid the isolation of 'aesthetic' and 'moral' qualities in poetry, to achieve a fusion of these into a new wholeness." (p. 191).

Stead also suggests that in Eliot, and to a lesser degree in Yeats, a definite change may be observed as a function of changes in the audience's expectations. "To an audience trained to criticize a poem by the 'ideas' that can be extracted from it . . . , the poet can only insist that there are *no* ideas, that the poem has a being but no meaning," as Eliot did in his early criticism. But once a new audience has begun to appear, willing "to take modern poetry on its own terms rather than on the terms of Kipling or Henry Newbolt, the aesthetic attitudes begin to relax." Eliot gradually shifts "from the symbolist towards the discursive in poetry, from the aesthetic towards the moral in criticism, and generally from the esoteric towards the popular." (p. 118).

Kermode's presentation of the poetics of the Image in the morbidly fascinating context of decadence and the *fin de siècle* makes it seem much more peculiar—more mysterious, occult, and eccentric—than it seems in the prosaic context of patriotic and complacent rhetoric that Stead supplies. Kermode seems to me to exaggerate the difference between the doctrine of the Image and the "great tradition" of poetic theory, or perhaps it would be better to say that he ignores the considerable area of overlap between them. Thus he speaks of the "commonplace modern conception of the work of art as some sort of complex image, autotelic, liberated from discourse, with coincident form and meaning." But any mimetic critic must call the art-work an "image of life" (Dryden's description of a play) or some equivalent; to use the metaphors to which M. H. Abrams gave new currency in his *The Mirror and the Lamp* (1953), if a work of art is a mirror, then what it contains or reflects must be an image. Aristotle, we remember, said that the key power of the poet is that of making metaphors, and Dryden that "Imaging is, in itself, the very height and life of Poetry." Autotelism is not a new doctrine, nor is the notion of a "logic of imagination" or "thinking in images" as novel or peculiar as Kermode makes it sound. Few critics, in fact, have seriously maintained that a poem has exactly the same kind of structure and meaning as a prose discourse or that form and meaning are independent of each other.[4] To take the poem as statement is, to say the least, no improvement over taking it as image. The New Critics spent an immense amount of effort in attempting to mediate between these extremes through considering the poem as drama, as gesture, as symbolic action, and the like. To abandon all this and go back to the assumption that the poem has the same kind of discursive meaning as prose would be, it seems to me, to retrogress enormously.

Kermode sometimes tends to suggest that a kind of conspiracy is at work, with the moderns smuggling in those contraband notions from the French; though he also notes that many of them are to be found in seventeenth-century English poets, in Boehme, Blake, and the English Romantic tradition. He seems to assume that the doctrines are all totally false, and hence must be accounted for as inventions and influences. But some of them were discovered, not devised. To cite the most obvious non-literary examples, Freud's dream-interpretation described genuine thinking in images—highly significant mental processes that are totally non-rational—and Jung revealed the awesome and mysterious powers of images in many times and places. Sometimes Kermode seems to lump together without much distinction everything

4. Yvor Winters is perhaps the only important modern critic who equates poetry with statement. *Image* need not have the magical overtones that it does in Yeats, of course; though it seems to have religious connotations that provoke an iconoclastic zeal in some critics. The best accounts of the doctrines of modern critics on these matters are to be found in *Theory of Literature*, mentioned above, and in *Literary Criticism: A Short History*, by Cleanth Brooks and W. K. Wimsatt (1957). For lucid philosophical defenses of a similar position, see Philip Wheelwright's *The Burning Fountain* (Bloomington, 1954) and *Metaphor and Reality* (Bloomington, 1962), and *Creation and Discovery*, by Eliseo Vivas (N. Y., 1955).

other than the straightforwardly rational: the occult, the mystical, any form of supernaturalism.

This discussion may seem to have belabored at unnecessary
length every conceivable objection to *Romantic Image*. My justification is that the book is extremely important and influential,
part of a significant critical trend, and, in my opinion, seriously
misleading. But it is not paradoxical to say that even if its argument is as misleading as I think, the book is still valuable. There is
much brilliant interpretation of Yeats in illuminating contexts,
and there are fascinating accounts of the mystique of the Image
and especially of the Dancer. Yeats emerges as no follower of
Symbolist aesthetic: though swayed by the mystique, he writes
poetry that is traditional in structure and form and that has a firm
grounding in the external world, including the world of public
affairs. In this he is contrasted to Eliot, who sometimes is hinted
to be the villain of a concealed implicit drama of which Yeats is
the hero.

In *Puzzles and Epiphanies* (1962), a collection of his essays and
reviews during the four years subsequent to *Romantic Image*,
Kermode deals chiefly with the same basic questions of the nature
of modernism and its relation to Symbolism and Romanticism,
but also explores some of its relations to neo- or post-modernism.
He is disturbed by what he takes to be the hostility to science,
the rational intellect, and democratic politics of the great moderns. It would be an exaggeration to represent Kermode as obsessed by Symbolism, but he does return to it with great fre-
quency, to show that it is synonymous with Romantic primitivism, to consider its affinity with occultism and its consequent hostility to science and nature, which leads it to propound
a "second nature" as substitute, or to demonstrate that various
poets or critics have been Symbolists without knowing it.

In discussing David Jones, Kermode links together all these
phenomena under the general notion of primitivism. He describes
the massively learned critical works of Auerbach and Frye, with
their figural or typological approaches, as "very civilized primi-

tivism, devoted to the recovery of imaginative patterns and relations so subtle that we in our brutality have lost them." And he
goes on to sketch an "anatomy of modern primitivism":

> There would be many ugly categories of it: psychologistic,
> mythographic, imagistic, for instance. *L'homme qui médite est
> un animal dépravé.* The development of intellect is the true Fall
> of Man. This is the basic Romantic primitivism: the high valua-
> tion of primitive image-making powers. Under imagistic primitiv-
> ism would be included all modern doctrines of symbol, image,
> ideogram, *figura,* and type (pp. 32–33).

As examples, he cites Pound, Charles Feidelson's *Symbolism and
American Literature,* and the philosophy of Ernst Cassirer and his
disciple Susanne Langer. Cassirer, he says, "represents this variety
of primitivism in its purest and most self-conscious form; for,
well aware of its origin in Kant and Herder, he develops it to the
point where it becomes a philosophy of symbolic forms depending upon a theory of pre-logical conception and expression. For
him, human art, language and science are the very organs of reality; they alone make it possible, by way of symbols, to apprehend
'anything real.' Science is posterior to the other symbolic forms.
. . . But art requires a step back to 'mythical thinking,' in which
the name and the object are the same, where there is no distinction between thought and emotion." According to Cassirer, he
says, art is essentially "an atavistic activity, seeking a temporary
fusion of thought and feeling that is foreign to modern consciousness; yet it is justified as providing insights into the formal
structure of reality not only different from, but richer than, those
of science." This is, as Kermode notes, the "central myth of 'dissociation' in its linguistic aspect"; and he proceeds to contrast it
with the scientific world-view: "mythical, imagistic, organicist
thinking becomes as desirable for the artist as it is undesirable for
the scientist." With mild irony, Kermode describes the "myth-
kitty":

Nietzsche blamed Socrates for destroying myth, the province of human creative force. In the domain of myth we can short-circuit the intellect and liberate the imagination which the scientism of the modern world suppresses; and this is a central modern position. Myth deals in what is more "real" than intellect can accede to; it is a seamless garment to replace the tattered fragments worn by the modern mind, a hallowed and communal expression, as it were a liturgy, of the truths meditated by the modern artist. . . . The cult of it is an aspect of a great longing for primitive mentality, for unity of being, for the body that thinks, not deputing that function to a Cartesian mind (p. 37).

Myth is "too often the anti-intellectualist substitute for science," he says, and there is a pressing need for "a modification of this myth-science antithesis." The chief villain in the split between the literary and scientific cultures (as in so many other things) he finds to be Symbolism, with its notion of art as having access to a truth not available to the intellect and its affinity for the occult, which has been since the Romantic movement "the seductively obvious alternative to Science" (p. 147).

Kermode appears to have arrived at his convictions about these matters originally under the heavy influence of *Axel's Castle*, and he still gives this work complete endorsement. (It is clear from the essay celebrating Wilson in the later volume *Continuities* that Kermode regards him as a kind of model.) Thus he says that Wilson's "real achievement was to identify, even if he could not completely describe, the master-spirit of an age."

He grasped the relation between Romantic and Symbolist, the ivory tower and the cork-lined bedroom; he understood the role of various substitutes for science, and the persistent anti-intellectualism of the whole tradition; he saw how the Romantic cult of personality was turned into its apparent opposite, a cult of impersonality; he understood why English seventeenth-century poetry took on a special importance in the age of Symbolism; and he perceived that the arts of post-Symbolism had a special survival problem (p. 56).

Kermode goes further to observe that, "in view of the close relations of Symbolist and Romantic aesthetics, this can be taken to
mean that modern literature is still working out the revolutionary
theses of the first Romantics. The scope of the twentieth-century
revolution is thus greatly reduced. . . ." It is indeed, and if one
proceeds, as Kermode does in later essays, to argue that the neo-
modernism of recent years is merely a second wave of palaeo-
modernism, then one arrives at what seems an impoverishing kind
of reductionism, for one is reducing all the later movements to
nothing but smaller waves of the first great Romantic movement.

It is testimony to Kermode's excellence as critic—his fidelity to
the work and his freedom from dogmatism—that in spite of all
these misgivings about Symbolism he should write so well and
sympathetically about the one modern poet who is unquestionably a Symbolist: Wallace Stevens. Kermode's fullest treatment is
his book, *Wallace Stevens* (1960). Perhaps it is the complete
openness and obviousness of Stevens's relation to the Symbolists
that disarms Kermode, for Stevens not only follows the Symbolist aesthetic but writes about it as his principal subject. Belief in
the imagination as creating a Second Nature is fundamental to
Stevens, and Kermode is convinced that "Notes Toward a Supreme Fiction" is his greatest work. Of it he says, "The study of
this heavy difference brings Stevens not to a sophisticated acceptance of one of the dead myths, as it brought Yeats, Eliot, and
Pound, but to the creation of this new myth of the hero"
(p. 77). In the end, Kermode observes, Stevens's subject is "living
without God and finding it good, because of the survival of the
power that once made Him suffice." And, concerning "The Idea
of Order at Key West," he sums up thus:

> Such a poem may stand as a great, perhaps belated, climax to a
> whole age of poetry that begins with Coleridge and Words-
> worth; it celebrates the power of the mind over what they called
> "a universe of death." It will be a poem that means something
> so long as we have any kind of belief in the lamp which Coleridge
> substituted for the mirror of Locke (p. 58).

Kermode's *The Sense of an Ending: Studies in the Theory of Fiction* (1967), based on a series of lectures originally called "The Long Perspectives," is outside our scope insofar as it deals with prose fiction. As an interpretation of the apocalyptic aspect of modernism, however, it is relevant to our concerns. In general, Kermode's stance here, as in the review-essays on modernism published in his latest volume, *Continuities,* is that of a counter-counter-revolutionary, defending the original or "traditional" moderns against the more recent "anti-traditional" or nihilistic ones. For the former, "the mood was eschatological, but scepticism and a refined traditionalism held in check what threatened to be a bad case of literary primitivism"; for the latter, these checks are gone (p. 104). He rejects Rosenberg's *Tradition of the New* and the painters therein defended because "the forms of art—its language—are in their nature a continuous extension or modification of conventions entered into by maker and reader, and this is true even of very original artists so long as they communicate at all" (p. 102). With due acknowledgement to E. H. Gombrich, he maintains that the innocent eye sees nothing. For the moderns of the 1920s, the past is a source of order; for those of the 1950s, it is something that ought to be ignored. After describing the shift from literature which assumed it was imitating an order to one which assumes it has to create an order (i.e. from mirror to lamp), Kermode protests against the latest shift to the assumption that the consumer can be left to create his own order, as in random or aleatory art. Finally, Kermode draws an analogy between the relation to the past of the traditional and anti-traditional moderns and that of the Anabaptists and Anglicans: "The common topics are transition and eschatological anxiety; but one reconstructs, the other abolishes, one decreates and the other destroys the indispensable and relevant past" (p. 123).

Continuities (1968), a collection of pieces written between 1962 and 1967, complements *The Sense of an Ending* as *Puzzles and Epiphanies* does *Romantic Image.* In many ways, it seems to me Kermode's most impressive book. The first section, "The Modern," contains the three essay-reviews on modernism that we have discussed in Chapter One. After some pieces dealing with time, typology, and related matters, there are six remarkably fine essays on poets. Those on FitzGerald and Dowson are historical criticism at its best; the one on *The Waste Land* is a magnificent celebration of a kind of poetry that Kermode must disapprove of, as is the "Afterthoughts" on Wallace Stevens; and the final essay pays tribute to a new enthusiasm, Allen Tate. One of Kermode's critical virtues has always been that he values fidelity to the work above theoretical consistency, and that he can respond faithfully and generously to works of which he should in theory disapprove; but this collocation of poets, together with the fact that very little is said about the former *bête noire* of Symbolism, makes one wonder if a theoretical reformulation is in progress. A more obvious explanation, however, is that almost half the book deals with novelists, and especially with apocalyptic themes in them: the nature of fiction and its relation to truth, the nature of time and its relation to eternity; the analogy between the novelist creating a fictional world and God creating the real world, and the like. The most spectacular essays, perhaps because their subjects fit in so well with these preoccupations, are those on D. H. Lawrence and Muriel Spark; but there are excellent ones also on Golding and a wide variety of other novelists, including Henry Miller as type of the nihilistic modern who rejects history and art for apocalyptic expectations and is in every essential respect a contrast to Joyce and Lawrence.

VISIONARY COMPANY

The subtitle is not really intended to suggest Hart Crane's "visionary company of love" but merely critics who are sympathetic toward visionary poets. The hostility of Eliot and most other New Critics toward poets who claim a private religious vision was very marked; they tended to dismiss Blake, Whitman, and Hart Crane (to take conspicuous examples) as do-it-yourself

mystics doomed to futility, and their antipathy to Milton and
Shelley was probably based partly upon the fact that those poets
share to some extent in this tradition. In academic criticism and
scholarship, perhaps the most striking phenomenon of the post-
war years has been the correction of this prejudice. Taking the
writers mentioned above seriously both as artists and as seers,
critics have cast much light on their work and its background.
Frye's *Fearful Symmetry* (to be discussed in detail in a moment)
was a pioneering study of this sort in Blake, illuminating especially
the prophetic books; and F. A. C. Wilson and others have studied
Yeats's relation to the occult tradition and thereby shed some flick-
ering light on the plays. The failure of Crane's "The Bridge" to
sustain its explicitly Whitmanic vision was a favorite *exemplum*
of some New Critics to prove that the vision itself was non-via-
ble; but Leslie Fiedler and many others have campaigned to rehabilitate Whitman, and the small body of Crane's verse now sup-
ports an immense weight of sympathetic commentary.

 Harold Bloom sums up the doctrine of the neo-Romantic
academics in its simplest and most dogmatic form:

> Yeats and D. H. Lawrence in Great Britain, Wallace Stevens
> and Hart Crane in this country, are the legitimate inheritors of
> this Spenserian or Romantic line of poets, whose theme is the
> saving transformation that attends some form of humanism, and
> whose creative mode is the heterocosm, or the poem as an alter-
> native world to that of nature.[5]

Most of the New Critics were also poets, and hence concerned
with the condition of poetry as a living art. One reason they
were severe with Lawrence and Crane was that they thought
them to be very seductive and very bad examples, both artisti-
cally and morally. The later critics are academics, addressing not
aspiring writers but an academic and general audience, and con-

5. In *Modern Poetry: Essays in Criticism*, ed. John Hollander (N. Y., 1968),
p. 501.

cerned not to justify the kind of poetry they have written or want to write, or with advising apprentices, but only with the kind of responsibility felt by the intelligent reader. An exception, however, is Karl Shapiro, a poet of very considerable power and unusual attractiveness, and a critic whose increasing disaffection with criticism and affirmation of neo-Romanticism makes an interesting and perhaps representative story.

Shapiro made his reputation as poet during World War II, under the aegis of the New Criticism. Since the war he has been (after a term as Consultant in Poetry to the Library of Congress) a university teacher for most of the time and editor of *Poetry* magazine and then *Prairie Schooner*. He repudiated the New Criticism in the essays collected as *Beyond Criticism* (1953; reprinted in paperback as *A Primer for Poets*, 1965), and by *In Defense of Ignorance* (1960) he had made an explicit commitment to the visionary and occult tradition and had become increasingly vindictive toward his former allegiances. The thesis of this last volume is stated in the preface: "The dictatorship of intellectual 'modernism,' the sanctimonious ministry of 'the Tradition,' the ugly programmatic quality of twentieth-century criticism have maimed our poetry and turned it into a monstrosity of literature." The motto is "everything we are taught is false," and Shapiro apologizes for not being more rigorously anti-intellectual. The first three chapters denounce Shapiro's unholy Trinity, Eliot, Pound, Yeats; the fourth adds to them Auden, who started promisingly but retreated. The chapters then move to the positive side: W. C. Williams is praised as the "true contemporary," and then Dylan Thomas; Whitman is rehabititated as "the first white aboriginal" (Lawrence's phrase). After some more general chapters there is one called "poets of the cosmic consciousness" affirming the occult tradition as found in Whitman, Ouspensky, Wilhelm Reich, Jung's synchronicity, psi phenomena, and the like; this concludes with praise of *Cosmic Consciousness*, by Whitman's friend Dr. Bucke, and a brief paean to Robert Graves and his White Goddess. The final chapter celebrates as "the greatest living author"

Henry Miller, because he is an occultist, unmodern, pro-life, anti-intellectual and anti-literature, "clown and clairvoyant." "The ponderous absurdities of modern literature and the world it perpetuated dissolve in the hilarities of this almost unknown American author. . . ." Earlier, Shapiro has narrowed "modern poetry" down to a decade, 1915–25, and argued that this is not only the official poetry of the twentieth century but a "surrogate for religion." Considering together Pound, Eliot, Yeats, and Stevens, Shapiro observes that, though only Eliot makes a specific religious commitment, all four believe in some version of "the central religious doctrine of Original Sin":

> It is at this point that Modern Poetry differentiates itself from "Romantic" poetry, whether by Whitman, Blake, Lawrence, or Williams. It is also at this point that Modern poetry becomes anti-American and anti-twentieth century. . . . All four are anti-Humanist (therefore politically pessimistic). All are anti-"Rationalist" (that is, anti-Science) (p. 89).

And he complains that the modern poets are not Symbolist enough: "Eliot's religion is, in fact, a *descent* from Symbolism to a lower plane of poetic endeavor; for religion in Eliot is just another name for civilization" (p. 90). These quotations are sufficient to reveal Shapiro's thesis and to sample the manner of his tireless and uninhibited campaign against all criticism and modern poetry.

Kermode makes the suggestion that Yvor Winters might be considered the John the Baptist of the critical counter-revolution —and it is amusing to think of the outrage Winters would feel if his role should really turn out to be that of hailing a greater prophet than himself. It is clear by now that the Messiah in this analogy would have to be Northrop Frye. Unfortunately, the analogy will not really work: Winters and Frye take positions diametrically opposed on most matters, and Frye can be regarded as a fulfillment of the New Criticism rather than as one coming to overthrow it. The religious terminology is not, however, merely jocular as applied to Frye: he is an ordained minister who quite literally preaches Blake's gospel in all his work.[6]

As he has acknowledged on several occasions, Northrop Frye's other work all grows out of his study of Blake, and he may best be understood in the light of that study and its commitments. Frye is most explicit about his own convictions in his essay written for Blake's bicentenary in 1957 (the year his *Anatomy of Criticism* also, and surely not accidentally, was published). In this essay he stresses the close relation of Blake and later Romantics to English popular culture, with its Biblical apocalyptism; they thought of themselves, he says, as restoring the "normal native tradition" which the Augustan period had interrupted from 1660 to 1760. The "English Romantic tradition has close affinities with the individualism of the Protestant and the radical traditions." Further, English Romanticism "is greatly aided in its feeling of being central to the tradition of English literature by the example of Shakespeare"—by his unpretentious, inductive, and practical approach, which "is another aspect of its individualism." Frye protests that he is not saying that the "Protestant, radical, and Romantic" kind of English culture is better than other kinds, but only that it is and was genuinely popular. Hence the "Catholic, Tory, and Classical" elements have been a consciously intellectual reaction, strongest in the 1920s:

> Its most articulate supporters were cultural evangelists who came from places like Missouri and Idaho, and who had a clear sense of the shape of the true English tradition, from its beginnings in Provence and medieval Italy to its later developments in France. Mr. Eliot's version of this tradition was finally announced as Classical, royalist, and Anglo-Catholic, implying that whatever was Protestant, radical, and Romantic would have to go into the intellectual doghouse.[7]

6. Ordained in the United Church ministry in 1936.
7. *Fables of Identity: Studies in Poetic Mythology* (N. Y., 1963), p. 149.

The irony here is heavy indeed. Frye abandons any faint pretence of impartiality a few sentences later when he remarks that the "fashionable judgments" on Blake's tradition "consist so largely of pseudo-critical hokum." Frye's championing of "Miltonic, Romantic, liberal, and allied values" and his view of the Augustan period as an aberration under foreign influence, with the Eliotic period regarded as an implicit parallel, suggest very much the same outline of English literary history that used to be held by standard academics in pre-modern days, though the emphasis on class and politics is relatively new.

Fearful Symmetry (1947), Frye says in the preface to the paperback edition of 1962, was finished early in 1945, after ten years of work and five complete rewritings. Frye is perfectly explicit about its "connection with the critical theories that I have ever since been trying to teach, both in Blake's name and in my own." These theories are the application to literature of a religious commitment on Frye's part to Blake's whole doctrine, as he interprets it. According to Blake-Frye, "the product of the imaginative life is most clearly seen in the work of art, which is a unified mental vision of experience."

> It is, then, through art that we understand why perception is superior to abstraction, why perception is meaningless without an imaginative ordering of it, why the validity of such ordering depends on the normality of the perceiving mind, why that normality must be associated with genius rather than mediocrity, and why genius must be associated with the creative power of the artist. This last, which is what Blake means by "vision," is the goal of all freedom, energy and wisdom (p. 25).

The visionary is "the man who has passed through sight into vision, never the man who has avoided seeing, who has not trained himself to see clearly, or who generalizes among his stock of visual memories." Hence he is anything but an escapist: "Any portrayal of Blake as a mystical snail who retreated from the hard world of reality into the refuge of his own mind, and evolved his obscurely beautiful visions there in contemplative loneliness, can hardly be very close to Blake" (p. 29). Toward the end of the book Frye proposes the study of anagogy, which would supply us with "the missing piece in contemporary thought which, when supplied, will unite its whole pattern" (p. 425). This study will "lead us to a single visionary conception which the mind of man is trying to express, a vision of a created and fallen world which has been redeemed by a divine sacrifice and is proceeding to regeneration"; and while a "comparative study of dreams and ritual can lead us only to a vague and intuitive sense of the unity of the human mind; a comparative study of works of art should demonstrate it beyond conjecture."

These quotations are intended to suggest how stupendously ambitious and radical a conception this one of Blake-Frye's is, and why art is central to it. In religion, Blake's basic premise is that "Man is All imagination. God is Man & exists in us & we in him. The Eternal Body of Man is The Imagination, that is, God himself. . . . It manifests itself in his Works of Art (In Eternity All is Vision)." And Frye comments, "Man in his creative acts and perceptions is God, and God is Man. God is the eternal Self, and the worship of God is self-development" (p. 30).

To descend from these staggering heights to the world of history, it seems worth while to summarize very briefly Frye's placing of Blake in the tradition of "visionary Christianity" which began with such humanists as Erasmus, Rabelais, Agrippa, Thomas More, and Ficino, who wanted further reform of the Church, disliked scholasticism, and "upheld, for religion as well as for literature, imaginative interpretation against argument, the visions of Plato against the logic of Aristotle, the Word of God against the reason of man" (p. 150). Since the authority for interpreting the Word of God must be the imagination, many of the humanists are interested in occult sciences such as cabbalism or alchemy as a source of new imaginative interpretations of the Bible, helping to "understand the central form of Christianity as a vision rather than as a doctrine or ritual." Something of this was retained by the anarchic and apocalyptic Anabaptists, who acknowledged no authority but the scriptures and their own "inner light." "The Anabaptist leaven, working in Germany, produced Boehme, and through Boehme and its Quaker descendants it came into England." "All these movements of thought we have been tracing converge on Blake's identification of the artist's genius with the Holy Spirit." Frye notes that there was also a "thin but significant line of liberal visionaries" in the Anglican church, including Spenser, Vaughan, Traherne, and Christopher Smart. Milton's "liberty" is practically the same thing as Blake's imagination, Frye argues, and it is in *Areopagitica* that Milton is nearest to Blake.

> The release of creative genius is the only social problem that matters, for such a release is not the granting of extra privileges to a small class, but the unbinding of a Titan in man who will soon begin to tear down the sun and moon and enter Paradise. The creative impulse in man is God in man; the work of art, or the good book, is an image of God, and to kill it is to put out the perceiving eye of God. God has nothing to do with routine morality and invariable truth: he is a joyous God for whom too much is enough and exuberance beauty, a God who gave every Israelite in the desert three times as much manna as he could possibly eat. No one can really speak for liberty without passing through revolution to apocalypse . . . (p. 60).

Can this be the same Milton with whose God William Empson has been so grimly wrestling? And are these Anabaptists and other "visionary Christians" the same people described by Norman Cohn in *The Pursuit of the Millennium*—and by Swift in *Tale of a Tub*—whose crazy doctrines brought so much needless suffering upon themselves and others? But we must not stop to argue with Blake-Frye.

Frye's *Anatomy of Criticism* was published in 1957, the bicentenary of Blake's birth and of the Last Judgment as predicted by

Swedenborg. There is no need here to summarize the doctrines of this brilliant, complex, and extremely influential book; our concern rather is to attempt to describe the beliefs and assumptions upon which it is based, and to consider their relations to Symbolism and New Criticism. The difficulty is that Frye's beliefs, being seriously Blakean, are so very radical that they are hard to relate to less audacious philosophical and aesthetic positions. Kermode describes the essential doctrine as follows:

> A poem is an anonymous and autonomous verbal structure; literal meaning cannot be rendered in other words; literary form is spatial; the intention is defined in the text. Add to these beliefs a highly developed organicism, a primitivism which arrives at myth through archetype and . . . you have the latest, extraordinary development of Symbolist criticism. . . . Everything in the book points downwards, to preconscious ritual, which is the necessary base of the structure (*Puzzles and Epiphanies,* p. 72).

Let us look at the *Anatomy* to consider the accuracy and fairness of these statements. Frye calls the poem (as shorthand for "work of literary art") a *hypothetical* as distinguished from an *assertive* verbal structure (p. 99). Hypothetical verbal structures, or poems, have no single discursive or rational meaning; a poet's intention "is centripetally directed. It is directed towards putting words together, not towards aligning words with meanings" (p. 86). A poem is the product of unconscious as well as conscious processes; creation "seems to be an activity whose only intention is to abolish intention" (p. 89). Symbolism as a literary movement he describes as a special and temporary emphasis, a complement to extreme naturalism; its great strength was that it "succeeded in isolating the hypothetical germ of literature" (p. 80). The poem is not simply a description or expression of an emotion: "the real core of poetry is a subtle and elusive verbal pattern that avoids . . . such bald statements." In the history of literature "the riddle, the oracle, the spell, and the kenning are more primitive than a presentation of subjective feelings.

The critics who tell us that the basis of poetic expression is irony . . . are much closer to the facts." A literary structure is ironic "because 'what it says' is always different in kind or degree from 'what it means.' In discursive writing what is said tends to approximate . . . what is meant" (p. 81). So far, this is merely an exceptionally able exposition of lessons learned presumably from the New Critics. But as Frye continues, the distinction between discursive and poetic, assertive and hypothetical, begins to disappear: not only are poems not statements, but neither are statements, or only partly so. Since "all structures in words are partly rhetorical, and hence literary, . . . our literary universe has expanded into a verbal universe, and no aesthetic principle of self-containment will work" (p. 350).

The completeness with which Frye has abandoned mimesis is indicated by his analogy between literature and mathematics: both "proceed from postulates, not facts; both can be applied to external reality and yet exist also in a 'pure' or self-contained form. Both, furthermore, drive a wedge between the antithesis of being and non-being that is so important for discursive thought" (p. 351). Frye has previously protested against the high place the discursive reason has traditionally been given in Western culture; he argues that "nothing built out of words can transcend the nature and conditions of words, and that the nature and conditions of *ratio*, so far as *ratio* is verbal, are contained by *oratio*" (p. 337). As we have seen before, it is the conception of anagogy that provokes Frye's most daring imaginative flights, taking him to heights where there seems to be no troublesome "antithesis of being and non-being":

In the anagogic phase, literature imitates the total dream of man, and so imitates the thought of a human mind which is at the circumference and not at the center of its reality. . . . When we pass into anagogy, nature becomes, not the container, but the thing contained. . . . Nature is now inside the mind of an infinite man who builds his cities out of the Milky Way. This is not reality, but it is the conceivable or imaginative limit of desire,

which is infinite, eternal, and hence apocalyptic. By an apocalypse
I mean primarily the imaginative conception of the whole of
nature as the content of an infinite and eternal living body which,
if not human, is closer to being human than to being inanimate
(p. 119).

In the anagogic perspective, poetry "unites total ritual, or unlimited social action, with total dream, or unlimited individual
thought"; each poem is a "microcosm of all literature."

The anagogic view of criticism thus leads to the conception of
literature as existing in its own universe, no longer a commentary
on life or reality, but containing life and reality in a system of
verbal relationships. From this point of view the critic can no
longer think of literature as a tiny palace of art looking out upon
an inconceivably gigantic "life." "Life" for him has become the
seed-plot of literature, a vast mass of potential literary forms,
only a few of which will grow up into the greater world of the
literary universe. . . . "Tout, au monde," says Mallarmé, "existe
pour aboutir à un livre" (p. 122).

As to the religious significance of all this, Frye says:

The study of literature takes us toward seeing poetry as the imitation of infinite social action and infinite human thought, the
mind of a man who is all men, the universal creative word which
is all words. About this man and word we can, speaking as
critics, say only one thing ontologically: we have no reason to
suppose either that they exist or that they do not exist. We can
call them divine if by divine we mean the unlimited or projected
human (p. 125).

What this really means I confess that I find it impossible to say,
but I cannot think it very useful in understanding either literature
or life, if I may be permitted to revert to the traditional distinction. On the other hand, in *Fables of Identity* some brilliant and
illuminating results are produced by expounding these ideas in

Blake and considering how other writers, from the Romantics to Yeats and Stevens, share or do not share such beliefs. Perhaps the most impressive is Frye's assimilation of *Finnegans Wake* into the Blake tradition. "Blake's work is middle-class, nineteenth-century, moral, romantic, sentimental and fervently rhetorical, and these were the cultural qualities that Joyce, to the dismay of many of his critics, most deeply loved and appreciated" (p. 256). Frye proceeds to demonstrate the parallel between Blake's myth of Albion and Joyce's myth of Finnegan: in both, the "priority of the imaginative over the doctrinal Word" is assumed and in both the "concrete universal, the identity of individual and total man, is the organizing principle of the symbolism." After noting an astonishing number of parallels and a few contrasts between the two, Frye arrives at the conclusion that in *Finnegans Wake* it is the reader who is the hero who achieves the quest. "In Blake the quest contains the cycle and in Joyce the cycle contains the quest, but there is the same challenge to the reader, and the same rewards for him, in Joyce's 'mamafesta' that there is in Blake's 'allegory addressed to the intellectual powers' " (p. 264).

It is inevitable that we should conclude by reflecting upon some of the differences between Frye and Kermode, though nothing could be further from my intention than to suggest that we must keep only one and discard the other. Reviewing Frye's *A Natural Perspective: The Development of Shakespearean Comedy and Romance* (1965), Kermode notes that Frye's critical stance is a deliberate standing back, as one stands back to look at a painting. One step back enables you to see thematic or psychological patterns; a second allows you to see the work in its genre; the third gives you Frye's view: the work as myth, "frozen in space, devoid like myth, of temporality, and fit for inclusion in an all-embracing mythical system." [8] (Frye says flatly that "litera-

8. *Continuities*, p. 117. For a group of varied critiques of Frye, see the English Institute volume, ed. Murray Krieger, *Northrop Frye in Modern Criticism* (N. Y., 1966).

ture is a reconstructed mythology," [9] and Kermode quotes him as saying that it is part of the critic's business to "show how all literary genres are derived from the quest-myth," and that "the central myth of art must be the vision of an end of social effort, the innocent world of fulfilled desires, the free human society.") It is this matter of distance that Kermode finds to be crucial: the more a work deviates from the reality principle the better Frye likes it, just as he believes only in criticism which has "backed so far away from literature that all the little things that make one work different from another drop out of view." Hence Frye is "the critic of regress," ignoring the reality principle which makes literature different from myth. To prefer Shakespeare's romances to the tragedies on Frye's grounds "is to dismiss as irrelevant everything that constitutes the personal presence of a work of art, its existential complexities, all that makes it mean something *now* to a waking audience." And he concludes:

> It is the breath of Hermione, the presence of Perdita, that are lost to view as you stand back; you sacrifice them to a system and a myth. The conclusion seems obvious: when you hear talk of archetypes, reach for your reality principle (*Continuities*, p. 121).

To sum up, Frye's argument is that art is the most important of human activities, literature is the most important of the arts, and the literary critic is at least as important as the "creative" writer, since the critic, too, is creative, and understands literature far better than those who produce it. (One thinks of Randall Jarrell's anecdote ending "Go away, pig; what do you know about bacon?") Furthermore, his own dogmatic and absolute system is to be the basis for a new, genuinely progressive and cumulative science of criticism. All this is an outrage to common sense, as is Frye's postulate that the critic should have nothing to do with evaluation. In contrast, Kermode is always modest and sensible, very much concerned in a practical way with being useful to the

9. *Fables of Identity*, p. 38.

reader. Sometimes he elucidates a group of related ideas—the Romanticism-Symbolism aspect of modern poetics, or the apocalyptic fiction-time nexus—as they affect literature, and sometimes he focuses on a single work or author. At his best, he combines the virtues of Edmund Wilson and R. P. Blackmur, for he is both an admirable close reader and a historical critic, concerned both to see the work in its full historical context and to formulate responsible historical generalizations. Though he eschews pontifical judgments in the Leavisite manner, his purpose is centrally to make reasoned and documented evaluations. Frye, on the other hand, is in a sense quite uncritical: not only is his whole system, as he says, irrelevant to judgments of value, but his view of English literary history, with its denigration of the eighteenth century, is essentially an old-fashioned one. His defense of modernism, in *The Modern Century*, makes no distinction between the two kinds of modernism which Kermode is at such pains to discriminate, but would apply equally to both. (Actually, Frye does smuggle discriminations into his system, as well as highly perceptive comments on individual works; but these are against his principles.) Frye seems to appeal to many people who always resented the New Criticism. It seems refreshing at first to be called on to be a Distant Reader, after so many years of genuflection to Close Reading; and after observing the excesses of some critics the call to give up evaluation is seductive. Furthermore, there can be few tonics more bracing to the sagging academic ego than Frye's vision of the critic's importance. But the cost is high.

At their worst, Kermode and Frye represent a pulling apart of qualities that the best New Critics maintained in balance or tension. Kermode, especially in his earlier work, maintained what seems to me an excessively rationalist position, denying any essential difference between poetry and prose; Frye, on the other hand, is a complete irrationalist, whose only articles of faith are the occult "tradition" and the Imagination. (I spare the reader the thought that the antithesis might be formulated as Apollonian-Dionysian.) In many ways, however, they represent necessary advances over the position of most New Critics (advances also made by many of the New Critics themselves). Thus it was obviously desirable to rehabilitate Milton and the Romantics, as both these critics do; to be systematic about theory, as Frye does with a vengeance; to take the relation of literature to history seriously, as Kermode does. It would be foolish to think that either or both of them have superseded the New Criticism, but they have complemented it in important ways. The bright young instructor no longer tackles a poem with nothing but his bare hands; he knows from Kermode's example that he needs extensive and curious knowledge to explain its historical dimension, and from Frye's work that awareness of mythical patterns and of a general systematic context can add significance and interest. But there is no Newer Criticism.

CHAPTER SEVEN

POETRY SINCE
THE MID-CENTURY

THE TITLE of this chapter may be misleading, for it is not concerned primarily with the history of poetry since 1950. The question to which it is addressed is the narrower one of defining the movement sometimes called neo-, post-, or new modernism and its relation to the earlier form. Before considering poetry, however, it is necessary to look at developments in other forms of literature and in the other arts.

ABOLISHING THE CITY

In the mid-1950s a new revolution seemed to be taking place in all the arts. Much of the commotion was stirred up by the insatiable need of newspapers, magazines, and television for new movements to publicize, and there had been many a false alarm; but it is clear in retrospect that by 1957 major changes were genuinely under way. Like the first modernist revolution, this movement was international and involved conspicuous interactions of the arts. Two of the pioneers were a Rumanian and an Irish playwright—Ionesco and Beckett—living in Paris and writing sometimes in French, but gradually achieving success in London and New York. The most conspicuous difference from the earlier revolution was that art was no longer regarded as a precious object, static and outside time, but as immediate experience, part of the direct and changing relation between artist and audience. Audiences became larger and more responsive; spontaneity was valued over calculation; the distinction between the serious and the popular arts began to break down. Some of this was a reaction against the glumness and austerity of English life in these years and the hysterical conformity of the Cold War in the United States. But anti-art had been, as we have seen, a part of modernism from the beginning, aiming to destroy the conception of art as an enclosed entity, beyond or apart from life; Jarry's *Ubu Roi* of 1896 is as thoroughgoing an anti-play as one could wish, and the Dadaists by 1916 were exploring anti-painting and anti-poetry very systematically. Samuel Beckett, progenitor of the new movement in literature perhaps more than any other single writer, was for many years the devoted friend and disciple of James Joyce. In the earlier modernism, this tendency existed in a fruitful tension with opposing forces; in the movement of the 1950s, the anti-traditional, destructive, nihilistic forces often seemed to hold sway alone.

The spearhead of the second revolution, as of the first, was the art of painting. Because it is susceptible to exploitation as a commodity open to all the worst pressures of capitalism—affected by advertising and journalism, by the appetite for change, novelty, fashion, and obsolescence; purchased for completely non-aesthetic reasons such as prestige, status, speculative investment—painting has come to involve really large sums of money. It becomes hard, therefore, to distinguish between what is significant for the history of art and what is significant only in the history of commerce or popular taste. The distinction is made more difficult by the enthusiastic efforts of most of the artists to obliterate it: in reaction against commercialism or in affirmation of aesthetic continuity, they value not the art work as end product, but the process of producing or discovering it (as in *trouvage* or Raw Materialism). Thus much of the most-discussed painting has a significance largely contextual: it depends for its meaning on the past history of painting, which it is in the act of rejecting. The contextual gesture, as made by Tinguely, Duchamp, Rauschenberg, or Warhol, for example, is a paradoxical one, at once crude and sophisticated, primitive and decadent; it disowns the past, but would be meaningless without this context; hence if it accomplished its object it would lose its point. Such purely negative or nihilistic works may be said to have another kind of significance, insofar as they direct the spectator's attention back to life, as a Rauschenberg all-white or all-black canvas, or a Warhol soup can, presumably does. But Surrealism, from Cocteau and early Dali to the later masters Magritte and Delvaux (both of whom died in 1967), goes beyond this limited kind of significance to suggest a new way of seeing and a new apprehension of reality. Though Breton defined Surrealism as "pure psychic automatism," most painters of this school have in fact employed with great skill conventional techniques of representation; and this balance of vision and craftsmanship has probably been responsible for much of their power. Action painting, with its emphasis upon process and spontaneity, has remained important, as have various other types of abstraction; all have demonstrated their effectiveness in revealing kinds of reality closed to the rational mind and unrelated to figuration.

In music, the relation between the post-World War II and the pre-World War I revolutions seems particularly clear. Stravinsky says that "at the end of the war in 1945 a new period of exploration and revolution began precisely with the rediscovery of the masterpieces of 1912, and the music of Webern in general." [1] It is plain that the second revolution alters the emphasis of the first, while developing tendencies which were present in the original movement. Thus improvisation and other modes of spontaneity now receive great emphasis, and aleatory music allows the principle of randomness full play, sometimes even using a computer to

1. Igor Stravinsky and Robert Craft, *Expositions and Developments* (London, 1962), p. 123.

eliminate completely any human tendency toward pattern. John Cage has developed these principles with the most rigorous and unflinching logic, though Stockhausen, Boulez, and others share much of the same ground.[2] Cage is, however misguided one may think him, emphatically no fake, but a talented and dedicated man who might best be described as a philosophical anti-humanist.[3] Like the Raw Materialists and the practitioners of *trouvage*, Cage—in such pieces as his composition for piano which consists of a period of silence—intends to obliterate any discontinuity between art and life by placing before the audience a length of aural time, a piece of unplanned "life," in the art context of heightened awareness and concentrated attention. The aim is to increase awareness of life and to remove the human "set" which predisposes and censors our apprehension of reality. It is a joke, less bitter than those of Samuel Beckett's plays with their absolutely minimal characters, but exhibiting the same kind of ascetic anti-humanism. Once the basic gestures have been made, it is hard to see much future in this kind of thing; after only one or two compositions consisting of silence or randomly tuned radios, or paintings consisting of untouched canvases, the shock and the joke wears off.

All this is obviously in line with the Dionysian drive beyond the human and toward expansion of consciousness. So is the tendency in recent years to weaken the absolute distinctions between the audiences for serious, popular, rock, and folk music. Vast differences remain, of course, but few "serious" listeners or critics now fail to recognize, in spite of the weird costumes, psychedelic gimmickry, and hypnotic noise, the elements of inventiveness and creativity in some rock and pop groups and of authenticity and taste in some folk music. In rock, especially, the emphasis on vi-

2. Peter Heyworth argues that Stravinsky and Schönberg merely delayed the true and radical break with the whole tradition of Western music, which came in the 1950s with Stockhausen, Cage, and Boulez (*High Fidelity*, June 1968).

3. I am indebted for much information to Calvin Tompkins, *The Bride and the Bachelors* (London, 1965).

sion, possession, and ecstasy through hallucinogenic lights and other psychedelic effects, together with the hypnotic music itself, and the constant suggestion of complementary drugs to produce maximum effect, is clearly Dionysian, and the female votaries in their collective madness often act like bacchantes. This is, in a way, a manifestation of the same *rapprochement* of the arts that was characteristic of the first revolution. The Beatles may seem a curious successors to the Russian Ballet, but they, various other pop and folk and rock groups, and advanced dance groups like Merce Cunningham's, which often performs with Cage and Rauschenberg, do clearly serve some of the same functions.

In literature the second revolution, with its dominant impetus the breaking down of barriers between work of art and audience, seems to have produced, temporarily at least, a new hierarchy of genres. Drama, with its live and immediately responsive audience, has been central; the novel, traditionally loose and adaptable to black humor and social criticism, has followed; with poetry, even when spontaneously improvised in a coffeehouse to jazz backgrounds, coming in a poor third. True, Allen Ginsberg has had an enormous following, but more as guru than as poet; and Rod McKuen, advertised as America's best-selling poet, is singer and personality rather than poet in the old-fashioned sense. In any case, how can any poetry, even that composed for rock music, possibly compete with Living Theater, or Theater of Involvement, in which the audience is invited to come up on the stage and help make the play, often with the added inducement of undressing in order to mingle better?

In America, the early poetic manifestations were spectacular enough—Ginsberg's *Howl!* (1956) and other volumes published by Ferlinghetti's City Lights Bookshop, in the new cultural capital of San Francisco, amid a sudden efflorescence of beards and coffeehouses—but it seemed doubtful for some time that all this had much to do with poetry as previously understood. Gradually, signs of a new attitude became apparent on all sides. There was no such Establishment and class system as the British had to rebel

against; but a literary one was invented, presided over by Eliot
and dominated by Southern New Critics such as Ransom and
Tate, and this was attacked for aestheticism, political reaction,
and snobbery. William Carlos Williams was revived as culture
hero and father figure, to replace Pound and Eliot: he was democratic, thoroughly American, had stayed home and cultivated the
rhythms of colloquial American speech. Much was made, especially by transatlantic critics, of a genealogical line from him
(sometimes with Pound as co-father) to Charles Olson (of the
Theory of Projective Verse and Composition by Field), Robert
Creeley, and the Black Mountain group of poets, painters, sculptors, and composers, and thence on to San Francisco. I do not
mean to speak ironically of Williams, whose *Pictures from
Breughel* (1962) was a magnificent volume, fully deserving all the
attention it got, and whose personal kindliness made him willing
to serve as a father figure for anyone who wished so to regard
him; but some of the historical formulations involving him do
seem to be largely back-formations.[4]

By the end of the decade the American revolution had found
its Tom Paine in Karl Shapiro, whose *Beyond Criticism* (1953)
fanned the flames of rebellion and *In Defense of Ignorance*
(1960) collected his propaganda pieces. Shapiro, as we saw in the
last chapter, narrowed modern poetry down to a tight little con-

4. For example, Donald Hall's introduction to his anthology, *Contemporary
American Poetry*, 1962. Hall's thesis is that "an orthodoxy ruled American
poetry" from 1925 to 1955, derived from Eliot and the New Critics, and
working "through the literary quarterlies and the universities." "It asked
for a poetry of symmetry, intellect, irony, and wit." Against this he sets
up the underground poets, followers of W. C. Williams, who "had a hard
time of it until the fifties." It is true that Williams's anti-intellectualism had
a genuine influence on these poets. As late as 1968 Ginsberg is quoted as
prescribing Williams's "No ideas but in things" as advice to a young poet.
Ginsberg also makes explicit the attitude of the movement toward the
past: "All past consciousness is bunk. History is bunk. Like Henry Ford
said about technology—there's nothing to be learned from history any
more. We're in science fiction now" (*The New Yorker*, Aug. 24, 1958,
p. 41).

spiracy of one decade, 1915–25, and denounced it; the heroes he celebrates in contrast are Williams, Dylan Thomas, Lawrence, and most of all "the greatest living author," Henry Miller. He also professes allegiance to the "cosmic consciousness" and the occult in general, especially as found in Ouspensky, Wilhelm Reich, and Robert Graves. In the same year Donald M. Allen's *New American Poetry 1945–1960* canonized forty-four poets, most of whom had previously been underground.

In England, as we saw in the last chapter, the most prominent movement in the mid-fifties was that represented by Robert Conquest's *New Lines* (1956), containing Amis, Wain, Davie, Gunn, Larkin, and others. This trend, somewhat absurdly called The Movement, was a reaction from the heady influence of Dylan Thomas and other irrationalist poets back to reason, strict form, and wit. As someone wittily said, the choice presented by the Movement seemed to be between Philip Drunk and Philip Sober; many of the better poets, such as David Jones and R. S. Thomas among the older, and Charles Tomlinson and Ted Hughes among the younger ones, were completely outside all this. At any rate, anthologies since *New Lines* have reversed the emphasis, quite openly under American influence: thus *The New Poetry* (1962), edited by A. Alvarez, puts the Americans first, and uses "Beyond the Gentility Principle" as a subtitle in the introduction.

OPEN POETRY

Though some of the propagandists for the second American revolution in poetry seemed really to want to make it a Terror, with no mercy to the Old Regime and reputations rolling in the streets like decapitated heads; and though the genealogies with which they supplied the new rulers seemed very dubious, we must leave the details of these matters to the historians. Dropping the overworked metaphor of Revolution, we can say that there was a fundamental change of attitude toward the writing and reading of poetry, beginning about the middle of the decade and rapidly gathering momentum. It is apparent not only in the work of young poets and in the fashionable or lunatic fringe, but in the work of most of the established poets of older generations.[5] (Pound's *Pisan Cantos*, 1948, anticipates the trend; Eliot's last play, *The Elder Statesman*, 1958, illustrates it, as does the change in the work of William Carlos Williams, Warren, and Auden, to cite a few obvious examples.) In general, the change is a reaction against any form of aesthetic discontinuity, against the poem as in any sense autonomous, against any esoteric quality or unnecessary difficulty; against tight or elaborate forms; and against irony. The qualities newly emphasized are openness, simplicity, directness, colloquial language, the accents of psychological truth as the poet reveals (often) the most sordid, humiliating, and intimate details of his life. Instead of being self-sufficient autonomous units, each equipped with a *persona*, the poems tend to come in sequences, with the poet himself as undisguised speaker. I prefer the terms "open poetry" or "poetry of experience" to spicier alternatives such as "confessional" or "naked" poetry; but "poetry of involvement" is also a good phrase, suggesting both the poet's involvement in experience and the increased emotional involvement in the poetry expected of the reader. Poetry of experience is often poetry of madness, both in the Blakean sense of prophetic truth that the world will think mad and in the clinical sense of an anguished awareness of mental and emotional disorder.

The chief early monument of open poetry, which confirmed its existence and brought it wide attention, and has since had an enormous influence, was Robert Lowell's *Life Studies* (1959). By surprisingly early general consensus, Lowell had been recognized as the dominant talent since the war; and *Life Studies* had such an impact because it marked a radical change in style and subject from his earlier volumes (*Land of Unlikeness*, 1944, *Lord Weary's Castle*, 1946, and *The Mills of the Kavanaughs*, 1951). Where these had been packed, convoluted, extremely allusive and

5. See the statements in *Poets on Poetry*, ed. Howard Nemerov (N. Y., 1966).

difficult—the end of the line in dense rhetoric, it was said—the new poems were loose, open in texture, nakedly personal in subject, with a long prose sketch about the poet's childhood and especially his sad and feckless father interposed among poems about his marital difficulties, his confinement in jail as a conscientious objector to the war, and his confinement in mental institutions later.

The extremists of the new movement (post- or anti-traditional moderns) often suggest that Lowell returned in this volume to the tradition of W. C. Williams, perhaps via the Black Mountain group. Lowell, however, emphatically denies this: in an interview with A. Alvarez in 1963 he said that he liked Williams but had not been influenced by him. His own verse, he said, is "much more formal, much more connected with older English poetry. . . ." [6] Ransom and Tate, he observed, made poetry more formal than Pound and Eliot did; and they—especially Tate—were Lowell's early masters. By the 1950s, he felt that he had to get away from formalism, but it was still in his blood. In writing "Skunk Hour," the earliest of the poems in *Life Studies*, the only influence he was aware of was that of Elizabeth Bishop, to whom the poem is dedicated. Lowell has described the circumstances of composing this poem vividly, and since the occasion was one of some importance in literary history, it seems worth while to quote his account. The time was 1957:

"Skunk Hour" was begun in mid-August . . . and finished about a month later. In March of the same year, I had been giving readings on the West Coast. . . . I was in San Francisco, the era and setting of Allen Ginsberg, and all about very modest poets were waking up prophets. I became sorely aware of how few poems I had written, and that these few had been finished at the latest three or four years earlier. Their style seemed distant, symbol-ridden and willfully difficult. . . . I felt my old poems hid what they were really about, and many times offered a stiff, hu-

6. *The Review*, No. 8, August 1963.

morless and even impenetrable surface. I am no convert to the
"beats." I know well too that the best poems are not necessarily
poems that read aloud. Many of the greatest poems can only be
read to one's self, for inspiration is no substitute for humor,
shock, narrative, and a hypnotic voice, the four musts for oral
performance. Still, my own poems seemed like prehistoric mon-
sters dragged down into the bog and death by their ponderous
armor. I was reciting what I no longer felt. What influenced me
more than San Francisco and reading aloud was that for some
time I had been writing prose. I felt that the best style for poetry
was none of the many poetic styles in English, but something like
the prose of Chekhov or Flaubert.

When I returned to my home, I began writing lines in a new
style. No poem, however, got finished and soon I left off and
tried to forget the whole headache. Suddenly, in August, I was
struck by the sadness of writing nothing, and having nothing to
write, of having, at least, no language. When I began writing
"Skunk Hour," I felt that most of what I knew about writing
was a hindrance.[7]

There can be no question of the openness and nakedness of this
kind of poetry, but some readers have felt doubtful whether or
not it really is poetry. In the same volume, that most artful poet
Richard Wilbur makes this comment:

Some have said that the poems of *Life Studies* are dilute and
artless by comparison to Lowell's earlier work. They look so only
if one has been so conditioned by the latter as to be irresponsive
to new techniques from the same poet. "Skunk Hour" . . .
cannot be read passively . . . one must participate in the lines,
discovering their implicit emotional value and generalizing from
their relatively dead-pan specificities. . . . There is art enough,
and density enough, in "Skunk Hour"; it is a more flexible poetry

7. Anthony Ostroff (ed.), *The Contemporary Poet as Artist and Critic*
(Boston, 1964), p. 108. Lowell here cites as sources, in addition to Elizabeth
Bishop, Hölderlin's "Brot und Wein" and another German poem by An-
nette von Droste-Hülshoff.

than Lowell has ever written; it admits a greater range of feeling, and in particular it liberates the author's excellent sense of humor (p. 87).

Roethke and Berryman, among Lowell's older contemporaries, had both exploited material of this kind, and we will have a few words to say about them shortly. W. D. Snodgrass had studied with Lowell, and perhaps influenced his teacher; his *Heart's Needle* was published in the same year as *Life Studies*, and won the Pulitzer Prize. Its themes—mental and emotional difficulties, the breakup of a marriage—were very similar to Lowell's. Anne Sexton and Sylvia Plath both studied with Lowell at Boston University in 1958–59, and obviously were influenced by him; Anne Sexton's *To Bedlam and Part Way Back* (1960) and Sylvia Plath's *Ariel* (published in 1965, two years after her suicide; its best known poems are "Lady Lazarus," about her previous attempts at suicide, and "Daddy," about the relation that lay behind them) mark the full flowering of the open or experiential movement. Obviously, however, far more than literary influence is in question; as we have already seen, there is a parallel tendency in the work of most older poets, in response to the same pressures that affected Lowell and the others. (Even in the realm of literature alone, it is probably safe to say that reaction against a kind of poetry that begins to seem irrelevant is more important, for most poets, than any influence.)

From the nakedness of self-exposure and self-revelation in *Life Studies* it is hard to see how poetry could go further in the same mode. In his subsequent work what Lowell has done is to balance the personal and confessional aspect of the poetry by writing—deliberately, it would seem—in modes that take him far outside himself and into the City of culture. (How much Lowell is a poet of the City in his earlier career, we have seen in Chapter Three.) No poet was ever farther from being a propagandist; but he has a powerful moral and political concern, a sense of responsibility for civilization, and specifically American civilization, that permeates his poetry. Certainly the wide and rapid acceptance of Lowell as the leading poet of his generation resulted in part from his commitment to the obligation of taking a public stand on politico-moral issues. But to return to the specific matter of the genres in which Lowell has written since *Life Studies*. The most striking of these is the imitation, which he has resurrected and which he employs very much as Pope or Johnson did: he writes, that is, poems that are somewhere between a very free translation of the original and a modern poem on the same theme. Lowell is, in fact, rather more strict than his eighteenth-century predecessors in that he never substitutes modern examples and allusions for the original ones (possibly because he knows that he cannot be sure, as the earlier poets could, that the reader knows the original and will get the point of ironic parallels and contrasts). Although he feels free to add lines and stanzas on occasion, and to drop lines and stanzas at will, the imitations consist mostly of actual translation, both rigorous and imaginative. Lowell's imitations are based not only on poems congenial to the modern taste but on those of many periods, styles, and languages, many remote from any obvious modern affinity: for example, Racine's *Phèdre* (1961) and, in the volume *Imitations* of the same year, Homer, Sappho, Villon, Pasternak, Leopardi, Hebel, Heine, Hugo, Ungaretti, Montale, as well as the more predictable Baudelaire, Mallarmé, Rilke, and Valéry; and in the latest volume, *Near the Ocean* (1967), Horace, Juvenal, Dante, Quevedo, and Gongora. *Lord Weary's Castle* contains several imitations, and it seems clear that Lowell has practiced the genre from the beginning as a kind of discipline. As Ben Belitt notes,[8] he never uses the alien poem as a mirror to reflect himself, or as an opportunity for histrionic mimicry, but (in spite of his disclaimers) is engaged primarily in practicing the translator's art of entering into another personality and another world. And his practice has grown closer to translation, rather than farther from it, with the years.

8. In the *Salmagundi* special issue on Lowell (Vol. I, No. 4, 1966–67): "*Imitations:* Translation as Personal Mode," pp. 44–56.

A second direction in which Lowell has moved is toward the drama, which imposes its own discipline and kind of impersonality, besides its special advantage of direct relation with an audience. *Phaedra* was his first work for the stage; his trilogy, *The Old Glory*, based on two stories by Hawthorne and a novella by Melville, was produced in 1964, and his *Prometheus*, based on Aeschylus's *Prometheus Bound*, in 1967. (He has also translated the *Oresteia* trilogy of Aeschylus; so far as I know this has not been published.) All these plays are related to the genre of the imitation in that they are based on originals from remote times and places and in forms remote from the modern stage, and no contemporary allusion or reference is inserted; but each has a theme with an obvious contemporary relevance and each thus treats a contemporary problem or failing—sometimes a peculiarly American one, as in *The Old Glory*, and sometimes one universally applicable, as in *Prometheus*. Jonathan Miller, who directed the first production, said of *The Old Glory*:

In a period when America was going through the most radical reappraisal of her domestic and foreign demeanor, these plays offered for the nation the most central dramatization of her dilemma. Refracted through the work of Hawthorne and Melville, Lowell had caught a piercing Yankee insight into the character of his own country. . . . These plays are about the big-hearted energetic blindness of the American nation and they show quite clearly how the country's cardinal virtues can overgrow their own strength until they actually harden into the very vices which so disable the American pursuit.[9]

This kind of public theme, never missing from Lowell's work but reduced to a minimum in *Life Studies*, has counterbalanced the personal and experiential themes in the poetry since that volume. It is based on a very powerful sense of tradition and the past, buttressed by a formidable knowledge of history, American

9. "Director's Note" prefixed to *The Old Glory*, London, 1966.

and European, economic and religious as well as political, and brought alive by a passionate sense of its relevance to the present. Lowell feels deeply, both as citizen and as poet, his responsibility for committing himself to a position on political and moral issues. As he said of himself,

> In life we speak with many false voices; occasionally, if we are lucky, we find a true one in our poems. A poem needs to include a man's contradictions. One side of me, for example, is a conventional liberal, concerned with causes, agitated about peace and justice and equality, as so many people are. My other side is deeply conservative, wanting to get at the roots of things, wanting to slow down the whole modern process of mechanization and dehumanization, knowing that liberalism can be a form of death too. In the writing of a poem all our compulsions and biases should get in, so that finally we don't know what we mean.[10]

Stanley Kunitz, who quotes this, adds: "Though he is not a man of action, he has a great intuitive gift for symbolic gesture. And though he is more deeply committed to the past than most contemporaries, the charismatic touch of his poetry is on the nerve of the modern."

The re-emergence of this public dimension is very clear in *For the Union Dead* (1965). The volume begins with two poems addressed to the poet's wife, and proceeds to "Middle Age," an intensely personal codicil to *Life Studies*, addressed to his father: "At forty-five, / what next, what next? / At every corner, / I meet my Father, my age, still alive. // Father, forgive me / my injuries, / as I forgive / those I / have injured!" The poems are informed by a vivid and specific sense of a particular time and place—a Maine lobster-town, New York in midwinter. "Fall 1961" renders the fear of nuclear war in the crisis of that date; the collective theme derives its power from the private one already developed: "Our end drifts nearer, / the moon lifts, / ra-

10. *Salmagundi* special issue, p. 22.

diant with terror. / The state / is a diver under a glass bell. // A father's no shield / for his child. . . ." Circling from the specific contemporary crisis out and back to Hawthorne, Jonathan Edwards, Caligula and Imperial Rome, and other matters of significance at once personal and public, the volume builds up to the title poem. "For the Union Dead" was originally published, with a different title, as the concluding poem in *Life Studies* (and in Chapter Three we discussed it briefly in that context); but it finds its proper place here as the conclusion to this sequence. Jerome Mazzaro [11] may be right in seeing a pattern suggested by Lowell's nickname "Cal," as "Caligula" explicitly is: thus "Jonathan Edwards in Western Massachusetts" expounds the Calvinistic view of men as powerless and foredoomed, spiders for the fire, sinners in the hands of an angry God, and "The Neo-Classical Urn," with its picture of the poet as a child catching turtles and putting them in the garden urn to die, may be an allusion to Browning's "Caliban upon Setebos," where Caliban, threatening to maim the straggler crab with purple spots, resembles the Calvinistic God. The poems together, at any rate, reveal post-Christian man inhabiting a meaningless and dying world, prey of new forces of violence and brutality in the struggle for survival.

"For the Union Dead" begins with the memory of the "old South Boston Aquarium" and the still persistent longing "for the dark downward and vegetating kingdom / of the fish and reptile"; to this is contrasted the humanity of Colonel Shaw, painful and doomed though it was (he was dead, with half of his Negro infantry, within two months after marching through Boston): "He rejoices in man's lovely, / peculiar power to choose life and die. . . ." But the poet fears undistinguishing nuclear death for all; he fears the conquest of space, with the corresponding aggravation of the race problem. The end of the poem unites all these themes, tying up the non-human marine life of the Aquarium with the dehumanizing effect of modern life in the image of the enormous tail-fins that were a preposterous fashion of the time:

11. Ibid., p. 58.

. . . Space is nearer.
When I crouch to my television set,
the drained faces of Negro school-children rise like balloons.

Colonel Shaw
Is riding on his bubble,
he waits
for the blessed break.
The Aquarium is gone. Everywhere,
giant finned cars nose forward like fish;
a savage servility
slides by on grease.

The new title points up, I think, the fact that the poem is a kind of companion piece or counterpart to Tate's "Ode to the Confederate Dead." Like Tate's poem, it is not really about the Civil War at all but about modern man and the contrast between him and the heroes of an earlier time; again like Tate's poem, it does not arrive at any solution, but reveals the speaker as part of the age that he condemns.

The image of the City is explicit in *Near the Ocean* (1967). Lowell says in the introductory note, "The theme that connects my translations is Rome, the greatness and horror of her Empire. . . ." Surely he is teasing the reader when he adds, "How one jumps from Rome to the America of my own poems is something of a mystery to me." Lowell's translations (and it is significant that he is willing to use this word rather than "imitations") consist of three from Horace, Juvenal's Tenth Satire (which Lowell calls by its Johnsonian title, "The Vanity of Human Wishes," but manages otherwise to keep free of Johnson), the Brunetto Latini episode from Dante's *Inferno*, and four sonnets from Quevedo and Gongora called "The Ruins of Time," united explicitly by the theme of Rome as both cultural City and imperial power.

The title sequence of five poems, "Near the Ocean," is reminiscent of Auden's "New Year Letter" in tone and versification (mainly tetrameter couplets, loose and slant-rimed). It also parallels Auden's poem in attitude, for both confront a critical and near-catastrophic political situation, admitting the worst possibilities but retaining hope; both pay tribute to virtue, public and private; and both retain belief in the City of traditional culture (which Auden pictures as a secret City within the city). Lowell's first poem joins the great company, led by Stevens's "Sunday Morning," of modern poems about the loss of religious faith as embodied in the contrast between our Sunday mornings and those of the churchgoing past. Looking inward at himself, outward at the modern world, and back through history, the poet sees himself in "Waking Early Sunday Morning" as "squatting like a dragon on / time's hoard before the day's begun!"—like the legendary dragon, guarding treasure that he cannot use or understand. Religion becomes steadily more remote—"Each day, He shines through darker glass"—and the church's emblems are "sad, / slight, useless things to calm the mad." He worries about America as imperialist military power—"top-heavy Goliath in full armor"—and the ceaseless wars that afflict the modern world: "Wars / flicker, earth licks its open sores, / fresh breakage, fresh promotions, chance / assassinations, no advance. / Only man thinning out his kind / sounds through the Sabbath noon, the blind / swipe of the pruner and his knife / busy about the tree of life. . . ."

The second poem in the sequence, "Fourth of July in Maine," is addressed to his deceased maternal aunt, Harriet Winslow. Criticizing his New England heritage as usual, Lowell observes with ironic amusement the Maine Republican descendants of revolutionaries now maintaining their "Emersonian self-reliance" by defending the country against communists, socialists, and clerical advocates of Civil Rights. He makes short work of the Puritan heritage: "Blue twinges of mortality / remind us the theocracy / drove in its stakes here to command / the Infinite, and gave this land / a ministry that would have made / short work of Christ, the Son of God. . . ." The poet pays tribute to Harriet Winslow (his daughter's namesake) and looks at the future his daughter will face. He prays that she will "live through the millennial year / Two thousand, and like you possess / friends, independence, and a house, / herself God's plenty, mistress of / your tireless sedentary love." The next poem, "The Opposite House," describes a house physically opposite in being across the street and spiritually the opposite of Harriet Winslow's house. It is abandoned, guarded by policemen who, like priests of violence (one of them "counts his bullets like beads") practice "deterrent terror." "Central Park" contemplates the daytime lovers and nighttime opposed violences of that place: "We beg delinquents for our life. / Behind each bush, perhaps a knife; / each landscaped crag, each flowering shrub, / hides a policeman with a club."

The last poem of the sequence, "Near the Ocean," is dedicated to the poet's wife. It begins with the poet rejecting the role of Perseus or Orestes, archetypal slayer of the wife-mother, Medusa or Clytemnestra; the American ocean does not, like "older seas and deserts," "give asylum, peace / to each abortion and mistake." He accepts the Gorgon or Terrible Mother figure in his wife, confining himself to the present: ". . . The ocean, grinding stones, / can only speak the present tense; / nothing will age, nothing will last, / or take corruption from the past. / A hand, your hand then! I'm afraid / to touch the crisp hair on your head— / Monster loved for what you are, / Till time, that buries us, lay bare."

Lowell is fully aware of all the risks inherent in open poetry. With his usual candor, he remarks, "It may be that some people have turned to my poems because of the very things that are wrong with me, I mean the difficulty I have with ordinary living, the impracticability, the myopia." [12] And he never loses sight of the importance of technique, of the fact that writing remains inescapably an art, poetry as well as experience. In accepting the National Book Award for *Life Studies* in 1960, he said: "Writing is neither transport nor technique. My own owes everything to a

12. Ibid., p. 23.

few of our poets who have tried to write directly about what mattered to them, and yet to keep faith with their calling's tricky, specialized, unpopular possibilities for good workmanship." [13] Commenting on Sylvia Plath's work after her suicide, he observed: "In the best poems, one is torn by saying, 'This is so true and lived that most other poetry seems like an exercise,' and then one can back off and admire the dazzling technique and invention." [14]

To compare Lowell to his elder contemporaries Theodore Roethke and John Berryman, both of whom may well have had some influence on him, would be an interesting but elaborate exercise. Roethke and Berryman are both extremely complex and various poets, of whom it is hard to say anything sensible in a few sentences. But I will make a few generalizations that I hope are suggestive. The primary strength of Roethke's poetry—though he wrote some wonderful light verse, satire, and love poems—is in its deep inwardness and closeness to the Unconscious, as in "The Lost Son" (1948), which renders a psychic crisis in terms of childhood experience. His "vegetal radicalism," as Kenneth Burke called it, enables him to evoke with great vividness the greenhouse world of his childhood, and the non-human world of earth and plant life. His poetry is often close to nursery rhymes and nonsense verse, and he cultivates his affinity to earlier mad poets: Traherne, Smart, Blake, the mad old wicked Yeats. In this non-human visionary world of childhood fears and adult madness, the Dionysian element is very plain. But the weakness is also plain: the world of normal adult experience is so remote that, both in content and technique, the poetry is limited, tending to obsessive concern with certain experiences and to incoherence on the verge of real obscurity. Roethke apparently realized this, and in his later verse was moving out toward a wider range and clearer organization, as in "Four for Sir John Davies." But his

13. Ibid., p. 59.
14. Ibid., p. 70.

lack of any real sense of the City is one way of defining his difference from Lowell (who celebrates him in an elegy in *Near the Ocean*).

Berryman is closer to Lowell in age and in poetic stance: he, too, is learned, allusive, concerned with American history and aware of contemporary political and social questions. Furthermore, he has accepted one of the ultimate poetic challenges of our time: not content with producing an equivalent in a sequence of shorter poems (the common recourse of modern poets), he has been determined to write a long poem. (His account of his experiences in attempting to carry out this intention, in Howard Nemerov's *Poets on Poetry*, is exceptionally interesting.) Nevertheless, one is obliged to say that he does not seem to have found a satisfactory principle of order, either in *Homage to Mistress Bradstreet* (1953, published as a book in 1956) or in the *Dream Songs* which have been under way since that time. In the prefatory note, the poet described 77 *Dream Songs* (1964) as "sections, constituting one version, of a dream in progress. Its working title, since 1955, has been *The Dream Songs*." In 1969 308 more songs were published, with the title: *His Toy, His Dream, His Rest: 308 Dream Songs;* no unifying principles were discernible aside from those apparent in the earlier songs. As with any unfinished work, it is theoretically possible that an adequate principle of order is yet going to emerge; but it does not seem likely. The *Dream Songs*, as the title indicates, exist at a psychological level down close to the Unconscious, far from the rational and discursive. There are various recurrent devices that serve a unifying function. The most important is the character Henry, who is and is not the poet; many of the poems are about him, and he sings or speaks others. He carries with him a continuing dramatic situation: a minstrel show in which Henry, often in minstrel-show Negro dialect, carries on dialogue or makes jokes or sings songs. Sometimes he is addressed as Mr. Bones (one of the traditional interlocutors in the minstrel show), who often seems to represent Death. The minstrel show was both a genuine kind of folk art and popular entertainment in nineteenth-century America, and a crowning symbol of the oppression of the Negro because it reduced him to the role of comic sycophant. Berryman's use of it is effective because it brings up automatically both the American past and contemporary issues of race, civil rights, and the like; perhaps more important, it also represents the poet as exploited entertainer (though with multiple ironies, romantic and other), making jokes out of his gruesome and harrowing experiences.

The *Songs* are very varied and attractive, often dramatic, with much humor and a vivid awareness of the surfaces (as well as the depths) of contemporary life. There is a "Lay of Ike" and a "Strut for Roethke" and other satiric and nostalgic ones; and there are confessional poems about breakdowns, fears of nuclear war, and the like: "He lay in the middle of the world, and twitcht"; " 'No visitors' I thumb the roller to." But, as the title confesses, there is no unifying structure. In most of them, the method is essentially the same as that of *Homage*, a double point of view in which the poet is partially identified with the dramatic character in the past but also retains his focus on the present. But while with *Homage* there was the external narrative of Anne Bradstreet's life to serve as framework, with built-in aesthetic and larger relevances in the facts of her being the first American poet and a Puritan, there are no such points of reference in the *Dream Songs*.

Berryman's Sonnets (1967) was written "many years ago," according to the introductory note, but remained unpublished (except for one of the 115 sonnets). They tell very explicitly and attractively the story of an adulterous affair, and are of interest as a full-blown example of confessional poetry written (but not published) before confession came in vogue. Much of Berryman's earlier poetry was highly organized in every way: for an extreme example, "Canto Amor," in *Short Poems* (1967; originally published in *The Dispossessed*, 1948), is a Dantean poem in terza rima. Nothing could be more ludicrous than to think of him as a pure Dionysian, in spite of the pictures that appeared in *Life* magazine showing him as a bearded roisterer in Irish pubs. But neither he nor Roethke has Lowell's sense of public responsibility, his religious and historical roots; they are far closer than he to the Dionysian pole as opposed to the City, and hence their poetry is felt as less of a significant gesture, exhibits less tension.

Two of the most promising poets to emerge in the 1960s have been distinguished by a very powerful sense of the non-human, mysterious, Dionysian forces in nature. (I do not mean, of course, to suggest that they alone have shown such awareness; D. H. Lawrence rendered it with great power in his novels as well as his poetry, and Edwin Muir is another obvious example.) These are Ted Hughes in England and James Dickey in the United States. Hughes is often said to be the best younger British poet, sometimes in tandem with Thom Gunn (who is, in convenient accord with our scheme, a somewhat Apollonian type: a university teacher, now residing in California). *The Hawk in the Rain* (1957) was Hughes's first volume; subsequent ones are *Lupercal* (1960) and *Wodwo* (1967). Hughes is the reverse of a sentimental animal-poet: he does not interpret animals in human terms at all. Instead, he shows respect for other kinds of life, utterly different from humanity; thus he makes poetry less man-centered, but he is aware also of these mysterious forces as they enter human life. A good example is the treatment of a conventional sentimental situation in "Macaw and Little Miss": the vicious, fierce bird in the old lady's parlor is patronized by the granddaughter, who also, however, implicitly equates the bird with the warrior who will come "Smashing and burning and rending towards her loin." "All day he stares at his furnace / With eyes red-raw, but when she comes they close." Though she "caresses, whispers kisses," he doesn't respond, but when she "strikes the cage in a tantrum and swirls out: / Instantly beak, wings, talons crash / The bars in conflagration and frenzy, / And his shriek shakes the house." The cruelty and violence at the heart of love are vividly suggested. "The Horses" is most like Lawrence, conveying the same sense of the mysterious otherness of these animals, their power and mystery. "The Martyrdom of Bishop Farrar" is a fine embodiment of the theme of power and violence, the triumph of will over circumstance, the transfiguring of ordinary men by heroism: "When they saw what annuities of hours / And comfortable blood he burned to get / His words a bare honouring in their ears, / The shrewd townsfolk pocketed them hot." (Farrar had said, on being chained to the stake, "If I flinch from the pain of the burning, believe not the doctrine that I have preached.")

"Thrushes" catches beautifully the merciless perfect efficiency of these creatures, "more coiled steel than living": "No sighs or headscratchings. Nothing but bounce and stab / And a ravening second." The poet wonders about the source of "this bullet and automatic / Purpose? Mozart's brain had it, and the shark's mouth. . . ." But "With a man it is otherwise"; whether his are "heroisms on horseback" or at a desk, the distracting devils bother him. "Relic" evokes the alien ferocity of the sea: "The deeps are cold: / In that darkness camaraderie does not hold: / Nothing touches but, clutching, devours. . . ." The ending returns to the jawbone found at the sea's edge:

> Time in the sea eats its tail, thrives, casts these
> Indigestibles, the spars of purposes
> That failed far from the surface. None grow rich
> In the sea. This curved jawbone did not laugh
> But gripped, gripped and is now a cenotaph.

Wodwo, Hughes's latest volume, consists of poems, stories, and a radio play all "intended to be read together, as parts of a single work" (Author's note). The title is a word from *Sir Gawain and the Green Knight* that seems to refer to some kind of undefined monster; the last poem in the book, "Wodwo," expresses this lack of identity, for it presents the monster speaking: "What am I? Nosing here, turning leaves over. . . ." "But what shall I be called am I the first / have I an owner what shape am I what / shape am I am I huge. . . ." This is, in one sense, an animated word out of a Middle English glossary going through an identity crisis, seeking self-definition (it is, I believe, a nonce word); more seriously, it is another exploration of the common ground between mythical monstrosities of the dark woods and the gentle reader. The central theme of the volume seems to be the nature of horror and its relation to imagination and illusion. This is especially plain in the fine prose stories, such as "The Rain Horse," about the terror and threat of an apparently malevolent (insane? possessed?) horse felt by the young man while he is also threatened and subdued by the power of nature in a heavy rainstorm. Similarly, a radio play, *The Wound*, deals with the hallucinations of a wounded soldier involving witches and other strange goings-on, with the line between hallucination and reality left open. "Sunday" is a story on a level nearer the "normal," about the mixed feelings of his audience as a human rat-catcher performs on a provincial Sunday. There are many splendid poems about animals, such as "The Bear": "In the huge, wide-open, sleeping eye of the mountain / The bear is the gleam in the pupil / Ready to awake / And instantly focus." Others deal with the jaguar, the wolf, and with ghost crabs. There is a fine satirical "Vegetarian": "Fearful of the hare with the manners of a lady, / Of the sow's loaded side and the bear's brown fang. . . ." Those who complained of Hughes's "verbal belligerence" and rape of the reader's attention in his earlier volumes will find no grounds in this one.

James Dickey, who had been publishing poems in magazines for more than a decade before his first volume, *Into the Stone*, appeared in 1960, has since published three other volumes, the last of which, *Buckdancer's Choice*, won the National Book Award in 1966. His collection, *Poems 1957–67*, sums up his achievement to date. Dickey is a perceptive and entertaining critic (*Babel to Byzantium: Poets and Poetry Now*, 1968) and a popular lecturer and reader of his own verse. He has been a college football player, pilot of night-fighters, and advertising executive as well as poet, and he appeals to a wide audience; the mass media have covered some of his readings and published some of his poems.

Dickey's account of his poetic growth in the *Poets on Poetry* collection [15] is of exceptional interest, for, though it points up the highly individual quality of Dickey's conception of poetry, it also reveals the parallel between the movement we have called open or experiential poetry and Dickey's development. We should note first, however, since Dickey says nothing about literary genealogies and influences, that it is clear that W. C. Williams meant little to him and the Beats even less; in fact Dickey is at his most amusing in deflating the pretensions of fashionable bards: "*Howl* is the skin of Rimbaud's *Une Saison en Enfer* thrown over the conventional maunderings of one type of American adolescent, who has discovered that machine civilization has no interest in his having read Blake." [16] Roethke is his great enthusiasm; in 1961 he calls him "the finest poet now writing in English," and describes him thus:

> The powerful, almost somnambulistic statements of his observations and accountings come to us as from the bottom of the "deep well of unconscious cerebration" itself, from a Delphic trance where everything one says is the right, undreamed-of, and known-by-the-gods-all-the-time thing that should be and never is said. The best of Roethke's poems are very nearly as frightening and necessary as "darkness was upon the face of the deep," and as simple and awesome as "let there be light" (*Babel to Byzantium*, p. 148).

Roethke is clearly Dickey's principal model; this is the kind of poetry he wants to write. From other references it appears that

15. Ed. Howard Nemerov, 1966; included also in Dickey's *Babel to Byzantium*.
16. *Babel to Byzantium*, p. 53. The first piece in the volume is a devastating review of Donald M. Allen's anthology *The New American Poetry 1945–1960*.

D. H. Lawrence and Rilke, also great Empathizers and Awakeners, played a part, and probably Sir Herbert Read. What he values most is "the individually imaginative or visionary quality," as he says in the Nemerov anthology. Let us turn now to Dickey's account of his own development. He began, he says, trying to realize a particular sound: "an unusual sound of urgency and passion, of grave conviction, of inevitability, of the same kind of drive and excitement that one hears in a good passage of slow jazz." [17] He decided against rhyme, but needed a strongly marked rhythm, which he finally identified as anapestic; with this he was able to produce "a strange, incantatory sound, a simplicity that was direct without being thin, and a sense of imaginative urgency that I had never been able to get into verse before." With a line usually of three beats, in simple declarative sentences, and in poems with narrative basis, fusing inner and outer states (dream, fantasy, and illusion), he arrived at the mode of his first two books. The third, *Helmets* (1964), was "less pronouncedly rhythmical and less hallucinatory" and he began aiming at

> the "open" poem: a poem which would have none of the neatness of most of those poems we call "works of art" but would have the capacity to involve the reader in it, in all its imperfections and impurities, rather than offering him a (supposedly) perfected and perfect work for contemplation, judgment and evaluation. I was interested most of all in getting an optimum "presentational immediacy," a compulsiveness in the presentation of the matter of the poem that would cause the reader to forget literary judgments entirely and simply experience (p. 235).

The parallel with the whole movement of "open poetry" is obvious enough, and is continued in Dickey's further observation:

> Of late my interest has been mainly in the conclusionless poem, the open or ungeneralizing poem, the un-well-made poem. I hope in the future to get the reader more and more into the actions

17. *Poets on Poetry*, p. 230.

and happenings of the lines and require him less and less to stand off and draw either aesthetic or moral judgments (p. 237).

As I suggested earlier, one of Dickey's most obviously Dionysian qualities is his ability to identify with non-human creatures and with the mysterious forces that they embody. He quotes Lawrence, "We don't exist unless we are deeply and sensually in touch with that which can be touched but not known," and describes beautifully this quality in Roethke:

> His poems are human poems in the full weight of that adjective: poems of a creature animal enough to enter *half* into unthinking nature and unanimal enough to be uneasy there. . . . They are the cries of a creature in a landscape which is beautiful and filled with mystery and does not know that it is: the utterances of a perceiving mind which cannot enter wholly into nature and yet yearns to, set off from the mindless flow it would become by a mind that reflects and assesses. The balance, the tranquil awareness that comes occasionally and wonderfully from this state is in his case the product of a terrible tension not far from madness at times, not far from total despair, but also not far from total joy (*Babel to Byzantium*, p. 151).

In Dickey's own poetry, a good example is "The Shark's Parlor," describing an incident when, as a boy, the poet and others pulled a shark into a beach cottage:

The shark flopped on the porch, grating with salt-sand   driving back in
The nails he had pulled out   coughing chunks of his formless blood.
The screen door banged and tore off   he scrambled on his tail slid
Curved   did a thing from another world   and was out of his   element and in
Our vacation paradise   cutting all four legs from under the dinner table

With one deep-water move   he unwove the rugs in a moment
    throwing pints
Of blood over everything we owned   knocked the buck teeth
    out of my picture
His odd head full of crushed jelly-glass splinters and radio tubes
    thrashing
Among the pages of fan magazines   all the movie stars drenched
    in sea-blood.

The intrusion of the alien deep-sea world into the familiar, trivial,
human world, and the humans' puny efforts to control the forces
they have unleashed, make for very powerful contrasts. "A Dog
Sleeping on my Feet," in a much lower key, shows the poet entering into the dog's dream of chasing a fox; "The Movement of
Fish" evokes once more the sense of alien depths in which fish
live. There are other fine ones about owls ("The Owl King"),
snakes ("Goodbye to Serpents"), wolverines ("For the Last
Wolverine"), foxes ("Fox Blood"), lions ("Encounter in the
Cage Country"), and even the imaginary monster, "The Sheep
Child":

> Farm boys wild to couple
> With anything   with soft-wooded trees
> With mounds of earth   mounds
> Of pinestraw   will keep themselves off
> Animals by legends of their own:

And one such legend, the poem continues, is that of the half-hu-
man half-sheep child in the museum in Atlanta. Most of the
poem consists of the sheep-child's speech; he unites man and animal:

> In the summer sun of the hillside, with my eyes
> Far more than human. I saw for a blazing moment
> The great grassy world from both sides,
> Man and beast in the round of their need. . . .

and exists as a rural myth:

> Dead, I am most surely living
> In the minds of farm boys: I am he who drives
> Them like wolves from the hound bitch and calf
> And from the chaste ewe in the wind. . . .

One of the remarkable things about this poem is the combination of the earthy, grotesque connotations of animal-human intercourse on the farm and the elevated imagining of the spiritual meaning of such unions of two natures in myths like those of the centaur or of Leda and the swan.

To make a radical simplification, the central impulse of Dickey's poetry may be said to be that of identifying with human or other creatures in moments of ultimate confrontation, of violence and truth. A good example is the last poem in his collected volume, "Falling," which imagines the thoughts and feelings of an airline stewardess, accidentally swept through an emergency door, as she falls thousands of feet to her death:

> . . . with the plane nowhere and her body taking by the throat
> The undying cry of the void   falling   living   beginning
> to be something
> That no one has ever been and lived through   screaming without
> out enough air
> Still neat   lipsticked   stockinged   girdled by regulation
> her hat
> Still on   her arms and legs in no world   and yet spaced also
> strangely
> With utter placid rightness on thin air. . . .

She plays the roles successively of airplane, of diver, of predatory bird; she becomes a goddess, embodiment of a myth: "The farm girls are feeling the goddess in them struggle and rise   brooding . . . dreaming . . . of what is really said by the moan / Of airliners passing over them at dead of midwest midnight"; she strips off

her clothes, "SOON   now will drop / In like this   the greatest thing that ever came to Kansas." The poem renders this metamorphosis very powerfully, from the vivid picture at the beginning
of the stewardess "In the galley with its racks / Of trays" moving
"in her slim tailored / Uniform . . ." to the long dying "lying still
in the field on her back   sensing the smells / Of incessant
growth try to lift her   a little sight left in the corner / Of
one eye   fading   seeing something wave   lies believing / That she could have made it   at the best part
of her brief goddess / State   to water   gone in headfirst
       come out smiling   invulnerable / Girl in a bathing-
suit ad   but she is lying like a sunbather at the last / Of
moonlight   half-buried in her impact on the earth. . . ."
Dickey's poetry, while often openly personal and autobiogra-
phical, has a large element of impersonality in this way. He has a
powerful sense of ritual and myth, which lies behind most of his
poems: a sense of the action as embodying powers larger than
life, forces beyond the will of the individual. Many poems show
tranced, exalted figures, seen from a distance, engaging in ritual
actions. The basic perception that lies behind the poetry is thus
often Dionysian, more than human. Though his central concern
is with vision, not form, he is aware that the problem of form is
inescapable; and we have seen how carefully he evolves the kind
of rhythmic structure that he needs. Dickey began as an extremely difficult and often obscure poet; his striving toward
greater openness and accessibility may be regarded as an Apollonian quality. For example, wit, totally lacking in the earlier poetry, supplies the whole basis for "Power and Light," based on a
series of topical puns: ". . . It is all in how you are / Grounded.
To bread I can see, I say, as it disappears and agrees / With me
       the dark is drunk   and I am a man / Who turns on. I
am a man." The narrative element in the later poems is often perfectly explicit, uniting past and present scenes: for example, "The
Leap," in which the poet, reading of a woman's suicide leap from a
window, recalls her leap at their first dance in elementary school;

or "The Bee" in which he recalls his football training when he must sprint to save his son driven by a bee into traffic—"Dead coaches live in the air, son   live / / In the ear / Like fathers, and *urge* . . ." When the basic Dionysian preoccupations (the sense of the more than human and the non-human; metamorphosis and transfiguration) operate in proper balance with the Apollonian elements we have been describing, the results can be very fine indeed. There are good poems about sex and women, such as the poignant "Adultery," and "Sustainment," in which, describing the woman whose horse fell on her and killed her when they fell from the bridle path into the creek, the poet reassures his love that they will not be destroyed by the power symbolized by the horse:

> . . . Know, love, that we
> Shall rise from here
> Where she did not, lying now where we have come
> Beneath the scrambling animal weight
> Of lust, but that we may sense also
> What it involves to change in one half-breath
> From a thing half-beast—that huge-striding joy
> Between the thighs—
> To the wholly human in time
> To die, here at this height
> Near the vague body-print of a being that struggled
> Up, all animal, leaving the human clothes. . . .

"The Fiend," about a Peeping Tom, shows the same ability as "The Sheep Child" to identify imaginatively with the more grotesque manifestations of sex and to give them human—and more than human—significance.

This discussion does not begin to do justice to the variety and power of Dickey's poetry; but it has, I hope, indicated how very fully it has responded to the same pressures as the work of the anti-poets while not abandoning traditional requirements. Introducing an anthology of young American poets in 1968, Dickey shows great sympathy for their passion and involvement, their desire to be "with and *in* human experience." He speaks candidly, as a "middleaged poet," of his own career:

> The aging process almost always brings to the poet the secret conviction that he has settled for far too little, that he has paid too much attention to the "limitations" that his contemporaries have assured him he has, as well as to literary tradition and the past. . . . The nearer he gets to his end the more he yearns for the cave: for a wild, shaggy, all-out, all-involving way of speaking where he (or, now, someone: some new poet) engage each other at primitive levels, on ground where the issues are not those of literary fashion but are quite literally those of life and death. All his lifelong struggle with "craft" seems a tragic and ludicrous waste of time. . . . [18]

What he yearns for is the Poetry of the Impossible, the burning bush, which could hardly have benefitted from a course in Modern Rhetoric.

And yet technique matters, even so. God uses it, for a buffalo is not a leopard; as my grandmother used to say, "He is made different." . . . All roads are long, as Allen Tate says, and in the end they lead to the problem of form.

And he gently suggests that some of these new poets "appear to have wandered into old or dead-end streets."

18. Paul Carroll (ed.), *The Young American Poets* (Chicago, 1968).

CHAPTER EIGHT

IN PLACE OF
A CONCLUSION

THIS CHAPTER will be neither a systematic recapitulation of the argument of the book nor an attempt to arrive at further conclusions. At this point I feel some misgivings about the book's thesis, since it is too large and coarse a net to use for fine discriminations. Inevitably, I have given most space to poets who best exemplify the thesis, and have had no occasion to mention many other good poets; if I were concerned primarily with evaluation, the picture would be a rather different one, with more poets in it. At any rate, I do not want to risk distortion by further simplification of the argument or putting it in abstract terms. Instead, I would like, in closing, to return to some of the principal topics that have recurred throughout the book and add a few final reflections and afterthoughts.

MODERNISM AND RELATED TERMS

The relation between modernism and Romanticism is remarkably difficult to state properly—so difficult that perhaps we must content ourselves with avoiding the worst kinds of misstatement. The problem is basically a semantic one: those who discuss this relation are rarely neutral, and one has to look for concealed as

well as explicit polemics. In 1961 Eliot noted that he had been influenced, in his "recurrent theme of Classicism versus Romanticism," by Babbitt and later by Hulme and Maurras—all notable
polemicists; but the terms, he comments, "have no longer the importance to me that they once had." [1] The terms, however, seem
still to be very important to a considerable number of scholars
and critics. Many people obviously derive a special satisfaction
from "proving" that various moderns who professed classicism or
antipathy for Romanticism were deluding themselves and have
been romantic all the time. The assertion that modernism is a late
phase of Romanticism is undeniably true in a simple historical
sense, but it may mean very different things depending on the
context and intention of the argument. The most useful discussion in such terms is likely to be that which discriminates among
the various ways in which particular moderns are and are not related to specific romantic traditions. Pound, for instance, is one of
the most curious cases: stemming from Browning and Flaubert
(as he puts it himself), acknowledging Whitman too, having
much in common with Rossetti, Swinburne, Dowson, Lionel
Johnson, early Yeats, he combines his aestheticism with a kind of
romantic medieval muse-worship, with belief in metamorphosis
and visionary states, and with various occult strains. Yet he is in
many ways genuinely classical: a strong emphasis on poetry as
craft, not inspiration, and hence on the necessity of discipline and
learning for the poet; on impersonality; on the importance of culture, intelligence, wit, civilization. Much of his best poetry is in
the form of translation, "imitation," or extended allusion. In his
Imagist period, he and the other two original practitioners, H. D.
and Aldington, are quite literally neo-classicists, they being neo-
Hellenists while he imitates chiefly the Roman satirists and epigrammatists. A thoroughgoing rationalist by temperament, he becomes a most extensive practitioner of rhetorical discontinuity
(in the *Cantos*).

As to terminology, it has seemed best to follow what appears

1. *To Criticize the Critic*, p. 15.

to be the most widely accepted usage, attempting to clarify it rather than to change it in any important way. This means that the historical label *modern* designates primarily the movement that began about 1909, reached an early peak in the 1920s, and in essentials is still going on. The great nineteenth-century forerunners can when necessary be called pre-moderns, though there are more meaningful labels to attach to Baudelaire, Flaubert, Rimbaud, Hopkins, and so on in most contexts. The most vexatious problem, of course, is what to call the movement that began in 1957. (I have tried to resist the temptation to call it a mini-revolution.) In poetry, the ensuing decade seems to have simplified the problem: the only significant product of the movement has been what we have called "open" (or naked or confessional) poetry. None of these terms are entirely logical, for the Beats and anti-poets are wide open too, as naked and confessional as it is possible to get; but the terms have become associated firmly with the work of certain poets who first became known as extreme examples of the trend (Sylvia Plath, Anne Sexton, W. D. Snodgrass) and with the new phase in the work of such established poets as Lowell. Hence the term *neo-modern* seems rarely justified, its two components being more specifically designated as *open* and *anti*-poets. I am aware that I have said so little about these anti-poets as scarcely to be intelligible to a reader who has managed to escape the deluge of journalism about Beat, Hippie, Op and Pop, Projective Verse, Objectivism, Composition by Field, and the like; but I have assumed that there would be few such readers. There is something to be said for Ginsberg, Olson, Creeley, and possibly even Ferlinghetti, and much for Duncan and Snyder. But then a great deal has been said, in many places.

According to Langbaum, the dramatic monologue was invented by Tennyson and Browning about 1842, independently and simultaneously, as a reaction against the Romantic confessional style.[2] With increasing refinement, the dramatic lyric becomes the dominant form in modern poetry; and there is a similar

2. *The Poetry of Experience*, p. 79.

development of "literature of perspective" in prose fiction.[3] It is a curious and ironic fact that some 115 years later, the tradition of the dramatic lyric (and point-of-view fiction) should be attacked in the name of the Romantic confessional style once more. But the whirligig of time is not merely taking its revenges; good "open" poets, as we have seen in discussing Lowell and others, do not renounce their art.

DISCONTINUITIES

My formulations of the various types of discontinuities were intended as paradigms, short-cuts, models to help reduce complicated matters to manageable proportions so that their relations could be kept in mind more easily. In retrospect, these discussions seem desperately inadequate; but another book would be required to make them much better.

With regard to historical discontinuity, we have seen that most of the great moderns accept it only as myth or nightmare; they fear it, and see the present more vividly in its lurid light. Even Eliot, for whom the myth of doom had enormous appeal, rejected it when he confronted it explicitly in the *Quartets*: the times "seem unpropitious," but that is really "not our business"; trying to divine the future "becomes, in the popular mind, a means of disowning the past"; our proper concern is not with either past or future, but with the here and now, which is the only real and important thing.

If we say that rhetorical discontinuity (or spatial form, non-linearity, or simultaneity) is usually associated with modernism, we must remember that this is not an absolute distinction but a question of degree. This quality is present in all imaginative literature to some extent, though I think we must maintain the common-sense position that the differences in degree are important (unlike Frye, who argues that everything written in words is literature).

3. Cf. Allen Tate, introduction to *Modern Verse in English 1900–1950* (N. Y., 1958).

Discontinuity is, of course, of no value in itself, and is extremely easy to fake. Gertrude Stein is just as discontinuous as Joyce in *Finnegans Wake*, but immeasurably less interesting. The difference between rhetorical discontinuity and the notion of the poem as drama is clear in Ransom, who detests the former but accepts the latter.

As to any single principle as the basis of modernism—imagism, symbolism, spatial form—it seems better to explain what happened in terms of reaction to a specific historical context than in terms of any sort of esoteric doctrine. As Stead reminds us, the dominant poetry of 1909 consisted of patriotic and conservative rhetoric expressing "sound" moral opinions. In this milieu, Pound and the other incipient moderns (including Yeats) violently reject rhetoric and opinion, and they emphasize those qualities poetry shares with painting, sculpture, and music rather than those it shares with history, philosophy, the essay, and non-literary prose. Prominent among these is myth, as a means of bridging discontinuities and of achieving a deeper level and a community of consciousness.

In the revolution of the 1950s this emphasis was reversed, and there was a drive away from rhetorical discontinuity and back toward statement, toward poetry conceived of as not something uttered by a *persona* or a fragment of a drama but as direct confession or revelation or prophecy by the poet undisguised. The attempt, sometimes very artful, is to produce an impression of artlessness, and to involve the reader. The drive is toward openness, toward eliminating any aesthetic discontinuity; the poem is no longer timeless artifact, but designed to draw the reader into time, immerse him in immediate experience.

DISSOCIATION OF SENSIBILITY

However unfortunate the phrase itself may be, and however barbarous our addition to it of the prefixes *psychological* and *historical*, the phrase points to the central perception of the moderns about themselves and about the age. It is, in one aspect, part of modern self-consciousness: people in earlier times may have been more divided than they realized (though they realized enough: *odi et amo*, "passion and reason, self-division's cause," and all the other variations come to mind); but obsession with the theme is certainly modern. There is a dark clinical side, from Poe and "Dr. Jekyll and Mr. Hyde" through Bleuler's coinage of the word *schizophrenia* in 1911 and Freud's revelations of the power of the irrational, hidden side of the mind over the conscious and rational. As Freud and Jung suggested, and Lawrence proclaimed, both dissociation and our awareness of it are part of the price we pay for civilization and culture; and this is part of the motivation behind the modern fascination with the primitive. It is also, in metaphorical form, the reason for the modern literary preoccupation with the Fall as a central image, with psychological terms instead of moral and religious: Innocence is wholeness, unity, unself-consciousness, which we have lost forever.

The discovery of inner emptiness and deadness, of death-in-life, is one of the great themes of modern literature. In prose fiction, the protagonist becomes aware that he has never really been alive, having lacked the courage to be, to love, to define himself; among the great examples are Tolstoy, "The Death of Ivan Ilych" (1884), James, "The Beast in the Jungle" and *The Ambassadors* (both 1903), and Joyce, "The Dead" (1904). In poetry, Pound explores the theme brilliantly in "Portrait d'une Femme," *Mauberley*, and some of the *Cantos;* but the great master of the theme is Eliot. From "Prufrock" and *The Waste Land* through "The Hollow Men," it is central in importance, and in the *Quartets* it forms half of the basic contrast between meaning and unmeaning, life and death, time and timelessness, and the other varied and interweaving contraries which are the basis of the poem.

COMMUNITY AND BIPOLARITY

The basic conclusion seems to me dangerously near platitude, and yet important. The best aspect of the movement of 1957 and after is that it is a drive toward community. It rejects all discontinuities, seeks spontaneity, warmth, involvement, the breaking down of all barriers between audiences and between them and the artist; through the Absurd and its bitter humor, it unites all against oppression, cruelty, hatred. The dangers and liabilities of such an attitude are obvious, and many sentimental and silly works demonstrate them; but the ideals are admirable, and they complement earlier modernism. Earlier modernism must not, however, be discarded; bipolarity requires the City as well as Dionysus. The concept of bipolarity involves tension, not a simple compromise ending in a genteel academicism or popular fakery. For bipolarity to work, both poles must be fully charged, so that a dynamic, living tension is produced.

Hart Crane provides a good example of genuine bipolarity. Crane was very consciously modern and an explicit Dionysian, chiefly through the influence of Nietzsche but also through that of Rimbaud, Blake, Whitman, and others in the same tradition. As we have seen, he asserts Dionysus against Christ in "Lachrymae Christi" and embodies a Dionysiac aesthetic in "Sunday Morning Apples" and "The Wine Menagerie" most explicitly; he also put it in practice, as visionary and anti-rationalist dedicated to tragic joy and cosmic consciousness. He is probably the most highly gifted poet ever to adopt rhetorical discontinuity as an explicit principle. But Crane was also committed to the City, in all senses. Literally, he experiences the metropolis to the full, and he gets New York in his poetry as nobody else did (so Lowell remarked later). He has a profound allegiance to the metaphorical City of tradition and culture. The basic modern problem, as he sees it, is the establishment of meaningful relations to the past, and the task he sets himself is to build a bridge across the chasm between past and present through the conscious employment of myth. Thus he writes that in "For the Marriage of Faustus and Helen" he was "really building a bridge between so-called classic experience and many divergent realities of our seething, confused cosmos of today," and in *The Bridge* he was trying to assimilate the American experience in order to show "the continuous and living evidence of the past in the inmost vital substance of the present." [4] He struggles unceasingly to repair the deficiencies of his own education, being unwilling to think of himself as merely modern; he writes in 1921 that Dada is "nothing more to me than the dying agonies of this movement, maladie moderne" (*Letters*, p. 72). In his essay on "Modern Poetry," he argues that revolution is not enough, that poetry cannot be based on evolution or ideas of progress: "The poet's concern must be, as always, self-discipline toward a formal integration of experience" (*Complete Poems*, p. 260).

Since I recognize that some readers (especially British ones) do not find Crane a convincing example, let us return to the one modern poet whose greatness hardly anyone doubts. Balachandra Rajan sums up Yeats's achievement thus:

> Yeats's poetry achieves the self-conquest which he himself called style by a sensitive engaging of extremities, in which commitment to either extremity is avoided and the poem grows out of the creative tension between them. His poetry succeeds, in other words, because it is securely the poetry of the mainstream (*W. B. Yeats*, p. 124).

This is not a time for predicting the future. As I write in 1969, there are rumors of newer poets, in smudgier little magazines even farther underground than *Fuck You!* Avram Saroyan writes poems of one word—"oxygen"—or sometimes two—"silence / silence"—or even three: "cat / book / city"; his third book is "an untitled wrapped ream of typing paper stamped ' © Aram Saroyan 1968' " and published by the Kulchur Press.[5] The future is often said to belong to such Rock poets as Donovan, Bob Dylan,

4. Hart Crane, *Complete Poems and Selected Letters and Prose* (N. Y., 1966), pp. 217, 248.
5. *The Young American Poets*, p. 369. Two other anthologies of interest as showing recent tendencies are *Naked Poetry: Recent American Poetry in Open Forms*, ed. Stephen Berg and Robert Mezey (Indianapolis, 1969) and *The Poetry of Rock*, ed. Richard Goldstein (N. Y., 1969).

Ed Sanders; and even without his music the best-selling poet is the pop personality Rod McKuen.

And yet the fact remains that an astonishing amount of good poetry, of immense variety and range, is being written now. Poetry is at present, in spite of everything, possibly in a better relation to its audience than has been the case since the trial of Oscar Wilde in 1895. The revival of poetry as an aural and performing art has been important, and the restoration of a close relation between poetry and music. The bond of emotional participation among the audience and between them and performers, though commercially exploited, is part of a genuine and persistent movement. In England, the rehabilitation of the Professorship of Poetry at Oxford and the appointment of a respectable poet as Laureate were straws in the wind. In the United States, it is significant that the 1960s began with Robert Frost reading at the Kennedy inauguration and ended with James Dickey covering the moon landing for a mass magazine and a television network, writing a good poem for the occasion and reading it effectively on television. In both countries, the situation of poetry seems to justify hope. The openness, the hunger for communion and for immediacy and spontaneity among the young are immensely promising, so long as they do not cause the discharging of the other necessary pole: concern both for form and for meaningful relation to the past—of which the earlier moderns now constitute an indispensable part.

INDEX